An

Other

Tongue

Nation

and

Ethnicity

in the

Linguistic

Border-

lands

AN OTHER TONGUE

Edited

by

Alfred

Arteaga

DUKE UNIVERSITY PRESS *Durham and London 1994*

© 1994 Duke University Press

All rights reserved

Printed in the United States of America on acid-free paper ∞

Typeset in Trump Medieval by Tseng Information Systems, Inc.

Library of Congress Cataloging-in-Publication Data appear on

the last printed page of this book.

para paula,

ella que hizo

tres vidas

y que me

aguantó

por la mejor

mitad de

la mía

———————————

Contents

Contents

Acknowledg-

ments

Thus book had an unusually long period of gestation, which transpired over great distance too, occurring as it did in my moves from Houston to London to Berkeley. Two people at the extremes of the trek, and of the alphabet as well, merit special mention because of their interventions at key moments. In Houston at *An Other Tongue*'s conception, Lois Parkinson Zamora urged its abortion, declaring rightly that it would be simpler to write myself rather than to solicit and collect original work for an inchoate project. I ignored her words and instead chose to follow her example, which is that of a tireless editor dedicated to producing collective works. And in Berkeley at a time when I had given up on the project, all but sealing its sepulcher, Arturo Aldama's enthusiastic support animated its Phoenix-like revival. I am grateful to each of the contributors, especially so to two who are particularly responsible for the book's realization, Michael Cooke and David Lloyd. I am most sad that I cannot now share this with Michael Cooke who died two months after completing "A Rhetoric of Obliquity" for this publication. He was a patriarch in only the very best of senses, one who inspired the best by advice and by example. Very early on, I consulted with Michael about the little course of this book and the larger course of my academic career. He brought me, a rather young and unpolished scholar, to lecture at Yale and was the only contributor to request to be included in *An Other Tongue*. His kind spirit has served as guide for my efforts here. David Lloyd has the distinction of not only being the first contributor accepted for this book but of also taking the longest time to write. The latter is mediated in part by the fact that his essay is also the longest. David also introduced *An Other Tongue* to Duke University Press by introducing me to my editor, Ken Wissoker. For this alone David deserves praise, for Ken has proven to be an exemplary editor, the driving force in the transformation of manuscript to book. Further impetus was provided at especially critical junctures by Andrea Remi Solomon and two anonymous readers at the press. All of the essays were either newly written, revised, or translated for *An Other Tongue*. Tzvetan Todorov's "Dialogism and Schizophrenia" appeared in French in *Papers in Slavic Philology.* A shorter version of Jean-Luc Nancy's "Sol Cou Coupé" appeared in French and in English translation as "Cut Neck Sun" in *Le Démon des Anges* and as "Beheaded Sun" in *Qui Parle.* The essays by David Lloyd and Tejaswini Niranjana appeared in their own books, *Anomalous States*, Duke University Press (1993), and *Siting Translation*, University of California Press (1992), respectively, before *An Other Tongue* came to print.

x

Acknowleg-
ments

An

Other

Tongue

_____

The words in *An Other Tongue* describe the words by which we are marked subjects, particular subjects of particular states. The matter is one of interrogating the processes of subjectification that define selves and others as the subjects of nation and ethnicity. It is the contention of the essays here, in varying ways, that the articulations of languages (e.g., English or Spanish) and that of social discourses (anything from regional dialect to legalese) participate in the push and pull struggle to define some version of "self" over and against some "other." Similarly, it is a common contention that these linguistic and discursive relationships manifest active displacements of power, power that must be reinforced continually to maintain a particular image of the world and hierarchy of relationships. In extreme human relationships, such as slavery or colonialism, it is absolutely clear that those so skewed relationships have to be maintained by tremendous displacements of physical and discursive power. This has been noted in discussions of colonialism, in distinguishing the period of domination, when an army of soldiers kills bodies of natives, from the subsequent period

Alfred Arteaga

of hegemony, when armies of English teachers and religious leaders kill their minds. *An Other Tongue* addresses the discursive states of subjectification.

To do so, the essays consider the factors at play in the articulation of *nation* and *ethnos* that define subjects. "National," "native," and "ethnic" markers are juggled differently in the local articulations of nation and ethnos, as can be imagined in such very different contexts as Indian postcolonialism, postcommunist East European nationalism, West European unification, Quebecois separatism, Mohawk autonomy, and neo-Nazi nationalism. The contexts and experiences vary to such a degree that the difficulty of generalizing is obvious. And yet, the intensity and range of experiences makes just as obvious the imperative that we face the problems conceived of the discourses of nation and of ethnos.

Etymologically, the subject is born of a nation (from the Latin, to be born). In English, the birth of subjectivity according to *nation* and *ethnos* first appears in print in the fourteenth century. Originally from the Latin *(nasci)* and the Greek (εθνοσ), they are reconceived in the Judeo-Christian context so that the innocuous notion of a similar people is infused with that of heathen alterity. Nation, in the singular, in 1300 signified people of a common place, but nations, the plural, in 1340 signified heathen, that is, non-Jewish, non-Christian, peoples. Ethnic, from its first occurrence in 1375, so thoroughly denoted non-Jew, non-Christian, that ethnos was erroneously assumed the etymological root of heathen. The contemporary sense of the nation-state appears in English in the 1850s, after the 1844 publication of the Spanish Royal Academy's dictionary that supplements the definition of "nación" with the notion of state and, most significantly, with that of national language.

The history of definition provides significant context for essays in this collection, but it is not their primary focus: *An Other Tongue* is about the here and the now. The fifteen essays concern themselves with specific moment and particular place, with the spatial site and temporal juncture where discourse is articulated, the chronotope where one *is*, when one is subject. For despite the weight of linguistic and cultural histories, it is, after all, only in the here and now that we exist, that we become subjects. We fashion ourselves always in a present articulation of language, be it thought, dream, poem, or casual speech. And yet, perhaps ironically, it is an articulation of etymologies, of definitions, of histories: in the present, we make ourselves subject of the dead, of old tales and old tongues. This is our plight: to conceive selves and to bear others, subjects of some national chronotope, en route to some ethnic telos.

The title, *An Other Tongue*, speaks to these concerns in several ways. Because the conception of the subject of nation is predicated upon an attendant conception of alterity, upon the heathen connotation, it is an *Other* tongue. Because *language* tends to connote system more than physical articulation, it is *Tongue*. And because subjectification occurs at a specific historical moment and material site, because each articulation is present specific, individual, the title is singular. *An Other Tongue* recognizes that radical individuation marks each context of subjectification and makes no collective attempt to ascertain *essential* similarities. The self and other conceived at each site of different histories, different local cultures, are conceived by different processes of subjectification, engendered by different displacements of power.

The essays share this insistence on specific difference and often share similar methodology. For the common endeavor to understand subjectification born of *nasci* and εθνος, is itself born of a critique of the liberal humanist subject. This is why the essays again and again speak the tongues of Derrida and Bakhtin and share the general perspective of what can be called the critique of colonial discourse. *Différance*, for example, is employed to criticize hegemonic writing of Self as present over and above an absent Other. In this manner, the erasure of minorities from majority conceptual space can be revealed and deconstructed. And discussion of the interaction of stratified discourses is most often articulated in terms of "heteroglossia" and "dialogism." This permits the evaluation of the relative tendencies of competing discourses to support or undermine the hegemonic, authoritative discourse. Derrida and Bakhtin, as well as colonial discourse criticism, provide the methods of choice for the contributors precisely because their work locates itself in opposition to the occluded working of subjectification in fields of asymmetrical power relationships.

These matters of subjectification affect me personally in the manner in which I conceive myself in regard to *nation* and *ethnos*. I define myself as a Chicano. I was born in California and am a citizen of the United States, but my relation to that nation is problematic. U.S. Anglo-American nationalists define their nation to the exclusion of my people. Today in California, for example, the male Republican governor and the two female Democratic senators, collude in generating anti-immigrant (i.e., Mexican in the United States) hysteria: that I am rendered alien by U.S. jingoism remains a quotidian fact. My nation is not Mexico, yet I am ethnically Mexican and racially mestizo. But my people exist in the borderlands that traverse the national frontiers of the United States and Mexico. It is obvious for us here that the language we speak both reflects and determines our position in relation to the two nations. The subjectivity engendered by the discourses *nation* and *ethnos* is very plainly tied to linguistic utterance and equally plainly locates the speaker, dreamer, poet, lawyer, somewhere within the power plays of nation(s). Being Chicano in California at the end of the twentieth century means being constantly subjected Other within the discourses of race, ethnos, and nation in a racist, ethnocentric, and nationalist society.

Matters of subjectification are extremely pointed throughout the world in these times in which we live. This century will have to be remembered for its severity and diversity of genocide: recall for example the extermination, because of ethnic, religious, or political difference, of millions of Armenians, Russians, Jews, and Cambodians. It has been a century of violent revolutions, violent suppression of revolutions, "world wars," and yet also, the League of Nations and the United Nations. The establishment and maintenance of the Soviet Union required tremendous physical and discursive power in order to produce and deploy both tanks and ideology. And when the union broke up, tremendous power was unleashed and great violence erupted in the quest to define nation, ethnos. The breakdown revealed repressions that had been occluded (the retarded in Romania, for example) and enabled intense nationalisms and "ethnic cleansing." And as Western Europe moves toward unification (economically, at least), nationalist sentiment emerges in ethnocentric hatred of the other: Germany provides the most noted example because of the recent history of the holocaust, but the fear and hatred of the encroaching Other is characteristic of Europe. After so much history, how can we still have South Africa, English and Spanish postimperial royalty, mass deportations from Israel, and institutional racism in the United States? In many ways, all of this points to the intensity of subjectification, to the many ways *nation* and *ethnos* are written as an oppression of "heathen" Others.

This is perhaps most evident in the subject of colonialism. This century is witness to two great decolonizations, Ireland and India, the former, because of the overthrowing of hundreds of years of colonial occupation, the latter, because of hundreds of millions of colonized people. And there are other colonial contexts, such as the internal-colonization of the other Indian, the American natives to whom full citizenship was delayed even longer than to blacks or women. Still other contexts emerge from the alteration of traditional colonial rule, from slaves to anxious economic immigrants, natives somehow rendered foreign in their own land, and migrants whose sense of home is transnational. Clearly great power is expended to establish and maintain these relationships, as it must be to subvert them. To know *how* one is, it is necessary to know how power is used and by whom.

This is the goal of *An Other Tongue*. It discusses different subjectifications in their specificities, identifies the expenditures of power, and evaluates the discursive factors that promulgate the subject. This is undertaken in the spirit of a dialogue, or rather a polylogue, with little in the way of working ground rules but with the effort to engage others, to listen to echoes, and to disagree. There is no question that each essay stresses the specific here and now of a specific material site, but in addition, each essayist undertakes some border crossing, that is, an attempt is made to negotiate the disjunction between diverse subjects. As such, these essays are particularly suited to consider multinational, diasporic, postmodern, postcolonial traffic.

An Other Tongue speaks in various tongues about the material conditions of subjectification. At times and in places, the essays discuss the styles of discourses and relations of power. At other times and in other places, they discuss the content of those discourses, especially the literature, history, and language. The essays discuss "texts" ranging from street ballads, translations, quadralingual poetry, and miscegenation to national languages. There are similar concerns and similar passions and senses of outrage, but their similarity is like metaphor (to use a simile for a metaphor) in that the worth of the perceived similarity rests on the recognition of difference. And so here too: Gayatri Chakravorty Spivak, for example, discusses postcolonial India and considers the internal colonization of the Chicano; she does this not so much in an endeavor to read one in terms of the other, but rather, to interrogate difference, to interanimate a Bengali accented English with a Chicano accented one.

And so these essays dialogue in a disharmony of tongues, each essay bearing its particular accent. That is, beyond the external dialogue of essay and real world referent, there is an intertextual, internal dialogue, among the contributors. Several of the essayists cite each other, and some direct their work as commentary on another essay in the collection. There is also another dialogue, one that was central to my original conceiving of *An Other Tongue:* that is the intercourse of Chicanos with the world. In the small world of this book there is, nevertheless, opportunity for meaningful interaction. Chicanos writing about themselves and about others interanimate with others writing about others and Chicanos. A pleasant manifestation of this small world interanimation is the French writers' reflection on mestizaje, a trope central to the conception of Chicanismo.

The collection begins with three essays, Chicano, (East) Indian, and Irish, each of which posits some type of hybridity in response to *nation* and *ethnos*. In "An Other Tongue," I focus on the interlingual, hybridized poetics of Chicano poetry. Tejaswini Niranjana, in "Colonialism and the Politics of Translation," suggests that postcolonials live "in translation" at the "site of translation." David Lloyd considers the hybridized street ballad, English infused with the background of Irish, and the problem of Irish nationalism, the nation, and the national epic. Each of these essays works in the spaces between competing languages where the forces of colonialism cleave the subject.

In his "Seeing with Another I: Our Search for Other Worlds," Eugene Eoyang delineates the subjective myopia, or the monocular vision, that characterizes the perception and conception of the Other. Jean-Luc Nancy undertakes a very subjective reading of distant Others, as the French philosopher considers the process of coming to be Chicano. He ponders linguistic, cultural, and racial hybridity and muses on the immensity and ultimate unknowability of the process of mestizaje. Norma Alarcón gives a critical reading to the various postmodern ideas of alterity and criticizes Nancy's conception of mestizaje. Gerald Vizenor's "Ruins of Representation" rings in many ways as a Native American rewriting of Derrida's essay, "Différance." In his self-consciously postmodernist problematization of the representation of the "true" Indian subject, Vizenor's notion of the "shadow" comes close to a Native American translation of *différance*. For Michael Cooke, the use of Derrida is less supplemental than it is contentious. He begins his essay taking aim at Derrida and suggests "obliquity" as the factor of differentiation between female and male Caribbean writers. Cordelia Chávez Candelaria, on the other hand, relies on *différance* to consider the representation of ethnic communities.

One way to consider the five essays that begin with Tzvetan Todorov's "Dialogism and Schizophrenia" is that they twist and turn, commenting and arguing on related grounds. Todorov narrates his life as a Bulgarian born, French intellectual, living in two languages, speaking both equally well but not being bilingual. For Todorov, Bulgarian and French exist hierarchically and function better in different spheres; he is therefore schizophrenic; his two languages exist in a dialogic, power differential. Ada Savin, a Romanian-French intellectual, takes Todorov to task and argues that the "chosen" dialogism of the willing immigrant differs from the "forced" dialogism of the incorporated minority, in this case, the Chicana poet, Lorna Dee Cervantes. But where Savin finds a necessary dialogic to Chicano poetry, Bruce-Novoa interjects the discourse of nation to argue that beneath the surface dialogism, there runs a nationalist monologue. Luis Torres takes a different approach and documents the presence of nineteenth-century Chicano poetry. Then, as if in supplement to the poetic dialogism envisioned by Savin and Bruce-Novoa, Torres evaluates social satire of bilingual verse. Edmundo Desnoes affirms that English and Spanish are essentially different, that speaking Spanish configures the speaker in certain ways that are profoundly characteristic.

Finally, *An Other Tongue* concludes with the interview I conducted with Gayatri Chakravorty Spivak, "Bonding in Difference." Like Todorov's and Desnoes's essays, it is a highly personal, subjective reflection on being in and between particular languages. I find it fitting closure to the book, for I was there at its occurrence and can attest both to its singularity and to its dialogism. And perhaps to bond in difference is what the ensuing essays seek to accomplish.

Berkeley
Summer 1993

7

Introduction

An

Other

Tongue

_____

Alfred

Arteaga

When I write about Chicano poetry, one of the first examples that comes to mind is José Montoya's "El Louie." I'm sure this is so because the poem strikes me as being thoroughly Chicano. It is, after all, about the high life and tragic end of Louie Rodríguez, exemplar of urban youth subculture; it is an elegy for a pachuco. And outside Chicano barrios, there exists nothing quite like the pachuco. Louie would dance both mambo and boogie and conflate the cultures from both sides of the border.

Yet more vital than Louie's story for me, as a poet and critic, is the language of Louie's story. And the language of "El Louie" matches its content: the verse is as thoroughly Chicano as is Louie's life. It begins, "Hoy enterraron al Louie / and San Pedro o sanpinche / are in for it . . ." [loosely, *Today they buried Louie / and heaven or hell / are in for it* . . .]. "El Louie" mixes languages in the style of popular Chicano speech: there is Spanish, there is English, and there is hybridization.

This style of multilingual hybridization is pushed to the extreme in a poem by José Antonio Burciaga. "Poema en tres idiomas y caló"

delineates the linguistic tensions embodied in the Chicano and is written in an interplay of languages, Spanish, English, Nahuatl, and the
Chicano hybridization, caló. Each of which is present in the following
two lines, "Mi mente spirals al mixtli, / buti suave I feel cuatro lenguas
in mi boca" [*My mind spirals to the clouds, / so smooth I feel four
tongues in my mouth*]. "Poema en tres idiomas y caló" acknowledges
the style of Chicano discourse and reflects the intercultural dynamics
at play in constructing Chicano identity. Being for Chicanos occurs in
the interface between Anglo and Latin America, on the border that is
not so much a river from the Gulf of Mexico to El Paso and a wire
fence from there to the Pacific but, rather, a much broader area where
human interchange goes beyond the simple "American or no" of the
border check. It is the space to contest cultural identities more complex than the more facile questions of legal status or images in popular
culture.

"El Louie" and "Poema en tres idiomas y caló" are born of a linguistic interplay that finds its central analog in the porous frontier.
Mexicans negotiate the border like no others, north and south, south
and north, realizing simultaneous cultural fission and fusion. It is this
border context that differentiates the styles of linguistic interplay of
Chicano poetry from other styles of polyglot poetics. The poetry of
Eliot and Pound, for example, incorporates other languages, from the
Italian of Dante to German conversation to Chinese characters. The
poetics of Montoya and Burciaga is similar to Eliot's and Pound's in
the fact of its linguistic hybridization, but the fact of the border contributes to a different emphasis in the styles of that multilingualism.
In Eliot and Pound there is much greater emphasis on quotation and
literary allusion, while in Montoya and Burciaga, poetic hybridization
tends to replicate the polyglot style of quotidian Chicano discourse.
The former often focuses on the content of that form (e.g., Dante's *In-
ferno*) and interlards "significant" texts; the later focuses on the form
of that form (e.g., caló, hybridization itself) and implements discursive
interaction.[1]

Because Chicano verse actualizes the discourse of the border and
embraces a broad range of difference, comparing the styles of linguistic interplay becomes a prime method of considering Chicano poetics.
One way that the styles of interplay can be compared is by juxtaposing the sizes of the linguistic units that play in the works of various
authors.[2] That is, from the macro to the micro, the monolingual unit
ranges from genres to texts to poetic and grammatical units to individual words and to morphemes, phonemes, and graphemes. Lucha

Corpi, for example, differentiates language at the level of genre: poetry is Spanish, *Palabras de mediodía* and *Variaciones sobre un tempestad* are two collections, while the novels are English, *Delia's Song* and *Eulogy for a Brown Angel*. For the poet, Juan Felipe Herrera, the monolingual unit tends to be the book. *Rebozos of Love* and *Akrilica* are primarily Spanish books, while *Exiles of Desire* and *Facegames* are English. Barbara Brinson Curiel, *Speak to Me from Dreams*, and Francisco X. Alarcón, *Cuerpo en Llamas* and *Snake Poems*, tend to vary language within the book, so that the monolingual unit is the poem, the stanza, or the phrase. Both José Montoya and José Antonio Burciaga alternate languages within the verse line and even within the individual word. In "El Louie," the word *shinadas* is a hybrid of English and Spanish, the English verb *to shine* is written as a Spanish past participle. This hybridization is a type of double voicing, as in "Poema en tres idiomas y caló," where Nahuatl infuses Spanish (*loco* becomes *locotl*) and English (*English* becomes *Englishic*). In Alurista's *Nationchild Plumaroja*, even the typeface speaks difference: the poems are printed in the script of barrio graffiti.

Border discourse contextualizes Chicano poetry to such an extent that even essentially monolingual verse is read within the larger framework of a multilingual poetics. Lorna Dee Cervantes's *Emplumada* is basically an English book, although it does have one Spanish language poem and Spanish words and phrases in others. Yet against the relative English consistency is manifested a subject matter of intercultural conflict. And it is a Spanish title that effects the unifying tropes of the text: *Emplumada*, that is, pen, feather, pen flourish, plumage. Even very monolingual texts, such as Lucha Corpi's *Palabras de Mediodía* and Bernice Zamora's *Restless Serpents*, are read as Chicano texts at the extremes of Chicano discourse but not beyond. Because the degree to which the discourse is polyglot, another language is implied, and such discourse imbues *Palabra* and *Serpent* with internal dialogue.

The border as discursive and existential fact does something to the interpretation of Chicano writing. It removes the discussion of the styles of linguistic interplay from the realm of the aesthetic alone because the border is a space where English and Spanish compete for presence and authority. It is not the site of mere either/or linguistic choice but one of quotidian linguistic conflict where the utterance is born at home in English and in Spanish and in caló. Here, verse is born of and sustained on conflict that has real world consequence. In the broad interface between Anglo and Latin America, the operative tropes, the definitions, the histories and logics and legal codes, the semantics and the epistemes are contested daily. Because of this, the study of literary style is inextricably bound up with that of discursive practice. And as Chicano discourse demarcates the realm of the poem, so it does the Chicano subject. Chicanismo occurs in the very nexus of languages and is continually marked by utterances in the linguistic borderlands.

In poem and in daily speech, English and Spanish bestow different levels of authority on text and speaker. The relative imbalance in authority grows daily in the present era of increasing legislative suppression of languages other than English. English carries with it the status of authorization by the hegemony. It is the language of Anglo America and of linguistic Anglo Americans, whether or not they be ethnic Anglos. Further, it is the language of the greatest military and economic power in the world. Spanish is a language of Latin Americans, south of the border and north. Across the border, Spanish is a Third World language; here it is the language of the poor.

Today as I write in Santa Cruz, California, the local newspaper carries an article that illustrates contemporary linguistic relations in the United States. It is an interesting variant to an otherwise common story in Chicano neighborhoods: the story of deportation. The article begins, "School and city officials expressed outrage this week over the Border Patrol's arrest of three Hispanic students outside an English as a Second Language class." Needless to say, the three were deported to Mexico. They were denied presence in "America" while trying to learn "American." Reading this from my Chicano perspective, I am struck by the irony of it: irony, not only that "officials expressed outrage" at so typical an INS action, but irony also, that the story made it into print in the first place.[3] For we have been trained to know that, despite the fact that we make up perhaps one in four in the state, what Mexicans, Chicanos, and Latinos say and do in our language is not worthy of print.

To speak, or even to attempt to learn to speak, sparks a display of power from the dominant group. It is within this system of unequal discursive relationships that Chicanos speak and write. This is evident, institutionally, in examples that range from the sixteen states that are officially English only, to the four English national language bills introduced into Congress *last year*, to the American Academy of Poets policy that the national Walt Whitman award be for English only verse. And from the congress to the academy to the streets, over and over, incessantly, an unequal struggle goes on in which Anglo America strives to inhibit dialogue, marginalize Chicanismo, and silence other tongues, and by synecdoche, silence other people.

But the United States is not a space where homogeneous speakers articulate a single language. It is, rather, the site of polyglossia, where multiple national languages interact. English is neither the sole nor original language. Yet, U.S. American culture presents itself as an English language culture; it espouses a single language ethos; it strives very actively to assert a monolingual identity. This is to say, its overriding tendency is toward the assertion of a monolingual authority and the complementary suppression of alternate languages. In Bakhtin's terms, this tendency is monologic, espousing the monologue of a dominant, authoritative discourse, eschewing dialogue with others. This monologic bias, from the English Only movement to the writing of U.S. history, valorizes English and suppresses expression both in and about Spanish.[4] English is elevated from the status of one language among languages, albeit the dominant one, to that of sole and pervasive language in general. This is coupled with the simultaneous erasure of Spanish through the restriction of its use and the interdiction of dialogue.

Because internal dialogue is so contributing a factor in the making of Chicano discourse, the dynamics of language are especially foregrounded in the verse and in the subjectification of the Chicano. Both come to be within a matrix that includes English, Spanish, and caló. This matrix, which Bakhtin calls heteroglossia, is the context of historical, interlingual, and interdiscursive factors that come into play in, and affect the meaning of, any utterance. Chicano poem and cultural subject acknowledge heteroglossia; this is what Chicano means: intercultural heteroglot. "American," according to the Anglo American's selective application of the continental name, means the suppression of heteroglossia and the selective recognition of only that set and sequence of factors that enhance the Self and that mark the alterity of Others. Distinctions of language, color, and religion are but some of the markers employed to subjugate. For Chicanos, linguistic practice has been the legal criteria to classify, to differentiate: Spanish Speaking, Spanish Surnamed, White Hispanic. Chicano subjectification is never far from the competition among languages.

The role of discursive activity in the creation and maintenance of identity can be neither disinterested nor indifferent. Each articulation is a taking of sides and a demarcation of subjects. There can be no objective disinterest within a situation of constantly unequal subjectification, for even to choose not to choose tacitly supports the status quo. It is comparable to the border check point question, "American or no?" Anything other than a prompt "yes," even a slight pause, causes suspicion and casts the American status of the speaker in doubt. For Chicanos it is patently clear: each utterance and textual manifestation identifies and aligns, promulgating one version of self, one dimension of space.[5]

So what does the Chicano discourse, does the Chicano poem do? First, in the common senses of language use, other than poetry, the mere presence of Chicano discourse resists Anglo American suppression of heteroglossia, much as the background noise of menials jars a social gathering. The presence of difference undermines the aspiration for an English-only ethos. And inasmuch as Chicano discourse is specifically multilingual and multivoiced, it further undermines the tendency toward single language and single-voiced monologue, that is, it undermines Anglo American monologism. It undercuts claims of prevalence, centrality, and superiority and confirms the condition of heteroglossia. It draws the monologue into dialogue. In short, it dialogizes the authoritative discourse.

And the poem? It is often maintained that poetry is a personal form of discourse, the particular discursive act of an individual poet. Bakhtin argued a generic distinction that poetry was formally monologic, the single-voiced discourse [edinogolosnoe slovo] of the individual poet.[6] He felt that it could not articulate the double-voiced discourse [dvugolosnoe slovo] of the polyglot novel. Bakhtin eventually reduced the absoluteness of his epic/novel differentiation, yet he nevertheless maintained that it was novelistic discourse that enabled the dialogues among social discourses, as well as that between character and author.

But clearly there is a tradition of poetry that is, at least in form, multilingual. Eliot and Pound emphasize the content of that form in the creation of poetic pastiche in poems that blend polyglot quotation and allusion with lines of English language, modernist verse. Eliot's quoting Dante, for example, by the simple fact of including Italian, does make for a bilingual poetry, and one that is, in a sense, double-voiced. But to the extent that the work is resonant with the authoritative discourse, whether it be Anglo Catholic Royalist or Mussolini Fascist, such bilingualism is not disharmonious with English or Italian nationalist tendency toward single-voiced monologism. This is to say that in this fashion, literary citation and allusion function in a manner that does not oppose the national narratives; indeed, such literary hybridization functions as a self-referential and tautological affirma-

Alfred
Arteaga

tion of the national telos: the hailing of the great dead establishes the continuity of cultural transmission to the latter day.[7]

This, I realize, is a generalization that here only serves to contrast a very different poetics undertaken by Montoya and Burciaga; it ignores completely, for example, Eliot's or Pound's incorporation of common and quotidian speech. Nevertheless, it remains obvious that the two Chicano poets do not cite in the same manner but instead implement an interlingual style that emphasizes the form of the form. Their caló is multilingual and double-voiced in its eclectic hybridization. Its style opposes standard English and opposes the canonical literary telos. It conflicts with the authoritative discourse; it is dialogic. It is in this sense that the simple contrast of styles is possible.[8] The strategy of Eliot and Pound can be understood to emphasize the selective drawing from the treasure house of texts central to Western culture, texts that constitute the authoritative discourse. The strategy of Montoya and Burciaga can be understood to emphasize the style of linguistic hybridization of the present-day border context, hybridization that dialogizes the Anglo American monologue. That Chicano poetry upsets the authoritative lines of American literature and of the American Self makes for a type of poetry that requires the consideration of the discourse and power relations that form its context.

The study of discursive practices that specifically subjugate and subjectify colonized peoples overlaps with Bakhtin's more general work in the shared focus on the work of language by which one group fashions authority over another. It specifically examines the process of subject formation within the context of a gross imbalance of power. The relationships between Britain and India or between Britain and Ireland, for example, are overdetermined by colonial contexts. Still today, the colonial language, English, figures prominently in the construction of Indian and of Irish identities. Colonial discursive practices are more immediately tied to displays of physical power than are the literary discursive practices that Bakhtinian analysis is usually employed to describe. Each colonial situation is unique, yet common to all are the conquest and domination of one people by another and a dominant, monologic discourse whose employment is linked to violence.

Colonial discourse criticism applied to internal U.S. relations would make manifest that the Chicano is *identified* as Other for the United States. The subjectification of the Chicano occurs within the context of an Anglo American domination that assigns marginality as a constitutive component. Within that context, each speech act is perlocutionary and differentiates in the act uttering. The Chicano subject is marginal because the signifier and signified "chicano" are marginal-ized in Anglo American discourse. The sign "chicano" and the sub-ject "chicano" are made alien by the centripetal forces of monologism that strive to locate the Self at the center and to locate the Other at the margins. The Other is contained, linguistically and spatially, on reservations, in barrios, in the colonies, far from the centers of the colonizer's Self and home and female body. "Chicano" exists, to the limited extent that it does exist, as a marker of difference, of inferi-ority and alterity. Being "chicano" is a process of continual remaking, a discursive process that is always negotiated within the context of the circumscribing discursive practices of the United States.

Any monologism, with its drive toward a unitary and self-refle(x/ct)ive discourse, discriminates Self from Other, but in the colonial situation, it radically differentiates the identities of colonizer and colo-nized. The extreme power differential prescribes literal subjectification through regimentation of semantics and prescribes physical subjuga-tion through regimentation of the body. The colonizer's language and discourse are elevated to the status of arbiter of truth and reality; the world comes to be as the authoritative discourse says. For discur-sive practice does not simply represent colonialism after the fact but rather functions as the means to order colonial relations and to estab-lish meaning of those relations, in short, to define the world for the benefit of the colonizer. It is this absoluteness of authority in the face of alternate discourses and other peoples that characterizes colonial relationships, relationships such as those between English and Irish, between Anglo American and Sioux, between white and black South African.[9]

The dominant discourse has such authority that it becomes adopted, in varying degrees, by the colonized subject. What begins during the conquest, in the precolonialism, as an externally imposed represen-tation, becomes, in colonialism per se and in postcolonialism, a self-imposed subjectification. The marginal Other autocolonizes himself and herself each time the hegemonic discourse is articulated. The utterance of English in Ireland or the use of a British-styled school system in India reinforces daily the colonizer's presence in the heart of the colonized. The authoritative discourse is, after all, a prescribed monologue structured to inhibit dialogue with the natives. Who would read these lines I now write, if they were written in caló? According to the monologue, the colonized subject is homogeneous and static, a silent text that can be written and read but never talked with. For this subject, discourse is itself textualized, a codified set of relationships

Alfred
Arteaga

and prescribed responses that delimit a fixed reality. The colonized subject becomes the (sub)altern Other prescribed by the dominant discourse in the act of articulating that discourse. The Other comes to be according to and, illustrates the validity of, an externally constructed social text.

Autocolonialism is perhaps most marked in those situations where the colonist never goes home, that is, in internal colonialism. In the United States, "internal colonialism" was first employed in the 1960s to describe the "colonization" of black Americans in white America.[10] Black nationalists and social scientists used it to describe a situation analogous to the colonial except that the colonized space was permanently encompassed by the colonizer space, that is, the colonist never left the colony. Within the confines of the United States, American Indians, Chicanos, and Puerto Ricans share the experience of conquest and continued occupation by Anglo America; blacks represent that special conquest, the forced immigration of the slave. None were originally English speakers.[11] But for them, after the decimation of conquest, enslavement, or genocide, the acceptance of the colonizer's linguistic practices has translated into an increase in life span and perceived human worth and a decrease in lynching and forced sterilization. The discursive relationships that constitute internal colonies are similar to those that constitute external colonies; the methods that describe the discursive processes that have subjugated and subjectified Indian, Irish, Algerian, and Aztec are methods that can illuminate the processes of internal colonialism within the United States.

In response to colonialism, there are several general reactions available for the colonized Other. Very generally, the reactions can be described according to different criteria as either autocolonial, nationalist, or hybrid, on the one hand, or as monologic or dialogic, on the other. The former describes the difference between the colonized's and the colonizer's discourse; the latter describes the relative tendency to engage in dialogue. Autocolonialism, in the extreme, requires the Other's adoption of the hegemonic discourse to the extent that the colonizer permits and to the extent that the Other is able to predicate it. The Other assimilates both discourse and the relationships it systematizes, so to the degree the discourse suppresses, the autocolonist effaces or denigrates him/herself from within. In the endeavor to mimic the monologue of power, the Other harmonizes with it and suppresses difference. Autocolonialism discourages dialogue. It is monologic.

Nationalism opposes the authority of the colonial discourse with the authority of an alternate discourse. Nationalist discourse defines itself in the related actions of rejecting the externally imposed system of representation and advancing an indigenous one. The alien, colonially defined world is rejected in favor of the native, nationalistically defined world. The articulation of difference would seem to dehegemonize colonial authority by its presence alone, and in a sense it does do this. The move to *select* one discourse over another is dialogic, but the content of that selection, the nationalist monologue, is monologic. Nationalism *combines* native elements into a privileged discourse, deaf *[gluxoj]*, as Bakhtin would say, to a deaf colonial discourse. Their "dialogue" is the clash of senseless monologues. Its overriding tendency is monologic.

Hybridization, or cultural mestizaje, differs from both autocolonialism and nationalism in that it is inherently polyglot. Hybridized discourse rejects the principle of monologue and composes itself by selecting from competing discourses. Further, there is no detritus of difference; distinct elements remain so, relating in a dialogue of dissimilarity. Hybridization asserts dialogue by articulating an alternate discourse and by organizing itself in internal dialogue. It is born of the struggles for discursive dominance and relates within itself and with other discourses according to the principle of dialogue. It is dialogic because it is so multivoiced.

The discursive actions, which authorize colonialism's stringent monologue and extreme power displacement, prescribe antithesis as the ordering factor of differentiation. Antithesis engenders a propitious rhetoric of difference that opposes the favorable representation of one people to the radical marginalization of a homogeneous and alien Other. Colonial and monologic discourse transpires through the rhetorical fashioning of what, from the dominant viewpoint, is a fortuitous reality. There can be no objective, disinterested discourse in colonial relationships.

Antithetical subjectification and radical differentiation are rhetorically determined as the dominant group employs its available discourses (e.g., science, religion, law, art) in order to constitute, codify, and read its literal power. Scientific discourse has been used to quantify and qualify, to prove (empirically or logically, for example), the *essentially* different nature of the Other. Examples range from the Victorian biologists' fetishization of the female, especially black female, buttocks and genitals[12] to the more contemporary gender and racial discrimination through ostensibly objective intelligence testing. Religious discourse defines the good and the bad, the right and the wrong.

Alfred
Arteaga

Even in seemingly moderate form, it identifies the heathen and heretic and is typically employed in the rhetoric of genocide, be it of Jews or Armenians this century or of American Indians before. The law, of course, defines citizen, alien, slave and constrains woman, child, Indian. Presently, it determines who is countable in the census and what languages can be spoken at the workplace.[13] Art differentiates the beautiful from the ugly, the civilized from the primitive, art from kitsch, the subject from the nonsubject. For not only does artistic discourse fashion the representation of peoples, it also discriminates who is to be represented and who represents.[14]

These and other discourses designate alterity by denoting essential and characteristic distinctions, differentiae such as race, region, nationality, ethnicity, religion, language, as well as those of class, time, age, and gender. These features are read as antithetical differentiae that prove the marginality that they designate. Tautologically, art confirms superior racial beauty and a higher degree of civilization; science, superior intelligence, and the transcending of superstition; religion and law, superior soul and body; history, the correct sequence of ascendance to that superiority. Historical discourse is especially significant in that the hegemonic history is the dominant narrative, the official version of reality to date as well as the plot for the future.

The rhetoric of monologic colonial discourse can be observed to proceed as follows. Subjectification of the Other is realized by the rhetoric of antithesis and synecdoche. The centripetal forces of antithesis exteriorize the Other. The colonial Self is present, here and central, the Other, there and marginal, absent. The Self differs *in essence* from the Other. *They* are not like *us:* they are not our color; their god is not God; their beliefs are not true, not science, etc. Antithesis allows for an open troping by which the Other can be relegated to anything beyond the borders of Self: the Other is colored, pagan, superstitious; the Other is primitive, savage, beast.[15] The more intense the monologism, the more open the troping, the more extreme the alterity.

Within the range of potential antithetical tropes, synecdoche functions to locate the troping of the Other within a narrow band of essential homogeneity. The rhetoric of antithesis restricts heterogeneity to the dominant Self, and synecdoche acts to disallow individuation to the Other. To know one is to know all. The characteristics of the group are the characteristics of each individual. Within acceptable and well-defined parameters, the Others are all the same. And yet, there is the occasional interstice in the homogeneity, when the rhetoric is forced to recognize an "individual" Other: the good slave, the Indian scout, the token "spook who sat by the door." But the number of such individuals must be severely restricted in order to maintain the image of homogeneity, that image that ensures the verisimilitude of the antithesis.

Not only is subjectivity fashioned through, and are actions informed by, the rhetoric of the dominant discourse, but identity and action are legitimated through a strategy of ultimate referentiality. Colonial discourse aspires toward a system of representation in which word is linked contiguously with reality, in which hegemonic story is true history. For the aspiration of monologue is the aspiration for the single language, single voice, and single version of social relationships.[16] Monologic authority is vested in the metonymic organization of discursive elements into the correct combinations that constitute the true history and the real political borders. Colonial discourse emphasizes referent and content, appropriating the epistemes of "truth" and "reality" in an endeavor to surpass metonymy and achieve the status of mirror, where the word reflects exactly and uniquely the world. This is to say, the hegemony envisions so contiguous a discourse that the troping collapses from consciousness and the power of discursive representation is rewritten as the power of literal presentation. It eschews the chaotic relativities of dialogue and the substitution of metaphors and aims, instead, at apodictic reference to the world.

This so referentially "true" discourse is not, however, aphasic discourse, as Jakobson would describe a solely metonymic discourse, but rather, a *phasic* one that oscillates between the axis of combination (metonymy and synecdoche) and the axis of selection (metaphor and irony). The contents of the ethnocentric and racist trope can range from "cannibal" and "redskin" to "animal" and "noble savage." But the form of relating those tropes, the organizing strategy, is combinatory rather than selective, syntagmatic rather than paradigmatic, and metonymic rather than metaphoric. Alternate versions of social relationships, that is, alternate paradigms, are proscribed through the prohibition of dialogue. Instead, the monologue of the mirror presents the authorized versions of reality, truth, telos. Rhetoric is refashioned as logic, and tropes disappear in a semantics of reference in which the meaning of the Other *is* the trope for the Other. The monologue strings together discourses favorable for the physical domination of a people, from the writing of stereotypes, to the creation of slaves, to the making of genocide.

These "truths" shape the "reality" in which the relative presence and absence of the Other is juggled. Antithetically, the Other is generally rendered absent, exteriorized from the central and present Self. But at times, the Other is brought into dangerous proximity. During physically violent encounters, as in the conquest, the Other is at once vividly represented as a dangerous presence and is effaced of full humanity. A present body, absent voice, absent humanity. Necessary for conquest, and for genocide, is the "truth" that the colonized is in some ways both dangerous and inferior, perhaps as wild beasts. The Other is a homogeneous menace, significant yet generalized, dangerous yet never humanly present.

In contexts of relatively diminished physical force, the Other is more fully relegated to the realm of absence. The more fully realized the physical subjugation is, the less is the need to represent a dangerous proximity, and so the less the Other need be envisioned present. Further, the Other is denied discursive presence, both in the sense that the Other is relatively absent from the vocabulary of the dominant discourse and in the sense that the Other is absent as an agent of discourse. The Other becomes nondiscursive and noninteractive and approaches the status of text: static, extant, "true." The hegemony restricts access to active discourse to itself. The Other is textualized, and according to traditional Western metaphysics, the written text, the literal Other, is denied presence: the Other is exteriorized, frozen, inscribed. Effectively, the Other is silenced, existing only as defined by a rigid and prescribed alterity or not existing at all.

Chicanos are products of two colonial contexts. The first begins with the explorer Colón and the major event of the Renaissance: the "old" world's "discovery" of the "new." Spanish colonization of the Americas lasted more than three centuries, from the middle of Leonardo da Vinci's lifetime to the beginning of Queen Victoria's. The first century is marked by conquest and true genocide: in Mexico alone, the indigenous population is cut down 96 percent, from 25 million to 1 million. The modern Mexican and Chicano descend from the miscegenation of Spaniard and Indian and the cultural encounter of conquistador and native. The second colonial context begins with the immigration of Austin's group from Connecticut to Texas, Mexico. Within one generation of Mexico's decolonization from Spain, two wars were waged in which Anglo America conquers Mexico and acquires its northern half. People were acquired with the lands, and the "Americanization" of natives in Texas, New Mexico, and California is analogous to that of natives in Manhattan, the Dakotas, Puerto Rico, or Hawaii. But because only half of Mexico was acquired, immigration can still figure largely in the constitution of the Chicano. Conversely, the territory of the Navajo, as that of the Puerto Rican, is entirely circumscribed by the United States; there can be only internal migration.[17]

Yet, for the Chicano, as for the Indian, the history of subjugation at home delimits the process of subject making. For both groups, alterity has coincided with the erasure of the Other domain, the Other space having been assimilated by the United States: Chicanos and Indians are rendered aliens from and in their own lands, internally colonized. The colonizer never left Indian nor Chicano space, neither Manhattan nor San Francisco. Shaping the original conception of the conquests, its subsequent rationalization, and its eventual erasure from U.S. consciousness, colonial discourse represented and continues to represent Chicanos and Indians as marginal and inferior Others.

Both are not real Americans in many senses, including the linguistic, and for both "being" "American" remains problematic. To a large degree, both the colonial Indian and Chicano subjects are constructed according to the representation of their linguistic practices. The Indian, at the time of the conquest and when compared to the middle-class WASP archetype upheld as the American national Self, is relatively less literate. Anglo America is both deaf and blind to Indian expression. This is read as "proof" of inferiority. Indigenous languages had no words for Jesus, for money, for opera, ergo, the Indian is uncivilized, savage, and quite likely, subhuman.[18] And by extrapolation, Indians can only benefit from conquest, that is, it renders Indians civilized, genocide and colonialism save Indians' souls, and further, Indians are so worthless in their "wild" stage that the world would loose little at their elimination. Such is the rhetoric that forgets the complete extermination of some Indian people and the suppression of the rest.

A threshold marked by the ability to write separates Civilized Man from the savage beings, and among the literate, human worth is appraised, at least in part, according to the relative values ascribed in a hierarchy of languages. The Chicano subject may be subaltern, but in so far as, and to the degree that, the subject is Hispanic, the Chicano is human. And since Spanish is relatively close to English in the linguistic hierarchy, the suppression of Hispanic America is more problematic and of a different order than the nearly absolute suppression of Algonquian, Athapascan, or Uto-Aztecan America.[19] The presence of an alternative, extant, and *literate* linguistic tradition causes a crisis for Anglo America: not only does it preclude the status for English as sole, unchallenged mode for civilized American discourse, but it also undermines several myths that are at the very heart of the self-image propagated by Anglo America.

Part of the inspiration, orchestration, and rationalization for New World colonialism lies in the troping of the Americas as a new world and in the paramount role envisioned for the Anglo American. Anglo American mythology would have it that the United States is so much more than a mere extension of Western Europe, that it is the first blank slate since Eden, the new and perhaps last chance to get things right. Anglo Americans met the challenge and performed that most elemental and significant of linguistic acts: the monologic, Adamic act of ascribing meaning, naming the new items in the new world. They inscribed themselves American Adams, invented new political institutions, forged new cities in the peopleless (not counting savages) wilderness.

History is a narrative, made story with plot, with telos, with heroes and villains. The United States locates itself at the climax and terminus of the trajectory of Western Civilization that began at the original Eden. The move West, from Eden to the thirteen colonies, traces not only the spatial relocation but, more importantly, the historical development of civilization proper, through Greece and Rome, the English 're-'naissance, and peaking at the American naissance of Adam Jr. Egypt, the rest of Africa, and the "Orient," of course, are ignored. And according to Western cartography, the West does not stop at Appalachia; there is a manifest destiny; civilization was destined to move as far West as possible, to the edge of that ultimate boundary with the East, to that ultimate "shining sea."

And en route west, the Anglo encountered Indian and Chicano, both of whom left traces in the dominant discourse. Indian names and words have been taken to describe American places, athletic teams, motor homes. The use of these terms evokes pride in the conquest, much in the same manner as a mounted animal head does for the hunter. After all, the actual people, the Indians, have been successfully contained: first their numbers have been thoroughly diminished, and second, those remaining are powerless, have the shortest life spans and highest infant mortality rates, and either are collected in remote areas far from Anglo Americans or are somehow invisible in the cities. The conquest of the "wild west" has been so efficient, the containment of the "redskins" so thorough, that contemporary mention of these peoples is read by Anglo America as allusion to the cast of colorful characters in American history, beginning with Pocahontas and ending with Geronimo. On the national level, the Indian exists as story, not as living human. There can be no dialogue with the Indian text; the Indian can only be written about or read. The Indian is thoroughly contained and can no longer pose a menacing threat.[20] Because of this, the second Wounded Knee can become a cause célèbre, Dennis Banks and Russell Means become inscribed beside Sitting Bull: the attack on Anglo America is so marginal and so contained that it can be romanticized; contemporary Indian resistance is understood through the narratives of nostalgia. After all, what *real* damage can those absent, silent, noble savages, those ecologically correct, happy campers, do?

But since the conquest of Mexican territory, there persists a stubborn linguistic trace that belies Anglo American image production and that is more difficult to contain than by simple appropriation for the naming of motor homes. Consider a particularly significant self-image: Anglo Americans epitomize their imperialist spirit in the cowboy: independent, powerful, free, implacable, and ever-moving westward through the vast wilderness, fashioning America. And as such, the cowboy represents the quintessential American. That cowboys appear only after the U.S. acquisition of northern Mexico is no mere coincidence: could the cowboy have occurred in Georgia or in Vermont, or in Surrey, at that?

And yet, the paramount Anglo American is thoroughly contaminated by a Mexican, a Hispanic, presence. Cowboy attire, tools, occupation, food, music, and most telling, his own lingo continually reveal this Other origin. The very language that marks the cowboy has a Spanish accent. Consider the cowboy lexicon and its context of Spanish language and border discourse: arroyo/*arroyo*; bukeroo/vaquero; canyon/*cañon*; chaps/*chaparreras*; cinch/*cincho*; cowboy/*vaquero*; desperado/*desperado*; hoosegow/*juzgado*; lariat/*la reata*; loco/*loco*; lasso/*lazo*; mesquite/*mesquite*; mustang/*mestengo*; pinto/*pinto*; ranch/*rancho*; renegade/*renegado*; rodeo/*rodeo*. But by selectively reading the heteroglossia, the cowboy icon is figured a singularly American and new phenomenon: the cowboy and his lingo are conceived as U.S. originals; the Spanish, Mexican, Chicano etymology is erased.[21]

The linguistic trace also persists in place names. When Anglo Americans finally acquired the western edge, California, they found existing cities already named: San Diego, Los Angeles, San José, San Francisco. The western "wilderness" had been already inscribed by Hispanics, much as the contemporary Chicano neighborhood is inscribed with barrio identifying graffiti placas. The new Eden had been denied Adam Jr.; things were already named, and worse yet, they had been *written* well before he and she arrived. Even California, the prize of the conquest and today's most populous state, especially California, undermines the myth: California was named in Spanish a century before the U.S.'s Anglo baptism, their first Thanksgiving.

The Chicano incarnates the Hispanic (i.e., literate, European, human, antecedent) inscription of America and makes evident the Anglo American rhetorical postscript. Unlike the Indian trace, the Chicano's remains threatening. There are so many more Chicanos than Indians. Los Angeles, for example, has the largest urban concentrations of both Indians and Chicanos in the nation. It is not rural New Mexico where Indians and Chicanos remain far from the national consciousness. Los Angeles is home to perhaps 80,000 Indians and perhaps 1.4 million Chicanos and other Latinos. In 1990 the population of Chicanos/Latinos in California alone is greater than the population of any of forty-two other states. Within California, Chicanos equal the combined total of all other minorities; in ten years, white non-Hispanics will fall from the position of majority, a position they hold, partially at least, when compared to Indians and Chicanos, because of a superior life span. In twenty-five years, the largest ethnic group in California will be Chicanos/Hispanics. In reaction to such rapid change, Anglo American rhetoric constructs a Chicano subject with minimal presence, with maximum absence. The growing discrepancy between rhetorical "truth" and existential fact works toward the impending "white shock" when Anglo Americans realize all in not as it seems. Witness the "shock" of Anglo Americans at the reaction of Los Angeles blacks to the acquittals of police in the beating of Rodney King, "white shock" at the intensity of black perceptions of a racist here and now.

In order to foster an image of an America born in the English language, it becomes necessary to propagate a story of contiguous and historical English precedence. Millennia of Native American presence is easily glossed over because Westerners read nothing of it. Hispanic America is more difficult to dismiss, but this is accomplished nevertheless. For example, history is not written chronologically but, rather, from East to West so that Spanish is encountered by the likes of Austin and Fremont during the Western expansion late in U.S. history, it appears *historically* after English. Spanish is made alien, an immigrant language, no more contiguously linked to America than is German or Chinese. There must be no Hispanicization of Anglo America, neither in its history nor in its future. Even cowboy lingo must be envisioned to arise from an English only monologue; it must not resemble an interlingual caló. These moves are advanced rhetorically and not logically. The history and contiguity of Spanish in the Southwest is denied in history book, popular culture, and through language laws.

A correlative of the displacement of Spanish is the illiteracy of the Chicano. Chicanos are depicted as nonwriting subjects who did not produce literature until taught English by Anglo Americans.[22] This erasure of a linguistic and literary tradition enhances the marginalization of Spanish, both from Anglo America and from the Chicano writer, and moves the Chicano from the pole of civilized Western European culture toward the pole of the illiterate savage. There is no Hispanic history of the Southwest and, besides, caló is no real language at all. Linguistically then, the Chicano speaks a language that has no real claim to the Southwest, speaks it poorly (it is not real Castilian) and worst of all, does not write it. In effect, the Chicano is like the Indian.

And in fact this is so declared: the Chicano is inscribed "savage," marginalized from the Eurocentric appellation "Hispanic." The Chicano is de-hispanized and written as dark, uncivilized Indian. The Spaniard is romanticized and relegated to the historical past: conquistador, mission padre, and aristocratic Californio. The historical link is broken because of racial difference (Caucasian versus hybrid mestizo), because of linguistic difference (Castilian versus Mexican Spanish and caló), and because of chronological difference (Spaniards of the past versus Chicanos of the present). The myth of Zorro contains the Spanish element in a safe, remote past; today's Chicano is not descended from Zorro and the other Spanish Californios, but at best, from their servants. In effect, the Chicano is located between Europe and indigenous America, marginalized from the Spaniard, moved partially toward the savage. Both Indian and Spaniard, the constitutive elements of the Chicano's mestizaje, are deferred to a safe past and are removed from consideration in the making of contemporary America. By envisioning both as "historical" and small in number, they pose little threat to American consciousness, and they can be romanticized and distantly acknowledged in Thanksgiving and Old California. But the number of Chicanos, the most rapidly increasing number, threatens the verisimilitude of the Anglo American vision.

The Chicano is not equated with the Indian because to do so would ascribe to the Chicano the status of native. Because of the border and Mexico, the Chicano can be envisioned as foreigner, so that after rhetorical gymnastics, the Anglo immigrant can write the Self as the undisputed original civilized human occupant. Therefore, the Chicano is not indigenous. Chicanos are foreign immigrants and illegal aliens.

The INS and the Texas Rangers attest to that.[23] Present-day Chicanos are divorced spatially from Mexicans south of the border, temporally from the Californio, and racially from the Indian. Chicanos are divorced from the Southwest and read, instead, as an immigrant labor force. Not the noble and savage Indian nor the genteel Californio Spaniard, the Chicano is the pest, is the bracero who had the audacity to stay and have children in gangs and on welfare.

One more point, a historical one: in order to project a narrative of the apex of democracy, the history of the U.S. military conquest of northern Mexico is written as a simple financial transaction. That Anglo America is superior and preferable must be self-evident, so there could not have been objection. The Chicano could not have wanted to resist colonization, let alone actually have done so. Therefore, the conquest of Northern Mexico was not imperialism; it was a bloodless transfer of title of an unpopulated territory. History simultaneously maintains that the Mexicans from California to Texas, who weren't there in the first place, welcomed U.S. incorporation in a very poor Spanish but not in writing.

In these ways, and in many, many other ways, Anglo American colonial discourse subjectifies and contains; it minimizes the presence of the Chicano Other. A heterogeneous group is represented as a marginal homogeneity. The authoritative discourse constitutes the colonist mythology and codifies the hegemony.

Chicano literary production can be read as the response to such discursive activity. Chicano poetry has opted for hybridization, a linguistic mestizaje, incorporating the languages and discourses at play in America. It tends to reject the monologue of either autocolonial, assimilationist, English-only verse or the monologue of nationalist Spanish-only verse. Instead, it opts for a multiple tongue, multivoiced literature of the border. The hegemony of Anglo American representation and subjectification is dialogized by a mestizaje of heteroglot texts that assert Chicano heterogeneity and American heteroglossia.

Such literature produces a subjectivity that opposes hegemonic subjectification: the alternate subjectification of the Other challenges the authoritative subjectification of the dominant Self, juxtaposing a literary representation with a literal representation. For it is in the realm of the literary that orders other than the literal can be first envisioned.[24] And this literary dialogism is characteristic of Chicano poetry.

Consider the poem "Poema en tres idiomas y caló"[25] by José Antonio Burciaga. It plays among four languages and clearly works in an other tongue:

Poema en tres idiomas y caló

Españotli titlan Englishic,
titlan náhuatl titlan Caló
¡Qué locotl!
Mi mente spirals al mixtli,
buti suave I feel cuatro lenguas in mi boca.
Coltic sueños temostli
Y siento una xóchitl brotar
from four diferentes vidas.

I yotl distictamentli recuerdotl
cuandotl I yotl was a maya,
cuandotl, I yotl was a gachupinchi,
when Cortés se cogió a mi great tatarabuela,
cuandotl andaba en Pachucatlán.

I yotl recordotl el tonatiuh
en mi boca cochi
cihuatl, nahuatl
teocalli, my mouth
micca por el English
e hiriendo mi español,
ahora cojo ando en caló
pero no hay pedo
porque todo se vale,
con o sin safos.

Poem in Three Idioms and Caló

Spanish between English
between Nahuatl, between Caló.
How mad!
My mind spirals to the clouds
so smooth I feel four tongues in my mouth.
Twisted dreams fall
and I feel a flower bud
from four different lives.

I distinctly remember
when I was a Maya,
when I was a Spaniard,
when Cortez raped my great great grandmother
when I walked over the Southwest.

I remember the sun
in my mouth sleeps
woman, Nahuatl
temple my mouth,
killed by the English
and wounding my Spanish,
now I limp walk in fractured Spanish
But there is no problem
for everything is valid
with or without safeties.

Notes

1 I am, of course, speaking of relative differences. But it is worth contrasting Eliot's "The Waste Land" with Burciaga's "Poema en tres idiomas y caló" (the complete text of Burciaga's poem is appended to the end of this essay). Clearly the styles of their multilingual poems differ sharply, and it is worthwhile to ask of these poems what discourses come into dialogue and who are the participants in dialogue

2 Bruce-Novoa noted the qualitative differences in the styles of multilingualism in his seminal contrasting of "bilingualism" and "interlingualism" in "The Other Voice of Silence: Tino Villanueva," *Modern Chicano Writers*, ed. Joseph Sommers (New York: Prentice Hall, 1979), 133–40.

3 I wrote these words on January 12, 1990, the day that "Border Patrol's School Raid Outrages Officials" (Kimura A3) appeared in the *Santa Cruz Sentinel*. In addition, there was another "chicano" article four pages later, "Has Law Led to Discrimination?" (Bishop A7), which begins, "A state panel has concluded that the 1986 immigration law has resulted in widespread job discrimination against Hispanic residents and others." It too strikes me as dramatically ironic.

4 Of course, other languages are also suppressed. Language marginalization can be accorded by degree of dissimilarity, linguistic Anglos valuing more highly German than Vietnamese, for example, and by a variety of other factors of perceived worth. French or Latin can be valued more highly than Yiddish or Gaelic for reasons of imagined cultural purity, aesthetics, or antecedence.

5 The distinction between "making an identity" and "making a space" can be considered to be the difference in conceiving subjectification either a metaphoric or a metonymic relation of discursive elements. The perception of subjectification as the creation of identity, if "creation" is seen as a choice from potential identities, would emphasize selection and paradigm. Finding a space, as the border, for example, would seem relatively more dependent on spatial context, on contiguity, syntagma.

6 As Bakhtin says, "The world of poetry, no matter how many contradictions and insoluble conflicts the poet develops within it, is always illumined

by one unitary and indisputable discourse. Contradictions, conflicts and doubts remain in the object, in thoughts, in living experiences—in short, in the subject matter—but they do not enter into the language itself," *Dialogic Imagination* (Austin: U of Texas P, 1981), 286. And yet this is qualified. Todorov observes that in his later writing, Bakhtin blurs the absolute distinction between the genres, "Should poetry attempt to avail itself of this resource [multiple voices], it is immediately drawn to the side of the novel. Bakhtin constantly cites Pushkin's *Eugene Onegin* as an example of the novel, not of poetry," *Mikhail Bakhtin: The Dialogic Principle* (Minneapolis: U of Minnesota P, 1984), 64.

7   I take up this issue at greater length in another context. In "Tricks of Gender Xing," *Stanford Humanities Review* 3.1 (1993), I examine the gender and racial politics of the imperial Spanish telos and how its narrative line is "crossed" by Sor Juana Inés de la Cruz in colonial Mexico.

8   There are other ways to consider the differences of these multilingual styles. One is to recall Bruce-Novoa's distinction between bilingualism and interlingualism so as to contrast Eliot and Pound's *alternation* of languages with Montoya and Burciaga's *hybridization*. Another way is to bring into consideration the border. Eliot and Pound were willing immigrants to countries they felt to be seminal to the course of Western Civilization. That Eliot became "more British than the British" and Pound preached Mussolini propaganda demonstrate a marked degree of assimilation. For Montoya and Burciaga, and Chicanos in general, the border is not so much a line to cross en route to becoming another but more of a zone where one lives and has to struggle to articulate an intercultural self. Following this differentiation, it is interesting to look at the essays in this volume by Todorov and Savin. Savin addresses Todorov's "Dialogism and Schizophrenia" in her "Bilingualism and Dialogism: Another Reading of Lorna Dee Cervantes's Poetry" arguing that there is a great distinction between the "chosen" bilingualism of the willing immigrant and the "obligatory" bilingualism of the nonimmigrant minority.

9   Clearly, the colonial relationship requires an extreme exercise of power, yet there are other relationships that require a tremendous amount of power; class and gender relationships are two obvious examples. Exhaustive and continual discursive activity is required to establish and maintain those relationships and the unequal distributions of power that structure them. In addition, the marginalization of those at the extremes of the human age range and those with low mental or physical capabilities, requires huge expenditures of energy. Then too, the expenditures of energy in maintaining the psychology, for example, of "superiority" are significant.

10   The seminal text is Robert Blauer's *Racial Oppression in America* (New York: Harper, 1972). Chicano historians who employ the internal colonial model include Rodolfo Acuña, *Occupied America* (New York: Harper, 1981), and Mario Barrera, *Race and Class in the Southwest* (Notre Dame: Notre Dame U P, 1979). In *Internal Colonialism: The Celtic Fringe in British National Development, 1536–1966* (Berkeley: U of California P, 1975), Michael Hechter cites the popularization of the term "internal colonialism" among U.S. black nationalists in the 1960s but traces its earlier

use by Lenin in *The Development of Capitalism in Russia* and by Gramsci in "The Southern Question."

11 Compared to Indians and Chicanos, blacks are linguistically more auto-colonized: they speak English; they are the most "Americanized"; their cultural production is most integrated into Anglo American culture. And yet, they remain extremely marginalized. While the former slaves may have assimilated the master's language, they have reworked it in the process. By rewriting Standard American English, black English dehegemonizes it.

12 A very good discussion of this is Sander L. Gilman's "Black Bodies, White Bodies: Toward an Iconography of Female Sexuality in Late Nineteenth-Century Art, Medicine, and Literature," ed. Henry Louis Gates, *"Race," Writing and Difference* (Chicago: U of Chicago P, 1986), 223–61. Noteworthy is the reliance of scientific discourse on synecdoche: one part of the black female anatomy signaled the essential difference of the black race; the size of Sarah Bartmann's buttocks "proved" the subhumanity of all blacks. And still today, the physical artifact, that is, the scientific "proof," the dismembered flesh of the most famous raceme, Sarah Bartmann's buttocks and genitals, remain on display for scientific study in the aptly named Museé de l'homme in Paris.

13 The enumeration and distribution of Chicanos is currently a hot topic in U.S. law. The census question of counting "illegals" embraces several concerns: the definition of "illegal" (read Mexican), the relative value (does one illegal equal one legal?), the significance of as accurate a count of illegals as for legals. States like Texas and California demand that illegals be counted. Cities like New York and Los Angeles demand accuracy so that none be missed. At the same time, Los Angeles is being sued for gerrymandering district lines to restrict Chicano representation in the city council. These points illustrate the borders which exist north of the border.

"Legal" language, that is, language use permitted by law, remains a major concern for Chicanos. Corporal punishment has been regularly employed throughout the Southwest for the speaking of Spanish in public schools. The beating of children has recently been outlawed in California but remains appropriate behavior in Texas. On the other hand, it is currently illegal in California and Florida, for example, to speak any language other than English while on the job at certain workplaces.

14 Art cultivates racism in two related ways: first, artistic discourse denies the Other presence and second, to the limited extent that is does represent the Other, it denigrates. Art as racist representation is the subject of two contemporary reviews. Richard Dorment considers black absence in *Times Literary Supplement* (September 15–21, 1989): "Can it really be true that the earliest recorded painting to deal with the subject of slavery was painted as late as 1788, the year George Morland exhibited "The Slave Trade" at the Royal Academy? Like so many questions raised by *Slaves and Liberators*, the first part of Hugh Honour's two-volume study *The Image of the Black in Western Art*, the answer demonstrates the impossibility of ever separating art from its social and historical background. For until the subject of slavery and its abolition existed as a social question, it could not

exist as a subject for the arts—even (surprisingly) in paintings illustrating the lives and legends of the saints. And right from the beginning, from the moment when Morland broached the theme, art mirrored all the evasions, stereotypes, velleities, and falsifications that permitted the institution to continue in the West." Several points are worth considering. One is the absence of slavery in artistic discourse and from artistic representation. Another is the converse of Morland's declaration of the dependency of the artistic subject on the social subject, that is, perhaps the social question of slavery could not exist until the artistic subject did. Then again, perhaps the two are interdependent. Finally, the observation that art mirrors social reality indicates the extent to which art tropes itself as the mirror of the world. Michael Kemmelman observes in the New York Times (January 18, 1990): " 'Facing History: The Black Image in American Art, 1710–1940' is an exhibition that no thinking person can walk through without feeling a measure of both sorrow and anger. The 100 or so paintings, sculptures and drawings gathered at the Corcoran Gallery of Art testify to a racism so ingrained in the American consciousness that artists—the overwhelming number of them white, but some of whom were black— thought nothing about stereotyping blacks as 'grotesque buffoons, servile menials, comic entertainers or threatening subhumans,' writes Guy C. McElroy, the show's curator, in the exhibition catalogue." It continues, "It is the casualness of the cruelty that leaves the deepest impression on the viewer. Sometimes the methods of expression are sophisticated, the prejudices subtly masked." Perhaps most sorrowful is the participation of black artists in the casual cruelty.

15 The troping differs from context to context and is related to the quality and intensity of the monologism. But clearly, common to the various antitheses is the simple statement: Self is what Other is not. The Self has the positive characteristics the Other lacks. The Other has the negative characteristics the Self lacks. A double negative definition: the Self is the negative of the negative Other.

In "Forms of Wildness" and "The Noble Savage Theme as Fetish," Hayden White demonstrates the necessary definition of Self that accompanies the antithetical troping of the Other; European troping of indigenous Americans as "noble savages" differentiates them from Europeans and stresses their homogeneity. It simultaneously tropes the European upperclass as "savage nobles," thereby increasing difference within "European," enhancing its heterogeneity. Tropics of Discourse (Baltimore: Johns Hopkins U P, 1978), 150–82, 183–96.

16 For discussion of the mono-logic impulse of nationalism and the singlemindedness of the narratives of nation, see my "Beasts and Jagged Strokes of Color: The Poetics of Hybridization on the U.S./Mexican Border" in Bakhtin: Carnival and Other Subjects, ed. David Shepherd (Amsterdam: Rodopi, 1993).

17 It is worthwhile here to consider the Yaqui, whose territory straddles the Arizona/Sonora border, whose immigration situation is somewhat analogous to the Chicano's, but who have a history of repression by mestizo Mexicans.

18 There is a little gradation of relative Indian worth. For example, when Anglo Americans claim to have "Indian blood," it is most often claimed to be Cherokee, in great part, I believe, because Cherokees are perceived to be the noblest savages. In this regard, see Vine Deloria, *Custer Died for Your Sins* (New York: Avon, 1969), 3. Further, it is not mere coincidence that Cherokees more fully assimilated English than other Indians and learned Western writing sooner.

19 Considering that Colonial American slavery was based on an essential sub-humanity, at least partially demonstrated by absolute illiteracy, imagine what it must have meant to have to acknowledge that a slave girl could write and was publishing poetry in English. Phillis Wheatley's writing and its confirmation by the likes of John Hancock forced a reconsideration of the rhetoric and began the arduous rewriting of "black."

20 This is, of course, on the level of national consciousness and on the level of the individual for the majority of Americans who imagine themselves living far from reservations and centers of Indian population. Overt racism still thrives at the junctures of Anglo and Indian cultures; there the living "injun" is very much present.

21 This etymology can be metaphoric rather than literal as in cowboy/vaquero and other instances of English occurrence before American contact with Texas Mexicans. Yet even in those cases, it is clear that the cowboy usage is shaped by the metaphoric Spanish/Mexican/Chicano accent.

22 This is why archival work, like that of Luis Torres is so significant, both for Chicano and "American" literary histories. Torres has recovered a wealth of literature written by Chicanos and successfully demystifies the impression of illiteracy; see his "Bilingualism as Satire in Nineteenth-Century Chicano Poetry" in this volume and *The World of Early Chicano Poetry, 1848–1910* (Encino: Floricanto, 1993).

23 Among Chicanos it is observed that after Texan Chicanos said "mi casa es su casa," the gringo replies, "go back to Mexico."

24 That such a juxtaposition, a dialogism, of alternate subjectifications begins with literary writing is not insignificant. In "French Feminism in an International Frame," Gayatri Chakravorty Spivak observed of feminist rewriting of dominant culture, quoting Catherine Clément, "One would cut through all the heavy layers of ideology that have borne down since the beginnings of the family and private property: that can be done only in the imagination. And that is precisely what feminist action is all about: to change the imaginary in order to be able to act on the real, to change the very forms of language which by its structure and history has been subject to a law that is patrilinear, therefore masculine," *In Other Worlds* (New York: Methanc, 1987), 145. It is in the realm of imaginary writing that relationships other than those authoritatively prescribed come to be. This rewriting can begin with deconstruction (see Spivak's, "Bonding in Difference" in this volume).

25 José Antonio Burciaga, *Undocumented Love* (San José: Chusma House, 1992), 39–41.

Colonialism

and the

Politics of

Translation

———————

Tejaswini

Niranjana

I n the postcolonial context, the problematic of translation becomes a site where questions of representation and history converge as we attempt to account for the practices of subjectification implicit in the colonial enterprise. By subjectification I mean the construction of a "subject" through technologies or practices of power/knowledge,[1] technologies necessarily involving some notion of translation, a notion underpinned, I argue, by the classical Western concepts of representation, reality, and knowledge.

What I am suggesting, however, is that classical philosophical discourse does not merely engender a practice of translation as subjectification. Simultaneously, translation in the colonial context creates and supports a certain conceptual economy which works into philosophical discourse to function as a philosopheme. As Jacques Derrida points out, the concepts of metaphysics are not bound by or produced solely within the "field" of philosophy. Rather, they come out of and circulate through various discourses in several registers, providing a "conceptual network in which philosophy *itself* has been constituted."[2]

In forming a certain *subjectivity,* translation also brings into being overarching concepts of reality and representation which help render invisible the violence accompanying the constitution of "otherness." I shall use the term translation in two ways, to refer to (a) the problematic of translation which authorizes and is authorized by a certain classical notion of representation and (b) the problematic opened up by the poststructuralist critique of the earlier one, which makes translation always the "more" or the *supplement* in Derrida's sense.[3]

My concern is to discuss the political as well as the linguistic aspects of translation and to show how translation, overdetermined by violence, law, and subjugation, becomes a strategy of containment in the colonial context. The rethinking of translation becomes an urgent task for a postcolonial theory attempting to make sense of "subjects" living already "in translation" and seeking to reclaim the notion by deconstructing it and reinscribing its potential as a mode of resistance. Translation is bound up, I argue, with history writing; the poststructuralist critique of "history," therefore, undermines the project of translation-as-subjectification. I suggest that notions of translation as displacement and history as "effective-history" or historicity (history still working in the present) can explain the conjunctures of past and present in postcolonial space. Obviously, my discussion of translation does not propose yet another way of theorizing translation so as to enable a more foolproof "method" of "narrowing the gap" between cultures; it seeks rather to think this gap, this difference, to explore the positioning of the obsessions and desires of translations, and thus to describe the economies within which the sign of translation circulates. Using a translation from Kannada, a South Indian language, into English, I show how the rethinking of translation as un-nostalgic and nonessentialist makes translating a strategy of resistance rather than one of containment.

One of the most profound insights Derrida's work has afforded to postcolonials is the notion that *origin* is always already heterogeneous, that it is not some pure, unified source of meaning or history. It would be a mistake for historiographers to challenge colonial representations as "false" or "inadequate"; the striving for adequacy based on such a challenge would trap postcolonial writing in a metaphysics of presence, in what Derrida has called "the generative question" of the age, the question of the value of representation.

In "Speech and Phenomena," his essay on Husserl, Derrida says: When in fact I *effectively* use words . . . I must from the outset operate (within) a structure of repetition whose basic element can only be representative. A sign is never an event, if by event we mean an irreplaceable and irreversible empirical particular. A sign which would take place but "once" would not be a sign. . . . Since this representative structure is signification itself, I cannot enter into an "effective" discourse without being from the start involved in unlimited representation.[4]

What Derrida is claiming is that there is no primordial "presence" which is then re-presented. The "re-" does not *befall* the original. It is the concept of representation which, by suppressing the difference that is already there in the so-called origin, grounds the whole of Western metaphysics. This is a metaphysics of presence, of the "absolute proximity of self-identity" (*SP* 99) and of presence to oneself. Perhaps the predominant characteristic of the metaphysics of presence is the privileging of voice and speech over "writing" (*écriture*) that Derrida calls phonocentrism of logocentrism, wherein writing as a derived form, the copy of a copy, comes to signify a distant, lost, or broken origin, a notion Derrida contests by revealing that any concept of the simple, the center, or the primordial is always already characterized by an irreducible or untranscendable heterogeneity.

In a series of brilliant readings of Husserl, Heidegger, Saussure, Levi-Strauss and Rousseau, Derrida demonstrates how representation—and writing—already belong to the sign and to signification: "In this play of representation, the point of origin becomes ungraspable. . . . There is no longer a simple origin."[5] To deconstruct logocentric metaphysics, Derrida proposes we use the notion of writing as he has reinscribed it. Derrida's "writing" is another name for difference at the origin; it signifies "the most formidable difference. It threatened the desire for living speech from the closest proximity, it *breached* living space from within and from the very beginning" (*OG* 56). The sign of origin, for Derrida, is a writing of a writing that can only state that the origin is originary translation. Metaphysics tries to reappropriate presence, says Derrida, through notions of adequacy of representation, of totalization, of history. Cartesian-Hegelian history, like the structure of the sign, "is conceivable only *on the basis* of the presence that it defers and *in view* of the deferred presence one intends to reappropriate" (*SP* 138). Here Derrida points to historicism's concern with *origin* and *telos* and its desire to construct a totalizing narrative. "History," in the texts of poststructuralism, is a repressive force that obliterates difference and belongs in a chain that includes meaning, truth, presence,

Colonialism and
Translation

and logos. Derrida points out in *Of Grammatology* that "History and knowledge, *istoria* and *episteme* have always been determined (and not only etymologically or philosophically) as detours *for the purpose of the reappropriation of presence*" (*OG* 10). *Istoria* and *Episteme* claim to "represent" and therefore to translate. Colonialism, as I have been arguing, proposes representation (and translation) as adequate to a pre-given "reality," as being transparent in its providing of knowledge. This concept of translation functions as an originary philosopheme, for, according to Derrida, the notion of a transcendental signified takes shape "within the horizon of an absolutely pure, transparent, and unequivocal translatability."[6]

While postcolonial theory would willingly dispense with the historical narratives that underwrite the imperialist enterprise, that come into being with the denial of historicity to conquered peoples, that suppress history in order to appear as history, it is aware that the situation of the postcolonial "subject," who lives always already "in translation," requires for its articulation some alternative notion of history.

Influential translations (from Sanskrit and Persian into English in the eighteenth century, for example) used techniques of representation that reconstructed colonial subjects, legitimizing or authorizing certain versions of the Oriental, versions that then came to acquire the status of "truths" even in the countries in which the "original" works were produced. European translations of Indian texts prepared for a Western audience provided to the "educated" Indian a whole range of Orientalist images. Even when the anglicized Indian spoke a language other than English, the legitimacy conferred on dominant knowledges and languages ensured that the "native" gained access to his own past through the texts of the colonial rulers. The translations by Calcutta's Fort William College scholars from Indian languages into English, for example, provided representations of the "Asiatik" to generations of Europeans.[7] As Edward Said points out, what is important about such representations is that they "acquire the status of objects or representations *without* history." Because they seem to be abstract models, they "become models for doing certain things," and they become facts that have a certain force to tilt the balance of power in the colonies. Said cites the case of Thomas Macaulay, who by denouncing indigenous learning as outdated and useless, prepared the way for the introduction of English education in India.[8]

The point is not just to criticize Macaulay's characterization of the indigenous education as "inadequate" and "untrue"; one should attempt to show the complicity of the representation with colonial rule and its part in maintaining the asymmetries of imperialism. The post-colonial desire for "history" is a desire to understand the traces of the "past" in a situation where at least one fact is singularly irreducible: colonialism and what came after. Historiography in such a situation must provide ways of recovering occluded images from the past to deconstruct colonial and neocolonial histories. In India, for example, the Subaltern Studies group, which has initiated such a project of rewriting history, is grappling with the conceptual problems of essentialism and representation.[9] As Gayatri Spivak points out, the Subaltern historians use a notion like "consciousness" strategically, deliberately, and unnostalgically, in the service of "a scrupulously visible political interest" (*DH* 342), to refer to an "emergent collective consciousness" rather than that of the liberal humanist subject. The strategic use of essentialist concepts marks what Spivak, and Derrida, would call "affirmative deconstruction." A comment of Derrida's from *Of Grammatology* offers an important clue to the way in which postcolonial theory will have to situate itself:

> The movements of deconstruction do not destroy structures from the outside. They are not possible and effective, nor can they take accurate aim, except by inhabiting those structures. Inhabiting them *in a certain way*, because one always inhabits, and all the more when one does not suspect it. Operating necessarily from the inside, borrowing all the strategic and economic resources of subversion from the old structure, borrowing them structurally, that is to say without being able to isolate their elements and atoms, the enterprise of deconstruction always in a certain way falls prey to its own work. (*OG* 24)

How can theory, or translation, avoid being trapped in the order of representation when it uses the concepts it critiques? Derrida would say that it should aim to be the kind of writing that "both marks and goes back over its mark with an undecidable stroke," for this "double mark escapes the pertinence of authority or truth," reinscribing it without overturning it. This displacement is not an *event;* it has not "taken place." It is what "writes/is written."[10] The double inscription Derrida mentions has a parallel in Walter Benjamin's strategy of citation or quotation. For Benjamin, the historical materialist (the critical historiographer) quotes without quotation marks in a method akin to montage. It is one way of revealing the constellation a past age forms with the present without submitting to a historical continuum, to an order of origin and *telos*.[11]

Derrida's double writing can help us challenge the practices of subjectification and domination evident in colonial histories or translations. The challenge, however, will not be made in the name of recovering a lost essence or an undamaged self. Instead, the question of
the *hybrid* will inform our reading. As Homi Bhabha puts it:

> Hybridity is the sign of the productivity of colonial power, its
> shifting forces and fixities; it is the name for the strategic rever-
> sal of the process of domination through disavowal (that is, the
> production of discriminatory identities that secure the "pure" and
> original identity of authority). Hybridity is the revaluation of the
> assumption of colonial identity through the repetition of discrimi-
> natory identity effects. It displays the necessary deformation and
> displacement of all sites of discrimination and domination.[12]

Colonial discourse, although it creates identities for those it trans-
fixes by its gaze of power, is profoundly ambivalent at the source of its
authority. Hybridity leads to proliferating differences that escape the
"surveillance" of the discriminatory eye. "Faced with the hybridity of
its objects," says Bhabha, "the *presence* of power is revealed as something other that what its rules of recognition assert" (*SW* 154). When
we begin to understand how colonial power ends up producing hybridization, "the discursive conditions of dominance" can be turned into
"the grounds of intervention" (154). The hybrid (subject or context),
therefore, involves translation, deformation, displacement. As Bhabha
is careful to point out, colonial hybridity is not a problem of cultural
identity that can be resolved by a relativistic approach; it is rather "a
problematic of colonial representation and individuation that reverses
the effects of the colonialist disavowal, so that other 'denied' knowledges enter upon the dominant discourse and estrange the basis of its
authority" (156).

Clearly, the notion of hybridity, which is of great importance for a
subaltern critique of historiography as well as for a critique of traditional notions of translation, is both "ambiguous and historically complex."[13] To restrict "hybridity," or what I call "living in translation,"
to a postcolonial elite is to deny the persuasiveness, however heterogeneous, of the transformations wrought across class boundaries by
colonial and neocolonial domination. This is not to present a metanarrative of global homogenization, but to emphasize the need to re-
invent oppositional cultures in nonessentializing ways. Hybridity can
be seen, therefore, as the sign of a postcolonial theory that subverts

Tejaswini
Niranjana

essentialist models of reading while it points toward a new practice of translation.

How then can we extend the meaning of representation while calling it into question? Meditating on the translation of *repraesentatio* into *Vorstellung, Darstellung,* representation, *représentation,* and *Repräsentation,* Jacques Derrida points out that before we know "how and what to translate by 'representation,' we must interrogate the concept of translation and of language which is so often dominated by the concept of representation" or a "presupposition or the desire for an invariable identity of sense."[14] Derrida asks if translation is "of the same order as representation," or whether "the so-called relation of translation or of substitution" escapes "the orbit of representation" (*SR* 297–98). To rethink a practice of translation regulating and regulated by the horizon of metaphysics involves a use of translation, I argue, that shatters the coherence of the "original and the invariable identity of sense." This coherence is constituted in part through the operation of History and Knowledge manifested, for example, in the production of translations in the colonial context. To deconstruct these essentializing discourses, therefore, is to disrupt "history" in the Benjaminian sense, to produce a translation of a translation.

To be able to reject the signifying systems of imperialism, we need "a cartography of imperialist ideology more extensive than its address in the colonialist space."[15] I turn, therefore, to an analysis of two postcolonial translations which, in their own ways, participate in the production of the Orient. I initiate here a practice of translation that is speculative, provisional, and interventionist.

I shall provide here the "original" in transliteration and three translations, the last one being my own.[16] The exemplary poem or *vacana*[17] is a fragment from a lengthy spiritual text "produced" in South India in the twelfth century but codified only in the fifteenth century. One of the reasons I choose a "sacred" poem to retranslate is to emphasize that what Benjamin would call a "profane" reading is of great significance in a context dominated by nationalist and nativist discourses that, in seemingly opposed but related ways, essentialize religions and thereby endorse communal violence. As Benjamin puts it, "In every era the attempt must be made anew to wrest tradition away from a conformism that is about to overpower it."[18]

Transliteration:

nimma tejava nodalendu heresari noduttiralu
    satakoti suryaru mudidantirdudayya!

miñcina balliya sancava kande;
    enagidu sojigavayittu!
Guhesvara, ninu jyotirlingavadare
    upamisi nodaballavarillayya.

Translation A

As I stepped back and looked
To see Thy light,
It seemed a hundred million suns
Came into sight;
A cluster of creeping lightnings I
With wonder saw.
O Guhesvara, if Thou become
The effulgent Linga, there be none
Thy glory to match!

Translation B

Looking for your light,
I went out:
it was like the sudden dawn
of a million million suns,
a ganglion of lightnings
for my wonder.
O Lord of Caves,
if you are light
there can be no metaphor.

Tejaswini
Niranjana

Translation C

Drawing back
to look at your radiance
I saw
the dawning of a hundred million suns.
I gazed in wonder
at the lightning's creepers playing.
Guhesvara, if you are become the *linga* of light
Who can find you figuration.

A brief introduction to the proper name that is usually designated as the author of this text: Allama Prabhu was a twelfth-century mystic, a revolutionary saint born in Balligave (in present-day Karnataka State), a small village in one of the kingdoms of South India. Allama was one of the "founders" of what became (and still is) a powerful sect devoted to the worship of the god Siva. Virasaivism launched an attack on the Vedic tradition of orthodox Hinduism, demanding the abolition of caste and gender distinctions in the access to worship. Its saint-poets disregarded Sanskrit, the dominant religious language of Hinduism, in favor of the local language, Kannada. In addition, the *vacana*-poets used for the first time the local "nonstandard" dialects of the areas they came from, whereas other poets of the time employed "a highly stylized archaic language."[19] For more than two hundred years, the *vacanas* circulated as part of a strong oral literature, until the Vijayanagar Empire revived Virasaivism in the fifteenth century and underwrote the codification of its sacred texts. So the text comes to us (even in Kannada) always already disarticulated, encoded.

The Virasaiva movement, commonly known in Karnataka as the *vacana* movement, has been examined primarily by students of religion or of literature. Very little material exists on the sociocultural history of the period, and even that which is available is a welter of contradictory assertions.[20] What appears certain, however, is that the Virasaivas or Lingayats came from different castes and occupations and successfully challenged both priest and king, or temple and palace—the traditional centers of power. Although the influence of Jainism, Buddhism, and Islam on the Virasaiva movement has been remarked upon, some writers see the Virasaiva movement as resulting in a reformed Brahminism strengthened by the adherence of different castes.[21] The *bhakti* movement (to give it its pan-Indian name) in general is seen by some historians as not really anti-Vedic and ultimately as performing the function of incorporating the non-Brahmin, non-Aryan population into the Vedic hierarchy.[22] However, a retranslation of the *vacanas* can show, for example, that *bhakti*, or Virasaivism, was neither monolithic nor homogeneous.

Given the lack of material on medieval Karnataka, we can only ask a series of questions: Why is it that the *vacana* movement did not come into being until the twelfth century in spite of Saivism being a strong religious current for four centuries before? Did the movement present a radical challenge to the established religious and economic order, or did it actually strengthen feudalism and the Vedic tradition? What was the significance of the participation of people from different castes? How did this undermine existing notions of caste boundaries? Why was the notion of ritual purity and impurity abandoned by the Virasaivas? Did a great number of women really take part in religious discourse, or was it just a highly visible minority? What is the relationship between the Virasaiva movement and social transformation in the twelfth century? What does the Lingayat consolidation of caste and socioeconomic power in later centuries tell us about the Virasaiva tradition/s impulses? How do questions like these inform our contemporary translations of the *vacanas*? My inability to provide even provisional answers forces me to devise other strategies of interpretation. These strategies, however, are marked profoundly by the questions I have just raised.

The parameters of my reading/translation of Allama's text are provided, on the one hand, by the consistent and disarticulated imagery of Saivite mystic poetry and, on the other, by my "theorization" about translation in the postcolonial context: that is to say, on the one hand by the notion of *figure* in Saivite poetry, which undoes the insistence on *linga*, meaning, and representation; and on the other hand by a consideration of the afterlife, the *living on* of a text, and the task of the translator.

In his attempt to assimilate the religious experience into everyday life, in his concern with propagating the new path to salvation, Allama emerges in this fragment and others as a poet deeply interested in issues of articulation and representation. The fragment comes from the *Sunyasampadane* (achievement/attainment of nothingness). A work written around Allama's life, the *Sunyasampadane* incorporates Allama's *vacanas* as well as those composed by the other Virasaiva saints and is presented as Allama's dialogue with those saints. It was first compiled by Sivagana Prasadi Mahadevayya in the early decades of the fifteenth century and included 1012 *vacanas*. The edition in use today is based on the fourth compilation, made by Gulura Siddhaviranarya, including 1543 *vacanas*.[23]

The fragment we read belongs to Allama's "spiritual autobiography." It is part of a dialogue with a saint-to-be in which Allama tries to convey a sense of the "ultimate" experience, the experience of the "void" or *sunya*. The eye of the god (Siva) has opened up the eye of fire in the sole of Allama's foot, and Allama sings the praises of this eye, calling it "radiance," "lightning," "a hundred million suns."

If we are to have a privileged "figure" for this text, it is the *linga*, which in fact offers itself as "originary" figure for the entire corpus of Saivite poetry. The *linga* is/is not Siva or god; it is a form for formlessness, a shape for shapelessness. It is an attempt to articulate that which cannot be articulated in the mystic experience, and in the poem fragment it eventually turns out to be an articulation of a disarticulation.[24]

Tejaswini
Niranjana

The thematization of light in Allama's poetry is always bound up with the possibility of articulation. And images of *light* are always connected here to those of *sight*. In the short space of six lines, Allama uses *look* or *see* three times; and light appears five times (radiance, suns, dawning, lightning, the *linga*). In Allama's spiritual biography there is a description of his meeting with the saint Animisa (literally, "one who does not blink," that is, a god; one who, therefore, sees steadily). Animisa *trans*mits the unutterable experience to Allama's heart through his eye alone. A single look *trans*forms Allama, and the *linga* on Animisa's palm is *trans*ferred to Allama's.

Allama has now experienced the "void" and is in a state of *Jivan-mukta* (free from life), which means to live in the world and be out of it at the same time, like "light in a crystal bowl." There are a number of light images in this part of the *Sunyasampadane*: burning charcoal, lighted camphor, lamps, fire, the refractive crystal. Allama has become form, though formless; he is body, though bodiless. He is *sunyamurthi*, void taken on form, image or figure of the void. *Jangama*, the saint, is himself *linga*, proclaims Allama. *Nodi kudi saiveragada/sukhavane-nendupamisuvenayya guhesvara!* asks Allama. How can I *figure* this joy of looking at and mingling with you? He adds: *Nimma suluhina sogasanupamisabaradu!* I should not/ought not *figure* the splendor of your passing. *Suluhu* can mean "motion," "turning," "going," or "passing." It shades off into "glimpse," "transitory perception," and eventually into "trace." I ought not figure the splendor of your trace. Suluhu can also mean *sign*.

The traces left by Allama's experience are always already there in the conception of this kind of experience in the *bhakti* or devotional tradition. The failure to find figures is an expected failure of language, a failure of articulation because of the disarticulation at the center of what demands articulation. Allama cannot finally believe that his figures *represent* his experience. "The undoing of the representational and iconic function of figuration by the play of the signifier"[25] is indicated by the *linga* (neither signified nor signifier, but that which can move with ease from one position to the other), which makes mockery of all attempts to figure its glory. These attempts are seductive insofar as they lead us to believe we have somehow captured in language the shadows of the cave (Guhesvara, Allama's god, is lord of the cave). But the movement of Allama's poem is a step beyond "traditional conceptions of figuration as modes of representation" and is therefore a movement toward "the undoing and erasure of the figure" (de Man 61). The arrest of articulation (recalling Derrida's speculations on Maurice

Blanchot's *L'Arrêt de mort*) is actually triumph, for the *jangama* is shown to be the *linga*, a death (or Benjamin's *mortification*) or attainment of the void is seen as survival or a living on.

Let us return to the different translations of Allama's poem, keeping in mind Derrida's comment that any translation contaminates the text with meanings, which it imports in turn and which rework the text. As he suggests, a text in translation trails more than one language behind it.[26] Because the poem has what Benjamin calls translatability, because it is not untranslatable, although it presses for constant deformation and disfiguration, there is an economy of translation—which does not exclude the political—regulating the flow of medieval Kannada into modern English.[27]

My contention is that Translations A and B fail to comprehend the economy of translation in this poem, because they fail to understand "the specific significance inherent in the original which manifests itself in its translatability."[28] Attempting to assimilate Saivite poetry to the discourses of Christianity or of a post-Romantic New Criticism, these translators reproduce some of the nineteenth-century "native" responses to colonialism. Accepting the premises of a universalist history, they try to show how the *vacanas* are always already Christian, or "modernist," and therefore worthy of the West's attention. Their enterprise is supported by the asymmetry between English and Kannada created and enforced by colonial and neocolonial discourse. This is an asymmetry which allows translators to simplify the text in a predictable direction, toward English and the Judeo-Christian tradition and away from the multiplicity of indigenous languages and religions, which have to be homogenized before they can be translated.

The first Western-style dictionary of Kannada was prepared in 1817 by William Carey, the polyglot colleague of William Ward and one of the most prolific of the Serampore missionaries.[29] The first translators of the *vacanas* were Christian missionaries in the 1860s,[30] attracted to Saivite poetry, according to Ramanujan, by its "monotheism" that "lashes out in an atmosphere of animism and polytheism" (*SS* 27). The missionaries are said to have made sarcastic references to the failure of the Virasaiva saints" prophecies that they would return from the "west," for *they*, the Christians, had arrived instead. Even according to the terms of the Saivites" own texts, they argued, the Christians represented a more evolved religion. We see here one of the typical moves of a colonial discourse that translates indigenous religious texts, castigates the natives for not being faithful to the tenets of their (translated) religion, then claims that the native religion is incapable of sustaining its devotees, and proposes "conversion" as a path to salvation. The missionaries even speculated that *"bhakti* attitudes were the result of early Christian influence" (*SS* 27, n. 4), another move that accommodates seamlessly the idea of a former Golden Age and the present fallen, degraded state of the "Hindoos."

Both European and Indian commentators persist in discussing Virasaivism in terms of Puritanism and Protestantism, suggesting that the poems of the Virasaiva saints are part of a Pilgrim's Progress. Speaking of the fact that these saints came from all classes, castes, and trades, Ramanujan adds in parenthesis "like Bunyan, the tinker" (*SS* 54). Ramanujan's version of the *vacanas* emphasize that they are "deeply personal" poems, that they use the language of "personal conversation," that they embody the conflicts of "real persons." There is a corresponding stress on the similarities between Virasaivism and European Protestantism: the privileging of "individual," "original," and "direct" experience; "monotheism" and "evangelism," and distrust of "mediators" like priests (*SS* 53–55). This combination of emphases allows Ramanujan to produce a post-Romantic translation of Allama's *vacana* that presents it as a "quest for the unmediated vision" (*SS* 52), a project deconstructed so skillfully in Paul de Man's "The Rhetoric of Temporality." This reading of Ramanujan's, I argue, cannot account for the instability of the "original."

Translations A and B both translate *teja*, the first significant noun in the *vacana*, as "light." I translate the word as "radiance," because the poem seems to be a movement *toward* the ostensible simplicity of light: Allama goes from "radiance" to "hundred million suns" and "light" before he approaches *jyotis* or "light" in the fifth line. The world "effulgent" in Translation A is superfluous for this reason. We cannot, however, gloss over the fact that *jyotis* is a Sanskrit word embedded in the Kannada poem and that *jyotirlinga* refers to a special kind of *linga*, a functioning therefore as a figure of condensation. Translation B has "light" for both *teja* and *jyotis*, since Ramanujan claims that Allama begins with a traditional metaphor of light and denies it at the end of the *vacana*. In the first place, the "original" does not suggest any such denial of light. Secondly, it seems to be in Ramanujan's interests to confer on the *vacana* a circularity of movement, or rather to suggest that the Saivite poets tell cyclical stories like those narrated by Ramanujan himself when he writes of protest against the "establishment" followed by its ultimate institutionalization, which is in turn followed by a new protest. This kind of narrative appears to have for its premise a metaphysical concept of history, associated, as Derrida points out, "with a linear scheme of the unfolding of presence, where the line relates the final presence to the originary presence according to the straight line or the circle" (*OG* 85). The concept of representation underwriting this notion of history participates, as I have argued, in colonial practices of subjectification.

Heresari in the first line is translated as "stepped back" by A and as "went out" by B. The dictionaries do not list the meaning provided by B, but add "drew back" or "drawing back" to "stepped back." I use "drawing back" since it seems to indicate more clearly the context where Allama looks at the eye on the sole of his foot. Why does B use "went out," almost completely contradicting the sense of *heresari*? One possibility is that B mistakes *here* (back) for *hora* (outside).[31] Or else the translator is playing a variation on the theme of linear "unfolding of presence," suggesting that it is only by a "going out" that Allama can see the figurative suns and lightning, in fact, the poet is made to go out "looking for your light." The notion of "drawing back" *in order to see* goes so much against his sense of what the poem means that he refuses to grant to the poem what it is saying.

Balli refers to "creeper," as in flowering vine, so the "cluster" in A is superfluous and the "ganglion" in B improbable. *Miñcina* qualifies *balli* and is adjectival, referring to the lightning. A key word that both A and B leave out of their translations here is *sancu* (as in *miñcina balliya sancu:* the lightning's creepers play), "flash or play." The play of signifiers sets in motion all the images of light in the *vacana*, and B responds by removing *gazed* and *playing* from the English version, setting in their place the word *ganglion*, taking the "play" from the realm of meaning and placing it firmly within the nervous system of the individual body.

Guhesvara is the name of Allama's god and remains untranslated in A as well as C. It is a name that recurs in every *vacana* that Allama wrote, and force of repetition allows it to function as a unique proper name that is not obscured by simple translation. Given that colonialism's violence erases or distorts beyond recognition (as witnessed in innumerable colonial texts) the *names* of the colonized, it seems important *not* to translate proper names in a postcolonial or decolonizing practice. Ramanujan's rationale for translating Guhesvara is oddly significant. He argues that since the god's names are "partly Sanskrit" (interestingly both *Guhe* and *esvara* would be of Sanskrit origin), and since "the transparent Kannada" ensures that the Sanskrit is "never opaque or distant for long," the etymologies quicken in the poem and demand the translation of "attributive proper names into literal

English" (SS 47). In attempting to smooth over the heterogeneous text, Ramanujan assigns to Kannada, and by implication to English, the ability to make and be "transparent."

I have already suggested that Translation A's use of an adjective in place of an noun, *effulgent* instead of *light*, does not work within the economy of the poem. B's version—"if you are light"—ignores the conception of *linga* which is not only crucial to this *vacana* but also to the entire Virasaiva tradition. Ramanujan's refusal to translate or inscribe the *linga* is, therefore, a refusal to interrogate the most significant image in Allama's text. My version translates *jyotis* as "light" and retains *linga* to complicate the notion of light as signification, since *linga* may be said to function in the *vacana* as the figure of dissemination that authorizes the use of "figuration" in the last line.

Translation B's trick of making verbs disappear is matched by its constant reducing and simplifying them. In the penultimate line, for example, *adare* ("it . . . are," in the sense of "to be" and also "if . . . to become") is turned into "are," and in the last line, *nodaballa* ("find," "to be capable of") is translated simply as "be." Translation A, on the other hand, retains only the sense of "become." In comparison, my version uses a somewhat archaic phrase—"if you are become"—in order to be able to translate both meanings, "be" and "become."

Trying to find a suitable translation for the crucial structuring statement in the *vacana, ninu jyotirlingavadare / upamisinodaballavarillayya,* A takes the easy way out by turning *upama* into a negative (*an-upama*) to mean "incomparable," or "matchless," so that "there be none / Thy glory to match!" This misses the problem entirely, for the question is not one of finding other gods or mortals to "match" the glory of *Guhesvara,* but one of finding someone capable of *representing* the *linga. Upama* is a figure of speech, simile, metaphor, never merely or simply "metaphor," as Translation B has it. B in fact turns the last line (which I translate as "Who can find your figuration") into "there can be no metaphor," thereby reinforcing its conception of the circularity of the *vacana:* "Sometimes in the vacanakara's [the author of the *vacana*] quest for the unmediated vision, there comes a point when language, logic and metaphor are not enough; at such points, the poet begins with a striking traditional metaphor and denies it at the end" (SS 52). Ramanujan refuses to acknowledge that the poet-saint *does not deny* the need for figuration. He merely recognizes its ineffectualness, marking thereby its possibility/impossibility, like that of representation or translation.

The deliberate roughness of my version of the *vacana* allows the text to "affect," as Benjamin would have it, the language into which it is being translated, interrupting the "transparency" and smoothness of a totalizing narrative like that of Ramanujan. Seeing "literalness" as an "arcade," I privilege the word over the sentence, marking thereby what Derrida calls in "Des Tours de Babel" a "displacement" from the syntagmatic to the paradigmatic level and inserting my translation into the attack against homogenizing and continuous narratives.[32]

The strategies of containment typical of colonial discourse operate in Translations A and B through the diction and "absences" of the former, and the insistence on the "light" motif and metaphor in the latter. The emphasis on metaphor seems to be "interpreted and over-determined" here as "a representation of representation" (*SR* 299). The use of "figuration" and the reinscription of *linga* in my version is part of an attempt to resist containment, to remark textuality, to dislodge or disturb the fixation on any one term or meaning, to substitute *translation* for representations in the strict sense. The *linga* functions as a "supplement" in my translation, exposing polysemy to what Derrida has called the law of dissemination, and the last line—"Who can find your figuration"—is neither a question nor an affirmation but both at the same time.

The *vacanas* "claim" the postcolonial translator by problematizing the issue of representation, which is crucial in a context where nationalist myths of identity and unity are collapsing. It seems more urgent than ever to be aware of the instability of the "original," which can be meticulously uncovered through the practice of translation. The arbitrariness of what is presented as "natural" can be deconstructed by the translator or her/his alter ego, the critical historiographer. The drive to challenge hegemonic representation of the non-Western world need not be seen as a wish to oppose the "true" Other to the "false" one presented in colonial discourse. Rather, since postcolonials already exist "in translation," our search should not be for origins or essences but for a richer complexity, a complication of our notions of the "self," a more densely textured understanding of who "we" are. It is here that translators can intervene to inscribe heterogeneity, to warn against myths of purity, to show origins as always already fissured. Translation, from being a "containing" force, is transformed into a disruptive, disseminating one. The deconstruction initiated by retranslation opens up a postcolonial space as it brings "history" to legibility.

Tejaswini
Niranjana

Notes

This chapter © 1993 by Regents of the University of California and is used by permission of the University of California Press.

1 "[Power] produces knowledge. . . . [They] directly imply one another," says Michel Foucault [in *Discipline and Punish: The Birth of the Prison*, trans. Alan Sheridan (New York: Vintage Books, 1979), 27]. He further suggests that the "individual" or the subject is "fabricated" by technologies of power or practices of subjectification.

2 Derrida, "White Mythology: Metaphor in the Text of Philosophy," in *Margins of Philosophy*, trans. Alan Bass (Chicago: U of Chicago P, 1982), 230.

3 In *Positions* [trans. Alan Bass (Chicago: U of Chicago P, 1981)] Derrida describes *supplement* as an "undecidable," something which cannot any longer "be included within philosophical (binary) opposition," but which resists and disorganizes philosophical binaries "*without ever* constituting a third term . . . ; the *supplement* is neither a plus nor a minus, neither an outside nor the complement of an inside, neither accident nor essence" (43).

4 Derrida, *Speech and Phenomena*, trans. David B. Allison (Evanston: Northwestern U P, 1973), 50. Cited henceforth as *SP*.

5 Derrida, *Of Grammatology*, trans. Gayatri C. Spivak (Baltimore: Johns Hopkins U P, 1974), 36. Cited henceforth as *OG*.

6 Derrida, *Positions*, trans. Alan Bass (Chicago: U of Chicago P, 1981).

7 For a fuller discussion of this, see my *Siting Translation: History, Post-structuralism, and the Colonial Context* (Berkeley: U of California P, 1992).

8 See Said's remarks in a discussion with Eugenio Donato and others, presented in *boundary* 2, 8.1 (Fall 1979), as "An Exchange on Deconstruction and History," 65–74.

9 Gayatri C. Spivak, "Subaltern Studies: Deconstructing Historiography," in *Subaltern Studies* 4 (Delhi: Oxford U P, 1985). Cited henceforth as *DH*.

10 Derrida, *Dissemination*, trans. Barbara Johnson (Chicago: U of Chicago P, 1981), 193.

11 For a discussion of Benjamin's conception of historiography, see my "Deconstructing Translation and History: Derrida on Benjamin," *Strategies* 1 (Fall 1988), 100–119.

12 Bhabha, "Signs Taken for Wonders: Questions of Ambivalence and Authority under a Tree outside Delhi, May 1817," *Critical Inquiry* 12.1 (Autumn 1985), 154. Cited henceforth as *SW*.

13 James Clifford, *The Predicament of Culture* (Cambridge: Harvard U P, 1988), 16.

14 Derrida, "Sending: On Representation," *Social Research* 49.2 (Summer 1982), 302–3. Cited henceforth as *SR*.

15 Benita Parry, "Problems in Current Theories of Colonial Discourse," *Oxford Literary Review* 9:1–2 (1987), 45

16 Translation A is from the *Sunyasampadane*, 5 vols., ed. and trans. S. C. Nandimath, L. M. A. Menezes, and R. C. Hiremath (Dharwar: Karnatak U, 1965), 1: 240; Translation B is from *Speaking of Siva*, trans. A. K. Ramanujan (Harmondsworth: Penguin, 1973), 168, cited henceforth as *SS*; Translation C is my own version.

17 Pronounced "vachana."

18 Walter Benjamin, "Theses on the Philosophy of History," *Illuminations*, trans. Harry Zohn (New York: Schocken,1969), 255.

19 Ramanujan, Introduction to *SS*, p. 46.

20 By far the most thought-provoking Kannada book on vacana poetry is Basavaraja Kalgudi's *Madhyakaaleena Bhakti matthu Anubhaava Saahitya haagoo Charitrika Prajne* (Bangalore: Kannada Sahitya Parishat, 1988).

21 See Romila Thapar, *A History of India* (Harmondsworth: Penguin, 1966), 1:216, for the influences of Virasaivism, and Louis Dumont, *Homo Hierarchicus: The Caste System and Its Implications*, trans. Mark Sainsbury, Louis Dumont, and Basia Gulati (Chicago: U of Chicago P, 1980), 190, for the notion of Brahminism being strengthened by a movement like that of Virasaivas. The problem with Dumont's theory is that it seems to rest on the same kind of essentialized and unchanging Hinduism and Brahminism that we find depicted in Orientalist texts.

22 M. G. S. Narayanan and Veluthat Kesavan, "Bhakti Movement in South India," in *Indian Movements: Some Aspects of Dissent, Protest and Reform*, ed. S. C. Malik (Simla: Institute for Advance Study, 1978), 45, 53. I am grateful to Gauri Dharampal for pointing out that the images of light, the void, and the cave, which are crucial to an understanding of Virasaiva poetry, are typical images in Vedic texts as well.

23 For more information about the different editions, see the translators' preface to the *Sunyasampadane*, ed. and trans. Nandimath, Menezes, and Hiremath, 1:xi.

24 Although Western commentators have suggested that the *linga* is a phallic symbol, there is no indication in any of the surviving *vacanas* that this was the case. A. K. Ramanujan explains that the *linga* is "the only symbol of Siva" and is "to be worn inseparably on his body by the devotee" (Introduction *SS* 32). Female devotees of Siva wear the *linga* too.

25 Paul de Man, "Shelley Disfigured," in *Deconstruction and Criticism*, ed. Harold Bloom et al. (New York: Seabury Press, 1979), 61.

26 Derrida, "Living On: Border Lines," in *Deconstruction and Criticism*, ed. Harold Bloom et al. (New York: Seabury, 1979), 76.

27 Medieval Kannada is comprehensible to a speaker of modern Kannada. A discussion of this, and of how the punctuation, syntax, and vocabulary of present-day Kannada has been affected by English is beyond the scope of this paper.

28 Walter Benjamin, "The Task of the Translator," in *Illuminations*, trans. Harry Zohn, ed. Hannah Arendt (New York: Schocken, 1969), 71.

29 Carey, *A Grammar of the Karnata Language* (Serampore: Mission Press, 1817).

30 I have not been able to locate these early translations of the *vacanas*. It would be interesting to speculate what direct or indirect influence they might have had on the diction of Translation A.

31 One of the Kannada versions available has *herasari* for *heresari;* this could be the source of the confusion.

32 Derrida, "Des Tours de Babel," in *Difference in Translation*, ed. Joseph Graham (Ithaca: Cornell U P, 1985).

Tejaswini
Niranjana

Adulteration

& the Nation:

Monologic

Nationalism

& the Colonial

Hybrid

_____

David Lloyd

I rish cultural nationalism has been preoccupied throughout its history with the possibility of producing a national genius who would at once speak for and forge a national identity. The national genius is to represent the nation in the double sense of depicting and embodying its spirit—or genius—as it is manifested in the changing forms of national life and history. The idea of the genius in play here could be reformulated quite accurately in terms derived from Kantian aesthetics: the national genius is conceived of as endowed with "exemplary originality."[1] That is to say, the national genius not only presents examples to a people not yet fully formed by or conscious of their national identity, but does so by exemplifying in himself the individual's ideal continuity with the nation's spiritual origins. True originality derives from the faithful reproduction of one's origins. Thus far, Irish nationalism represents, as indeed does Kant, merely another variant on the Enlightenment and Romantic critical tradition for which the originality of genius is understood as the capacity to reproduce the historical or individual sources of creativity itself. The Irish nationalist merely insists on a different notion of what is to be formed in the encounter with genius: not so much the intermediate subject of taste as the political subject, the citizen-subject, itself.

Unlike Kant, however, the Irish nationalist is confronted with a peculiar dilemma which Young Ireland's most influential aesthetician, D. F. McCarthy, quite succinctly expressed when he remarked that the great national poet was "either the creation or the creator of a great people."[2] The expression points to an impassible aporia for the doubly representational aesthetics of nationalism, since the poet must either be created by the nation which it is his (always his) function to create or create it by virtue of representing the nation he lacks. Neither a continuous national history, which could connect the individual to the national genius, nor even the nature, by the invocation of which in the form of Naturgabe the category of genius has traditionally been grounded, are easily available to the Irish nationalist.[3] For the nationalism of a colonized people requires that its history be seen as a series of unnatural ruptures and discontinuities imposed upon it by an alien power while its reconstruction must necessarily pass by way of deliberate artifice. Almost by definition, this anticolonial nationalism lacks the ground on which to base its representative claims and is forced to invent them.[4] In this respect, nationalism can be said to require an aesthetic politics quite as much as a political aesthetics.

Historically, this constitutive paradox of Irish nationalism has not been practically disabling, though in cultural terms it leaves the problem that virtually without exception Ireland's principal writers have been to a remarkable degree recalcitrant to the nationalist project. I have discussed that recalcitrance more extensively elsewhere in relation to the extreme demand for identification with the nation that nationalism imposes upon the Irish writer.[5] Here, I wish to explore more fully how not only the antirepresentational tendency in Irish literature but also the hybrid quality of popular forms constantly exceed the monologic desire of cultural nationalism, a desire which centers on the lack of an Irish epic. Both the popular and the literary forms map a colonial culture for which the forms of representational politics and aesthetics required by nationalism begin to seem entirely inadequate, obliging us to conceive of a cultural politics which must work outside the terms of representation. Incidentally, this colonial situation may also suggest the limits of the Bakhtinian formulations on which this analysis will in the first place be based.

David
Lloyd

I

At several points in *The Dialogic Imagination*, Mikhail Bakhtin isolates as a definitive characteristic of the novel its capacity to represent the heteroglossia internal to an apparently unified but nonetheless stratified national language.[6] Requiring the depiction of the conflictual, dialogic nature of social relations, this characteristic underlies the generic mobility and, at given historical moments, subversiveness of the novel which opposes it to the epic, as well as to other stabilized and "monologic" genres. The epic belongs to a closed and completed world and characteristically represents the unity or integration of that world and the integration of its exemplary heroes in that world (35). Typically, the epic casts backward to "an absolute past of national beginnings and peak times" (15), correlative to which is its stylistic closure: unlike the novel, the epic is a genre closed to development and therefore insusceptible to the representation of historical development (16–17). Intrinsic to Bakhtin's discussion of epic and novel is, accordingly, an historical periodization which derives the novel from the disintegration of the epic and its culture.[7] In the long term, the dialectic of the novel form leads to the disintegration of the myth of "a unitary, canonic language, of a national myth bolstered by a yet-unshaken unity" (370) and a concomitant displacement of the ideological by the human speaking subject.

Bakhtin, as that last citation serves to recall, posits the moment of unitary national culture in the past. The instance of a decolonizing nationalism, such as Ireland's throughout the nineteenth and early twentieth century, leads us to pose the question in slightly different terms. What if the epic of a nation has yet to be written and if the unity of the nation is desired as a prerequisite to the anticolonial struggle? In such a case, precisely what seems to be required is the monological form of the epic as a means to rather than a mere legitimating record of national unity while the function of the desired epic may be seen not only as the unification of a culture but also, in a quite specific sense, as the production of a dialogic subversion of the colonizing power. For these purposes, which are integral to the politically mobilizing project of cultural nationalism, the heteroglossic mode of the novel could be seen as distinctly counterproductive. Precisely that which, according to Bakhtin, the novel is constantly adapted to represent, the multiplicity of contending social voices, is what Irish nationalism must, for entirely coherent political reasons, seek to supersede in the form of a unified national identity. For the cultural nationalists of the nine-

teenth and early twentieth century, believing "that Irishmen were en-
slaved because they were divided,"[8] the principal task of nationalism
must be to overcome the sectarian, class, and ethnic affiliations that
divided Ireland. The task of producing representations of a common
identity was accordingly entrusted to literature, and to a literature
whose very rationale was monologic in so far as it was intended to
produce exactly the "national myth" which Bakhtin envisages to have
collapsed as the novel supplanted the epic.[9]

As I have argued elsewhere, the literary project of Irish nationalism, stemming from the Young Ireland movement of the 1840s, involves a quite sophisticated theory of generic development linked to
a universal history of cultural developments. In this argument, fully
developed cultures such as England's can rely on a political constitution which expresses the underlying unity of their conflicting social
forces, whereas underdeveloped cultures such as Ireland's must turn
to literary institutions for the same unificatory effects. Due, however,
to the apparently fragmentary and strife-ridden course of Irish history
and to the divided society of its present, that literature has yet to be
created. If, "rightly understood, the history of Ireland . . . had the unity
and purpose of an epic poem," that epic had yet to be written and
could not be prematurely forged. Before it could be written, the prior
stages of literary development must be passed through, permitting, as
if at accelerated tempo, the recomposition of all those ballads and folk
songs on which it was believed such epics as Homer's were founded.[10]
Hence the enormous quantity of ballads produced and collected in
nineteenth-century Ireland was not merely a question of propaganda
but directly concerned the constitution of an idea of Irishness which
could "contain and represent the races of Ireland."[11]

But this project of presenting to the Irish a single "spirit of the
nation" (to cite the title of one enormously popular collection) is confronted with peculiar problems as soon as it turns to extant ballads as
examples of that spirit. Collectors of Irish ballads classify them generally into three subdivisions: Gaelic or peasant songs, street ballads,
and literary or Anglo-Irish ballads.[12] To the latter class we will return,
since it is the problematic status of the first two which most acutely
confronts the cultural nationalist.

By the mid nineteenth century, the study of Gaelic language and
culture had proceeded little beyond the scarcely systematic amassing
of materials while distinctions between "high" and "low" literary productions remained relatively fluid and uncertain.[13] Collections were
recognized to be provisional and incomplete. Yet despite the, as it

were, objective grounds for the fragmentary corpus of Gaelic literature, nationalists who review it in order to distinguish and define Irish
identity time and again trace in that corpus a fragmentariness lodged
in the artifacts themselves. Thus when Davis remarks that "There are
great gaps in Irish song to be filled up," it is not to the state of research
that he refers but to the nature of the object, a nature that is for him, as
we shall see, historical and absolutely not essential. The "bulk of the
songs," he asserts, "are very defective": "Most of those hitherto in use
were composed during the last century, and therefore their structure is
irregular, their grief slavish and despairing, their joy reckless and bom-
bastic, their religion bitter and sectarian, their politics Jacobite and
concealed by extravagant and tiresome allegory. Ignorance, disorder
and every kind of oppression weakened and darkened the lyric genius
of Ireland."[14] The historical oppression of the Irish has contaminated
both the structure and the content of the Gaelic poetry, so that if it appears gapped, that gapping is internal to it, consisting in its "defective"
or "extra-vagant" deviation from the essential "genius" of the Irish
nation. There is something alien in the poetry, and the job of the popular editor is accordingly one of condensation: "cut them so as exactly
to suit the airs, preserve the local and broad historical allusions, but
remove the clumsy ornaments and exaggerations" (225–26). The perfection of the defective native Irish poetic tradition requires a process
of refinement which is, in principle at least, the antithesis of supple-
mentation, involving instead the purging of extraneous materials and
the unfolding of an obscured essence. Davis's formulation is characteristic of nationalist reception of Gaelic songs, which are similarly
perceived by D. F. McCarthy as "snatches and fragments of old songs
and ballads, which are chapters of a nation's autobiography."[15] In every
case the fragmentary autobiography is to be completed in the formation of a national identity properly represented in a national literature
imbued with its spirit rather than with the accidental traces and accre-
tions of its colonial history. Consistent with this general requirement
is an implicit rejection of the allegorical in favor of the symbolic: in
quite traditional Romantic terms, the extravagance of allegory is es-
chewed while historical and local allusion is promoted precisely as
"participating in that which it represents."[16] The aesthetic of nationalism accords with its political ends, subordinated at every level to the
demand for unity.

It is on the same grounds that the second class of street ballads is
criticized by nationalists, with only more vehemence than in the case
of their Gaelic language counterparts. Condemnation of the street bal-

lads, purchased widely by the already substantial portion of the people whose principal language was English, was virtually universal among Young Ireland critics who argued for their supplanting by ballads imbued with the national spirit such as those published in *The Spirit of the Nation* or in Duffy's and MacCarthy's collections of Irish ballads. Though their dismissals are fairly summary for the most part, it is possible to decipher the grounds for the antagonism. Most importantly, they are urban: "the mass of the street songs," remarks Duffy, "make no pretence to being true to Ireland; but only to being true to the purlieus of Cork and Dublin."[17] Nationalist antagonism to urban Ireland, which continues by and large to structure the nation's ideological self-representation, is by no means as simple and self-evident a phenomenon as its constancy has made it seem. It belongs to the constitutive contradiction of a modernizing ideology forced to seek its authenticating difference from the imperial culture on which it remains dependent by way of an appeal to a rural and Gaelic culture which is already in decay. Indeed, it is not, as we have seen, to that culture in itself that appeal is made, but rather to a "refinement" or "translation" of its essence, traced among the fragmentary survivals of an already decimated past life. The antagonism to the urban is, accordingly, an antagonism to the inauthenticity legible in its cultural forms. Cork and Dublin, along with Belfast, represent in mid-nineteenth-century Ireland, as already for several centuries in the case of Dublin, sites of cultural hybridization as well as centers of imperial authority and capital domination. Garrison as well as industrial or port cities, they represent concentrations of an English domination that penetrates every level of Irish social life. At the same time as they are nodes for the flows of English capital and imperial authority, they are also conduits for the contrary flows of a dislocated population, the points to which a dislocated rural population gravitates in search of employment or prior to emigration. The Pale area around Dublin had always seemed, to English eyes, under constant threat of contamination by Gaelic culture and by the transformation of old or new English into a settler population "more Irish than the Irish." But a rapid acceleration of the process of cultural hybridization, now more threatening to the nationalist than to the English, would appear to have taken place in the late eighteenth and early nineteenth centuries as an overdetermined consequence of the effects of the English industrial revolution, the serial crises in Irish agriculture after the Napoleonic wars and the gradual lifting of the Penal Laws in the decades preceding the Union of

Great Britain and Ireland in 1800. Simultaneously, the Irish language was perceived to be in decline.[18]

Even a quite casual collection of eighteenth- and nineteenth-century street ballads like Colm O Lochlainn's *Irish Street Ballads* will serve as a quite accurate gauge of the extent to which such works register, both thematically and stylistically, these processes as they are apprehended by the Irish population.[19] A very high incidence of the songs is devoted to migration or emigration, to conscription or enlistment in the British army, as well as to the celebration of the 1798 uprising and a range of rebel heroes. Even the many love songs are coursed through more by laments for grinding poverty, imprisonment under English law, or the necessity of emigration or vagrancy than by complaints of fickleness and inconstancy, a characteristic which is considerably at odds with their frequent use, by colonizer and nationalist alike, to ground the stereotype of pure Irish sentimentality. At the stylistic level, the street ballads at moments provide an even more intimate register of the processes of cultural hybridization. They are, most often, adaptations of traditional airs to English words, enforcing frequently a distortion of standard English pronunciation or syntax to fit Gaelic musical and speech rhythms, a trait in fact frequently celebrated in the more refined literary productions of translators and adaptors like Moore, Ferguson, and Callanan.[20] This primary hybridization is matched by varying degrees of incorporation of Irish language fragments into the predominantly English texts of the ballads. Usually phonetically transcribed by writers illiterate in Irish, these fragments can be whole refrains, as in "The Barrymore Tithe Victory" (1831), which retains as part of its refrain the words of the Gaelic ballad "A Dhruimfhionn Donn Dílis" whose tune it appropriates, but which it transcribes as "A Drimon down deelish a heeda na moe" and turns to a celebration of the popular hero and political leader, Daniel O'Connell. Others, by far the majority, seem little more than tags from the Gaelic, place names or mythological and legendary figures, that from the dominant perspective would appear as recalcitrant recollections of the culture which is in transformation but still politically and culturally resistant. From another perspective, however, that of the balladeers and many in their audiences, such tags would resonate with familiar and quite complex allusions to allegorical or historical figures from Gaelic culture, adding a richer, if occluded, dimension to the ballads' reception. Thus the refrain of "A New Song in Praise of Fergus O'Connor and Independence," celebrating the election of Chartist O'Connor as MP for Cork, runs "So vote for brave Fergus and Sheela na Guira," the Gaelic tag referring again to the original ballad, "Sighile Ni Ghadhra" from which the tune is borrowed, but probably subsisting as an allegorical figure for Ireland. Even less political street ballads, such as the later "Kerry Recruit," which relates the story of a young peasant enlisted for the Crimean War, uses fragments of Irish as well as of Anglo-Irish dialect as a means of linguistically dramatizing the experience of dislocation and the role of such institutions as the army in the transformation of the colonized population:

> So I buttered my brogues and shook hands with my spade,
> And I went to the fair like a dashing young blade,
> When up comes a sergeant and asks me to 'list,
> "Arra, sergeant a gra, put the bob in my fist."
>
> "O! then here is the shilling, as we've got no more,
> "When you get to head-quarters you'll get half a score."
> "Arra, quit your kimeens," ses I, "sergeant, good-bye,
> You'd not wish to be quartered, and neither would I."[21]

This last example, though somewhat later than the Young Ireland writings instanced above, draws attention to a further element of the street ballads which drew nationalist criticism, namely their frequently burlesque tone. Precisely because of the heterogeneity of the ballads, whether taken as collections or, indeed, as individual specimens, it would be impossible to posit a "typical character" for the street ballads or to fix their tone. In "The Kerry Recruit," for example, it becomes exceedingly difficult to specify the object of the mockery, the country gosthoon or the sergeant, peasant ignorance or British institutions. Tonal instability of this kind is common, as is a similarly vertiginous mixture of realism and burlesque, "high language" and slang. Two further examples will suffice, one, "Father Murphy," being an anonymous rebel ballad on the 1798 rebellion, the other, "Billy's Downfall," attributed to the most celebrated of Dublin street balladeers, "Zozimus" (Michael Moran), being a satirical commemoration of the blowing up of a unionist monument to William III on College Green in 1836:

> The issue of it was a close engagement,
> While on the soldiers we played warlike pranks;
> Thro' sheepwalks, hedgerows and shady thickets,
> There were mangled bodies and broken ranks,
> The shuddering cavalry I can't forget them;

We raised the brushes on their helmets straight—
They turned about and they bid for Dublin,
As if they ran for a ten-pound plate.

By brave Coriolanus and wiggy McManus,
By dirty King Shamus, that ran from the Boyne,
I never was willing dead men to be killing,
Their scurry blood spilling, with traitors to join.
For true-heart allegiance, without much persuadience,
Myself and all Paddies we're still at a call,
But to burke a poor king, 'tis a horrible thing,
Granu's sons never heard it in Tara's old hall.[22]

As both instances indicate, the processes of hybridization registered
in the street ballads proceed far beyond the integration of Gaelic into
English language forms. To the instabilities of tone that derive from
the refusal to differentiate the burlesque from the serious corresponds
a similar indifference to cultural registers. Military language can co-
habit with that of the racecourse, or classical references give way to
citations of ancient and modern history, folk heroes, and contemporary slang. Much of the pleasure of the street ballad, as with so many
"popular" forms, derives precisely from this indifference to cultural
hierarchies.[23] It may even be that the very adaptibility of the ballad,
as a kind of template transformable to fit any given locality or momentary reference, subserves not only the continual demand for the
"new song" as instant commodity, but also a more discrete function.
Beyond the cultural resistance they articulate, such ballads as "Father
Murphy" in their very descriptions of combat conceivably served to
preserve and transmit not merely the historical memory of insurrec-
tions but also the repertoire of means to resist, the tactical knowledge
of how and where to conduct armed struggle. For a rural audience,
"Father Murphy" may serve precisely the same function in terms of
tactical knowledge as John Mitchel's regular military lessons in the
United Irishman of 1848, themselves adapted from a British military
handbook.[24]

Such speculation aside, the stylistic elements of the street ballads
alone throw into greater relief the grounds for cultural nationalist criti-
cisms of them. The cultural nationalism that is developed within the
Young Ireland movement is quite strictly a Romantic nationalism and,
like its Unionist counterparts, derives much from English and German
high Romanticism. But the forces which a poet like Wordsworth seeks
to counteract, the spectacle of the city as a "perpetual flow/ Of trivial

objects, melted and reduced / To one identity, by differences that have no law, no meaning, and no end,"[25] are accentuated in the Irish case by the colonial encounter which both accelerates the processes of cultural disintegration and gives a specific political name, anglicization, to the phenomenon of "reduction to identity." What we have described, in the wider sphere of the Irish political economy as well as in that of the street ballads, as "hybridization" is necessarily grasped by nationalists as the paradoxically simultaneous process of multiplication or disintegration and homogenization. The flooding of the market with English commodities both disintegrates what is retrospectively constructed as a unified Irish identity and absorbs its residues into the single field of the British industrial and imperial empire. And since the only means to resist this process, in the absence of autonomous national political institutions, appears to be the formation of nationalist subjects through literary institutions, the field of popular literature becomes peculiarly fraught. For if the ultimate desire of the nationalist must be for the state (in every sense of the word "for"), that desire must in fact not first of all be for the state itself, as a body of specific institutions to be controlled, but for what the state in turn is held to represent, namely, the unity or reconciliation of the people. Hence the necessity for a cultural nationalism, not merely as a supplement to, but as a prerequisite for, a military nationalism, and hence the requirement that that nationalist culture be monological in its modes of expression. The representation as a desired end of an homogeneous Irish nation is a necessary preliminary to the political struggle in any form.

Accordingly, the aesthetic choices which oppose the nationalists' literary recreations of Irish ballad poetry to both the street ballads and to the Gaelic songs are also at every level political choices. Their collections are designed, as it were, to give law, meaning, and end to a specific difference which would constitute an Ireland independent of England and in opposition to the heterogeneous image of Irish social life and culture borne in the street ballad or in extant translations of Gaelic poetry. A national poetry must speak with one voice and, unlike those street ballads in which it is often difficult to tell if the hero is subject or object of the burlesque, must represent the Irish people as the agent of its own history, of a history which has "the unity and purpose of an epic poem." What this requires, as I have argued more fully elsewhere, is a "translational" aesthetic, in the sense that what must be constantly carried over is the essential spirit rather than the superficial forms of Irish poetry in either language.[26]

As Dennis Florence MacCarthy puts it in *The Book of Irish Ballads*:

"This peculiar character of our poetry is, however, not easily imparted. An Irish word or an Irish phrase, even appositely introduced, will not be sufficient; it must pervade the entire poem, and must be seen and felt in the construction, the sentiment, and the expression."[27] In the examples cited above, "Sheela na Guira" or the "Granu's sons" are juxtaposed in contiguity to Fergus O'Connor or Coriolanus, achieving an expansion—and complication—of referential range without requiring the subordination of the elements to one another. MacCarthy's aesthetic program, on the contrary, requires the subordination of the Gaelic element as a representative instance consubstantial with the homogeneous totality of Irish identity. In keeping with an antagonism to the allegorical tendency of Gaelic poetry and the street ballads in favor of a generally symbolist aesthetic, nationalist writing must perform a transfer from the metonymic axis of contiguity to that of metaphor. Where the metonymic disposition of popular forms lends itself to the indiscriminate citation of insubordinate cultural elements, the fundamentally narrative structure of metaphoric language seeks to reorganize such cultural elements as representative moments in a continuous epic of the nation's self-formation.[28]

MacCarthy himself provides us with an exemplary instance in his ballad "The Pillar Towers of Ireland" which, though by no manner of means the most celebrated of Young Ireland productions, almost self-consciously enacts the appropriation of historical Irish elements to a seamless representation of Irish destiny. The pillar towers become symbols of the continuing spirit of Ireland, both its products and its organizing representatives, giving shape and relationship to the several races which have passed through or settled the land in the course of its history:

> Around these walls have wandered the Briton and the Dane—
> The captives of Armorica, the cavaliers of Spain—
> Phoenician and Milesian, and the plundering Norman Peers—
> And the swordsmen of brave Brian, and the chiefs of later
>   years![29]

A persistent and resistant element of the Irish landscape, the round or pillar tower stands as itself a metaphor for the metaphoric process by which an initial perception of difference can be brought over time into a superior recognition of identity:

> There may it stand for ever, while this symbol doth impart
> To the mind one glorious vision, or one proud throb to the heart;

While the breast needeth rest may these grey old temples last,
Bright prophets of the future, as preachers of the past!
(*Book of Irish Ballads*, 128)

It is not necessary to be aware of the continuing exploitation of the Round Tower by the Irish Tourist Board and other such institutions to sense how rapidly this representation of an authentic Irish identity veers toward kitsch. Indeed, the constant gravitation of cultural nationalism toward kitsch is a virtually inevitable consequence of its aesthetic program, if not, indeed, to some extent a mark of its success. The commodification of style and the mechanical reproduction of standardized forms of affect that define kitsch have their close counterpart in cultural nationalism.[30] Here, the incessant injunction to produce representative ballads which will reproduce Gaelic styles by and large known to the producers only by way of representations is directed toward the homogenization of a political rather than an economic sphere. It similarly requires, nonetheless, the production of novelties which are always interchangeable, a condition of the principally journalistic sphere in which most nationalist ballads first appeared, and the immediate evocation of an affect which is the sign of identification with the nation. Congruent in most respects with Romantic aesthetics generally, the subordination of the nationalist ballad to a quite conscious political end denies it the auratic distance which is usually held, if often erroneously, to guarantee the critical moment of the modern artwork.

Ironically, what is properly, in Brechtian terms, an epic distance belongs more frequently to the street ballad than to the nationalist ballads which were intended to replace them. Self-consciously produced as commodities, and with the ephemeral aptness to momentary need or desire which is the property of the commodity, the street ballads often achieve an effect akin to montage in which the contours of an heterogeneous and hybridized culture can become apparent without necessarily losing political force. Indeed, a large part of the pleasure of the street ballad is political and lies in its use of "extravagant allegories": what it exploits is precisely the unevenness of knowledge which characterizes the colonized society. The variegated texture of colonized society permits to a remarkable degree an exploitation by the colonized of those elements which are unfamiliar to the colonizer, and therefore appear encoded, like the Gaelic tags cited above, as a means of at once disguising and communicating subversion, as message to the colonized and as uncertainty to the colonizer. The very inauthenticity of the colonized culture becomes the means to an unpredictable process of masking. Where the colonizer, whose proper slogan should be that "Ignorance is Power," seeks to reduce the colonized to a surveyable surface whose meaning is always the same, and where the nationalist responds with an ideal of the total translucence of national spirit in the people, the hybridized culture of the colonized offers only surfaces pitted or mined with uncertainty, depths and shallows whose contours vary depending on the "familiarity" of each observer. On this surface, demarcations of the borderline between damage and creative strategies for resistance are hard to fix. As we shall see, neither the damage nor the resistance lend themselves easily to assimilation.

Captured in the contradiction between its modernizing effects and its conservative appeal, nationalist culture on the other hand is drawn into a process of stylization, the representation of a style, which constantly returns it to an inauthenticity akin to though not identical with that of the street ballad it seeks to supplant. This effect of stylization is probably inseparable from the fundamental dislocation which colonization effects in any culture and which is the necessary prior condition for the emergence of any specifically nationalist resistance. In proceeding, it is only necessary to insist again that the dislocation of the colonized culture should not be thought of in terms of a loss of a prior and recoverable authenticity. Rather, authenticity must be seen as the projective desire of a nationalism programmatically concerned with the homogenization of the people as a national political entity.

II

Unsurprisingly, given the virtually aporetic status of its contradictions, the terms of mid-nineteenth-century nationalist cultural discussions are by and large reproduced half a century later in the Irish literary revival. James Joyce presents them prominently in *Ulysses* as a prelude to Stephen Dedalus's development of his own conception of genius out of Saxon Shakespeare:

> —Our young Irish bards, John Eglinton censured, have yet to create a figure which the world will set beside Saxon Shakespeare's Hamlet though I admire him, as old Ben did, on this side idolatry.
>
> Mr Best came forward, amiable, towards his colleague.
> —Haines is gone, he said.
> —Is he?
> —I was showing him Jubainville's book. He's quite enthusiastic,

don't you know, about Hyde's Lovesongs of Connacht. I couldn't bring him in to hear the discussion. He's gone to Gill's to buy it.

Bound thee forth, my booklet, quick
To greet the callous public,
Writ, I ween, 'twas not my wish
In lean unlovely English.

—The peatsmoke is going to his head, John Eglinton opined.

—People do not know how dangerous lovesongs can be, the auric egg of Russell warned occultly. The movements which work revolutions in the world are born out of the dreams and visions in a peasant's heart on the hillside. For them the earth is not an exploitable ground but the living mother. The rarefied air of the academy and the arena produce the sixshilling novel, the musichall song. France produces the finest flower of corruption in Mallarme but the desirable life is revealed only to the poor of heart, the life of Homer's Phaeacians.[31]

It is not merely that Joyce alludes here, in compressed fashion, to the principal concerns that continue to play through Irish cultural nationalism: the desire for the masterwork; the opposition between the spirit of peasant song, "racy of the soil," and the hybrid "flowers of corruption"; the turn to Homer as the figure who exemplifies the unification of the work of genius with the "genius of place." Furthermore, he indicates the complexity of the cultural transactions that take place in the thoroughly hybridized culture of "West Britain," where Irishmen discourse on English, German, and Greek culture while an Englishman, Haines, studies the Celtic element in literature and Hyde regrets the necessity which forces him to exemplify a Gaelic metre in lean, unlovely English.

Joyce's evocation of Hyde at this juncture allows us to grasp both the extent to which turn-of-the-century cultural nationalism recapitulates its earlier forms and the extent to which its terms had become at once more sophisticated and more problematic. Douglas Hyde, founder-president of the Gaelic League, was a principal advocate of the Irish language revival, a scholar, poet-translator, and folklorist. His most famous single essay, "The Necessity for De-Anglicising Ireland" (1892), resumes Young Ireland attacks on the penetration of Ireland by English culture as well as capital and on the consequent emergence of an entirely "anomalous position" for the Irish race, "imitating England and yet apparently hating it."[32] In large part, this essay presents a dismal catalog of hybridization which ranges through place and family names to musical forms and clothing. Its conclusion, that a de-anglicization of Ireland is the necessary prelude to and guarantee of eventual Irish autonomy, is prescriptive for Hyde's own laborious collection and translation of Irish folksongs and poetry. In these, as he had already argued in his essay "Gaelic Folk Songs" (1890), the Irish genius was properly to be deciphered: "We shall find that, though in their origin and diffusion they are purely local, yet in their essence they are wholly national, and, perhaps, more purely redolent of the race and soil than any of the real literary productions of the last few centuries."[33]

When it comes to deciphering that essence, nonetheless, Hyde is confronted with the dilemma which led to Young Ireland's translational aesthetic. There remain "great gaps in Irish song." For Hyde, however, as a scholar whose intimacy with the Gaelic material was far greater than Davis's or MacCarthy's, the question as to whether the "gapped" nature of Irish folk song was of its essence or an accident based upon the contingent, historical determinants of an oral culture, remains correspondingly more difficult to resolve. After citing a number of exemplary instances from Gaelic love songs, he pauses to remark on the necessity to cite in order to represent the nature of these songs in general. The ensuing reflections lead him to an unusually complex rendering of the "nature" of the Gaelic spirit, leaving him unable to decide between the historical and the essential:

It may appear strange, however, that I have only given stray verses instead of translating entire songs. But the fact is that the inconsequentness of these songs, as I have taken them down from the lips of the peasantry, is startling.

Many adjectives have been applied by many writers to the Gaelic genius, but to my mind nothing about it is so noticeable as its inconsequentness, if I may use such a word—a peculiarity which, as far as I know, no one has yet noticed. The thought of the Irish peasant takes the most surprising and capricious leaps. It's [sic] movement is like the career of his own goblin, the Pooka; it clears the most formidable obstacles at a bound and carries across astonishing distances in a moment. The folk-song is the very incarnation of this spirit. It is nearly impossible to find three verses in which there is anything like an ordinary sequence of thought. They are full up of charms that the mind must leap, elipses [sic] that it must fill up, and detours of movement which only the most vivid imagination can make straight. This is the reason why I have found no popular ballads amongst the peasantry, for to tell a story in verse requires an orderly, progressive, and somewhat slow sequence of ideas, and this is the very faculty which the Gael has not got— his mind is too quick and passionate. . . . But even this character- istic of Gaelic thought is insufficient to account for the perfectly extraordinary inconsequentness and abruptness of the folk-songs, as I have found them, I imagine that the cause of this peculiarity is not to be ascribed wholly to the authors of the songs, but also in great part to the medium which the songs passed through be- fore they came to us—that medium, of course, being the various generations of local singers who have perpetuated them. These singers often forgot, as was natural, the real words of the song, and then they invented others, but more frequently they borrowed verses from any other piece that came into their head, provided it could be sung to the same tune, and hence the songs as we have them now are a curious mixture indeed. What between the 'un- sequacious' mind of the original makers, the alterations of singers who forgot the words, and the extraneous verses borrowed from completely different productions, two out of three of the folk- songs which I have collected, resemble those children's toys of paper where when you pull a string you get a different pair of legs or a different head, joined to a different body. The most beautiful sentiments will be followed by the most grotesque bathos, and the tenderest and most exquisite verses will end in the absurdest nonsense. This has been done by the singers who have transmitted them. (113–14)

The folk songs appear here as at once the representation of an essence, the Gaelic spirit, and as the products of the specific and contingent conditions of their transmission. But if we take these representations as those of an essence, then the essence itself makes it impossible to define any essential character of the race, since a character, to have any identity at all, must be consistent, as Young Ireland and their fol- lowers in the Literary Revival consistently argued. On the other hand, the historical argument in its turn, recognizing the sheer contingency which has conditioned the forms and peculiarities of the folk songs, would make it impossible to derive a national character from them.

Despite the momentary hesitation which this acknowledgment of the overdetermined grounds for the "great gaps in Irish song" causes him, Hyde rapidly recuperates the Irish identity by offering, after citing one instance of a thoroughly adulterated verse, "one specimen of a comparatively perfect folk-song which has not been interfered with" (115). The song, "Mo bhron ar an bhfarraige" [Oh, my grief on the sea!], which concludes with the lines,

> And my love came behind me—
> He came from the south—
> With his breast to my bosom,
> His mouth to my mouth,

appears as a perfect because consistent expression of "genuine passion," lacking any of the marks, "the alliteration, adjectives, assonance, and tricks of the professional poet" (117). Hyde's "restoration" of the essential folk song requires, in other words, not only its purification from hybridization internal to the culture or derived from external influence, but even the representation of the work of the Gaelic bards as a deviation from the true passion of the people. Irish folk culture is transformed into an ahistorical ground on which the defining difference of "Irishness" can be established over against the homogenizing/hybridizing influence of "Anglicization."

It is more than probable that Joyce knew Hyde's essays and certain that he knew this particular song, if only from the only slightly revised version in *The Love Songs of Connacht*, since it appears transformed early in *Ulysses*. It reappears, however, not in the context of "genuine passion," but in the course of Stephen's "morose delectation" on Sandymount Strand as his thoughts shift back and forth between the cockle picker's woman passing him and the memory of his dead mother:

> She trudges, schlepps, trains, drags, trascines her load. A tide westering, moondrawn, in her wake. Tides, myriadislanded, within her, blood not mine, oinopa ponton, a winedark sea. Behold the handmaiden of the moon. In sleep the wet sign calls her hour, bids her rise. Bridebed, childbed, bed of death, ghostcandled. Omnis caro ad te veniet. He comes pale vampire, through storm his eyes, his bat sails bloodying the sea, mouth to her mouth's kiss. (*U*, 40)

The verses emerging here reappear somewhat later, in the "Aeolus" section, in a form closer to that given by Hyde:

> *On swift sail flaming*
> *From storm and south*
> *He comes, pale vampire,*
> *His mouth to my mouth.* (*U*, 109)

We may read in the transformation which the folk song gradually undergoes a representation at several levels of the processes of hybridization as they construct the individual consciousness. Many of the elements of that hybridization are superficially evident: the chain of foreign, or rather, "anglicized" words used to describe the cockle picker's woman, the phrases from Homer and from the Latin of Catholic ritual, or the parody of biblical invocations. The effect of hybridization, however, needs more careful analysis both at the formal literary level and at that of the representation of an individual subjectivity which it entails. The most familiar stylistic term in Joyce criticism used to describe the representation of subjective interiority is "stream of consciousness," a term which implies a certain consistency within the representation as well as implying a relative transparency and evenness among the elements. As such, the term is largely inadequate, even in the earlier sections of the novel, to describe the staccato or interrupted rhythms, the unevenness of accessibility of the allusions, whether to different readers or to the represented subject (Stephen or Bloom) or to the various levels of implicit "consciousness" that these stylistic effects constitute.

Equally inadequate would be any description of these effects in Bakhtinian terms as instances of "assimilation" or "appropriation." These are terms employed by Bakhtin in his description of the normative dialogical formation of the subject:

> As a living, socio-ideological concrete thing, as heteroglot opinion, language, for the individual consciousness, lies on the borderline between oneself and the other. The word in language is half someone else's. It becomes "one's own" only when the speaker populates it with his own intention, his own accent, when he appropriates the word, adapting it to his own semantic and expressive intention. (293)

> One's own discourse is gradually and slowly wrought out of others' words that have been acknowledged and assimilated, and the boundaries between the two are at first scarcely perceptible. (345n)

Despite the difficulties he acknowledges to afflict these processes, Bakhtin is clearly operating here with an at least residually Kantian subject, one existent as potential prior to any engagement with word or object and, perhaps more importantly, on its way to conformity with those maxims of enlightenment which for Kant define the autonomous subject: independence, consistency, and formal, universal identity.[34]

It is, of course, toward the production of such a subject, capable, for example of assimilating the alien English language to Irish identity or the equally alien Gaelic language to the English "mother-tongue," that Irish nationalism is directed. What it constantly diagnoses, however, is a subject-people always the object of imperfect assimilation to either culture, in a state, that is, of continuing dependence. It is for this reason that Joyce's "citational" aesthetic in *Ulysses* cuts so strongly at once against Bakhtin's description of the subjective processes which the novel typifies and against the translational aesthetic of Irish nationalism. One could, indeed, argue that Bakhtin's assimilation is itself a version of a generally translational aesthetic for which the subject is formed in a continual appropriation of the alien to itself just as translation, as opposed, for example, to interpretation or paraphrase, is seen as essentially a recreation of the foreign text in one's own language.[35] Joyce's, or Stephen's, version of this love song of Connaught rather insists on its heterogeneity in the course of an essentially "inconsequential" meditation or miscegenates it with an entirely different—but no less "Irish"— tradition of Gothic vampire tales.[36]

Accordingly, where the principal organizing metaphor of Irish nationalism is that of a proper paternity, of restoring the lineage of the fathers in order to repossess the motherland, Joyce's procedures are dictated by adulteration. Joyce's personal obsession with adultery is well-documented, and it is a commonplace that the plot of *Ulysses* itself turns around Molly Bloom's adulterous relationship with Blazes Boylan.[37] That the figure of the nineteenth-century leader of the Home Rule party, Charles Stewart Parnell, recurs from Joyce's earliest works as a victim of betrayal consequent on his adulterous relationship with Kitty O'Shea underlines the extent to which adultery is also a historical and political issue for Irish nationalism. The common tracing of the first Anglo-Norman conquest of Ireland in 1169 to Diarmaid Mac-Murchadha, King of Leinster's adulterous relationship with the High King's wife, Dearbhghiolla, establishes adulteration as a popular myth of origins for Irish nationalist sentiment. As the Citizen puts it, in the "Cyclops" chapter of *Ulysses:* "The adultress and her paramour brought the Saxon robbers here. . . . A dishonoured wife, . . . that's what's the cause of all our misfortunes" (266).

For the nationalist citizen, the identity of the race is adulterated by "la belle infidele" and, as in the old expression, the restoration of that identity by translation (traditore) is haunted by the anxiety of a betrayal (traduttore). This chapter, that in *Ulysses* in which issues of nationalist politics and culture are played out most intensely and in which the various elements of Irish culture are most thoroughly deployed, circulates not only thematically but also stylistically around adulteration as the constitutive anxiety of nationalism. For while the citizen is militant against the hybridization of Irish culture, the chapter itself dramatizes adulteration as the condition of colonial Ireland at virtually every level. Barney Kiernan's pub is at the heart of Dublin, but also located in Little Britain St., in the vicinity of the Linenhall, the Barracks and the law courts, and across the river from Dublin Castle, the center of British administration. Most of the characters who pass through the bar (already a parodic form of the legal bar, both being sites of censure and debate) are connected in one or other way with these institutions while the legal cases cited continually associate the influence of British institutions with economic dependency in the form of debt and that in turn with the stereotype of financial and cultural instability, the Jew.[38] The slippage among institutional, cultural, racial, and political elements is a function of a stylistic hybridization which refuses to offer any normative mode of representation from which other modes can be said to deviate.

These features of the "Cyclops" chapter have been noted in different ways by many commentators. What needs to be stressed, however, is that by and large the mingling of stylistic elements is rendered by critics in terms which reduce the process of hybridization to the juxtaposition of a set of equivalent representational modes, a reduction which, even where it refuses to posit the register of colloquial speech as an "original" of which all other modes are "translations," implies the essential coherence or integrity of each mode in itself. To do so is to leave fundamentally unchallenged the principle of equivalence on which the translational aesthetic is based. This is the case even in one of the most astute accounts of the chapter. After rewriting a passage from "Cyclops" in what is effectively parallel text, Colin Mac-Cabe comments:

> Ignoring for the moment that part of the second text which has no parallel in the first, what is important in this passage is not the truth or falsity of what is being said, but how the same event articulated in two different discourses produces different representations (different truths). Behind "an elder of noble gait and countenance" and "that bloody old pantaloon Denis Breen in his

bath slippers" we can discern no definite object. Rather each object can only be identified in a discourse which already exists and that identification is dependent on the possible distinctions available in the discourse.[39]

MacCabe's description of Joyce's procedures at this juncture is comparable to Bakhtin's general description of the novel as a genre:

> The novel can be defined as a diversity of social speech types (sometimes even diversity of languages) and a diversity of individual voices, artistically organized. The internal stratification of any single national language into social dialects, characteristic group behavior, professional jargons, generic languages, languages of generations and age groups, tendentious languages, languages of the authorities, of various circles and of passing fashions, languages that serve the specific sociopolitical purposes of the day, even of the hour (each day has its own slogan, its own vocabulary, its own emphases)—this internal stratification present in any given language at any given moment of its historical existence is the indispensable prerequisite for the novel as a genre. (262–63)

Adequate insofar as they go, neither description is capable of grasping the internal heterogeneities, the adulteration of discourses as Joyce constructs them in "Cyclops" and throughout *Ulysses*. This process of adulteration ranges from a phenomenon of colloquial Irish speech to which Oscar Wilde gave the name of "malapropism" to the ceaseless interpenetration of different discourses. Malapropism varies from casual misspeaking, sometimes intentional, sometimes based on mishearings of an improperly mastered English ("Don't cast your nasturtiums on my character" [263]), to deliberate and creative polemical wordplay (as in English "syphilisation").[40] As a larger stylistic principle, the adulteration of interpenetrating discourses is unremitting, blending, among other things, pastiches of Biblical/liturgical, medieval, epic (based in large part on Standish O'Grady's already highly stylized versions of old Irish heroic cycles), legal, scientific, and journalistic modes. Frequently, the legal and journalistic discourses at once contain and disseminate adulteration, representing as institutional formations material sites for the clash of heterogeneous languages and interests. The following example instantiates the possible modulations among different registers:

> And whereas on the sixteenth day of the month of the oxeyed goddess and in the third week after the feastday of the Holy and

Undivided Trinity, the daughter of the skies, the virgin moon being
then in her first quarter, it came to pass that those learned judges
repaired them to the halls of law. There master Courtenay, sitting
in his own chamber, gave his rede and master Justice Andrew, sitting without a jury in probate court, weighed well and pondered
the claim of the first chargeant upon the property in the matter of
the will propounded and final testamentary disposition in re the
real and personal estate of the late lamented Jacob Halliday, vint-
ner, deceased, versus Livingstone, an infant, of unsound mind, and
another. And to the solemn court of Green street there came sir
Frederick the Falconer. And he sat him there about the hour of five
o'clock to administer the law of the brehons at the commission for
all that and those parts to be holden in and for the county of the
city of Dublin. And there sat with him the high sinhedrim of the
twelve tribes of Iar, for every tribe one man, of the tribe of Patrick
and of the tribe of Hugh and of the tribe of Owen and of the tribe of
Conn and of the tribe of Oscar and of the tribe of Fergus and of the
tribe of Finn and of the tribe of Dermot and of the tribe of Cormac
and of the tribe of Kevin and of the tribe of Caolte and of the tribe
of Ossian, there being in all twelve good men and true. . . . And
straightway the minions of the law led forth from their donjon
keep one whom the sleuthhounds of justice had apprehended in
consequence of evidence received. (265)

Categorization of this and similar passages as "dialogical" would be
limited precisely insofar as what occurs here is not an opposition, con-
versational or polemical, between coherent "voices," but their entire
intercontamination. Indeed, precisely what is lacking or erased here
is voice which, as Bakhtin remarks, is a category fundamental "in the
realm of ethical and legal thought and discourse. . . . An independent,
responsible and active discourse is the fundamental indicator of an
ethical, legal and political human being" (349–50).

It is through the question of voice and its dismantling that we can
begin to grasp the complex ramifications of Joyce's deployment of adulteration as both motif and stylistic principle in *Ulysses*. Where nationalism is devoted to the production, in stylistic terms, of a singular
voice, and to the purification of the dialect of street ballads or Gaelic
songs, it produces equally what we might envisage as a matrix of articulated concepts which provide the parameters of its political aesthetic or aesthetic politics. Thus this singular voice correlates with the
formation of the Irish subject as autonomous citizen at one level and

with a collective Irish identity at another. That analogical relation between the individual and the national moments is permitted by a concept of representation which requires a narrative movement between the exemplary instance and the totality which it prefigures. Identification between the representative individual and the nation constitutes the people which is to claim legitimate rights to independence as an "original," that is, essential, entity. Consistent representation of that essence underwrites simultaneously the aesthetic originality, or autonomy, of the literary work which takes its place as an instance of the national culture. Such a self-sustaining and self-reinforcing matrix of concepts furnishes, as it were, the ideological verisimilitude of cultural nationalism, permitting its apparent self-evidence.

Joyce's work, on the contrary, deliberately dismantles voice and verisimilitude in the same moment. Even if, as MacCabe has suggested, particular discourses attain dominance at given points in the text, the continual modulations that course through "Cyclops," as indeed through the work as a whole, preclude any discursive mode from occupying a position from which the order of probability that structures mimetic verisimilitude could be stabilized. But even beyond this, the constantly parodic mode in which any given discourse is represented prevents their being understood as internally coherent, if rival, systems of verisimilitude. The double face of parody, at once dependent on and antagonistic to its models, constantly undercuts either the production of an autonomous voice or the stabilization of a discourse in its "faithful" reproduction.[41] Adulteration as a stylistic principle institutes a multiplication of possibility in place of an order of probability and as such appears as the precise aesthetic correlative of adultery in the social sphere. For if adultery is forbidden under patriarchal law, it is precisely because of the potential multiplication of possibilities for identity which it implies as against the paternal fiction which is based on no more than legal verisimilitude. If the spectre of adultery must be exorcized by nationalism, it is in turn because adulteration undermines the stable formation of legitimate and authentic identities. It is not difficult to trace here the grounds for nationalism's consistent policing of female sexuality by the ideological and legal confinement of women to the domestic sphere.[42] There is probably no need to rehearse here either the anxieties which Bloom raises for the citizen on racial as well as sexual grounds or the extent to which the narrative as a whole occupies aesthetic, cultural, and sexual terrains in a manner which continually runs counter to nationalist ideology.[43] What must be noted, however, is the extent to which its antirepresentational mode of writing clashes with nationalist orders of verisimilitude precisely by allowing the writing out of the effects of colonialism that nationalism seeks to eradicate socially and psychically. This, however, is not merely a matter of the content of a representation but also inseparably an issue of stylistics. Thus, for example, Bloom cannot be the exemplary hero of what might be an Irish epic not only because of his status as "neither fish nor fowl," to cite the citizen, but because *Ulysses* as a whole refuses the narrative verisimilitude within which the formation of representative man could be conceived. The aesthetic formation of the exemplary citizen requires not only the selection of an individual sociologically or statistically "normative" but also the representation of that individual's progress from unsubordinated contingency to socially significant integration with the totality. This requires in turn what Bakhtin describes as "a combining of languages and styles into a higher unity," the novel's capacity to "orchestrate its themes" into a totality (263). *Ulysses'* most radical movement is in its refusal to fulfill either of these demands and its correspondent refusal to subordinate itself to the socializing functions of identity formation.[44] It insists instead on a deliberate stylization of dependence and inauthenticity, a stylization, that is, of the hybrid status of the colonized subject as of the colonized culture, their internal adulteration and the strictly parodic modes which they produce in every sphere.

III

David
Lloyd

We will become, what, I fear, we are largely at present, a nation of imitators, the Japanese of Western Europe, lost to the power of native initiative and alive only to second-hand assimilation. (Douglas Hyde)

Everywhere in the mentality of the Irish people are flux and uncertainty. Our national consciousness may be described, in a native phrase, as a quaking sod. It gives no footing. It is not English, nor Irish, nor Anglo-Irish. (Daniel Corkery)

[The pachuco's] dangerousness lies in his singularity. Everyone agrees in finding something hybrid about him, something disturbing and fascinating. He is surrounded by an aura of ambivalent notions: his singularity seems to be nourished by powers that are alternately evil and beneficent. (Octavio Paz)

We Brazilians and other Latin-Americans constantly experience the artificial, inauthentic and imitative nature of our cultural life.

An essential element in our critical thought since independence, it has been variously interpreted from romantic, naturalist, modernist, right-wing, left-wing, cosmopolitan and nationalist points of view, so we may suppose that the problem is enduring and deeply rooted. (Roberto Schwarz)

"A European journalist, and moreover a leftist, asked me a few days ago, "Does a Latin-American culture exist?" . . . The question . . . could also be expressed another way: "Do you exist?" For to question our culture is to question our very existence, our human reality itself, and thus to be willing to take a stand in favor of our irremediable colonial condition, since it suggests that we would be but a distorted echo of what occurs elsewhere. (Roberto Fernandez Retamar)

The danger is in the neatness of identifications. (Samuel Beckett)

Riding on the train with another friend, I ramble on about the difficulty of finishing this book, feeling like I am being asked by all sides to be a "representative" of the race, the sex, the sexuality— or at all costs to avoid that. (Cherríe Moraga)[45]

Since there is insufficient space for a more exhaustive account, the above citations must serve as indicators of a recurrent and problematic set of issues that course through numerous colonial situations, and perhaps especially in those where an "original" language has been displaced by that of the colonizing power.[46] This problematic can be described as a confrontation with a cultural hybridization which, unlike the process of assimilation described by Bakhtin and others, issues in inauthenticity rather than authentic identity. To describe this confrontation as problematic is to insist at once that the experience of inauthenticity intended here is not to be confused with that of the celebrated postmodern subject, though clearly the overlapping geographical and historical terrain of each ultimately requires that they be elaborated together. For the aesthetic freedom of the postmodern subject is the end product of a global assimilation of subordinated cultures to the flows of multinational capital in the postcolonial world, and to fail to specify that subject is to ignore equally the powerful dissymmetry between the subject who tastes and the indifferent, that is, interchangeable objects of his/her nomadic experience.[47] It should be recalled that the experiences of colonized cultures such as Ireland's, with differing but increasing degrees of intensity, is to be subjected to an uneven process of assimilation. What is produced, accordingly, is not a self-sustaining and autonomous organism capable of appropriating other cultures to itself, as imperial and postmodern cultures alike conceive themselves to be, but rather, at the individual and national-cultural level, a hybridization radically different from Bakhtin's and in which antagonism mixes with dependence and autonomy is constantly undermined by the perceived influence of alien powers.

A complex web of specular judgments constructs this problematic. On the side of the colonizer, it is the inauthenticity of the colonized culture, its falling short of the concept of the human, that legitimates the colonial project. At the other end of the developmental spectrum, the hybridization of the colonized culture remains an index of its continuing inadequacy to this concept and of its perpetually "imitative" status. From the nationalist perspective, the perceived inauthenticity of the colonized culture is recast as the contamination of an original essence, the recovery of which is the crucial prerequisite to the culture's healthy and normative development. The absence of an authentic culture is the death of the nation, its restoration its resurrection. In this sense, nationalist monologism is a dialogical inversion of imperial ideology, caught willy-nilly in the position of a parody, antagonistic but dependent.[48]

These remarks need to be qualified, however, by reiterated stress upon the dissymmetry of the specular relation. Nationalism is generated as an oppositional discourse by intellectuals who appear, by virtue of their formation in imperial state institutions, as in the first place subjected to rather than the subjects of assimilation. Their assimilation is, furthermore, inevitably an uneven process: by the very logic of assimilation, either the assimilated must entirely abandon their culture of origins, supposing it to have existed in anything like a pure form, or persist in a perpetually split consciousness, perceiving the original cultural elements as a residue resistant to the subject formed as a citizen of the empire. Simultaneously, the logic of assimilation resists its own ideal model: since the process is legitimated by the judgment of the essential inferiority of the colonized, its very rationale would be negated in the case of a perfect assimilation of colonized subjects without remainder. Accordingly, it is at once the power and the weakness of assimilation as the cultural arm of hegemonic imperialism that a total integration of the colonized into the imperial state is necessarily foreclosed. Recognition of this inescapable relegation to hybrid status among "native" intellectuals formed by the promise of an ever withheld subjecthood is a principal impulse to nationalism at the same time as it determines the monological mode of nationalist ideology.[49]

We should recall, however, that the desire for the nation is not merely to be formative of an authentic and integral subjecthood, but also the means to capture the state which is the nation's material representation. This fact has crucial theoretical and practical consequences. The formation of nationalist intellectuals takes place through both the repressive and the ideological state apparatuses of the empire, the army and police forces being as instrumental as the schools or recreationary spaces. What this entails is that the space of the nation itself is constituted in the first place through these apparatuses which quite literally map it and give it its unity while, at the level of the individual, the formation of the citizen-subject through these apparatuses continues to be a founding requirement of the new nation state.[50] Hence the constant phenomenon of the postcolonial world, the reproduction in "independent" states of institutions analogous to those of the colonial states, is not merely an imposition of the defeated empires with a view to continuing external domination, but also a condition of anticolonial nationalism itself. By the same token, postcolonial nationalism is actively engaged in the formation of citizen subjects through those institutions and accordingly on the analogy of the metropolitan subject. This is an instance of the "modernizing" effect of the state as ensemble of institutions which ensures the continuing integration of the postcolonial state in the networks of multinational capital.

The terrain of colonial hybridization which we have been analyzing in the Irish context but which has its specific counterparts virtually everywhere in the colonial world falls in a double and, for the new nation, contradictory sense under the shadow of the state. Even where its most immediate instruments seem to be economic or cultural forces remote from the purview of the state, hybridization is impelled and sustained by the intervention of the imperial state—by its commercial and criminal laws, its institutions, its language, its cultural displays. Against this process reacts a monological nationalism which, though already marked by hybridization, seeks to counter it with its own authentic institutions. In the postindependence state, these very institutions continue to be the locus of a process of hybridization despite the separation out of a more or less reified sphere of "national culture" whose functions, disconnected from oppositional struggle, become the formal and repetitive interpellation of national subjects and the residual demarcation of difference from the metro-

politan power. In this respect also, the postindependence state reproduces the processes of metropolitan culture, the very formality of the
"difference" of the national culture ensuring that the interpellation of
its citizens always takes the "same form" as that of the metropolitan
citizen.

Consequently, the apparatuses of the state remain crucial objects for
a resistance which cannot easily be divided into theoretical and practical modes, not least because what determines both is an aesthetic
narrative through which the theoretical is articulated upon the practical and vice versa. What begins as a Kantian precept finds specific
material instantiation in postcolonial politics. For though the mode
of formation of the citizen-subject may appear as a merely theoretical issue, the narrative of representation on which it depends for the
principle by which individual and nation can be sutured determines
equally the forms of schooling and of political institutions adopted.
These in turn demarcate the limits of what can properly, in any given
state, be termed a political practice. For, like any other social practice, politics is an effect of an ideological formation obedient to quite
specific laws of verisimilitude. To have a voice in the sphere of the
political, to be capable either of self-representation or of allowing oneself to be represented, depends on one's formation as a subject with a
voice exactly in the Bakhtinian sense.

I have been arguing throughout that the processes of hybridization
that are active in the Irish street ballads or in *Ulysses* are at every
level recalcitrant to the aesthetic politics of nationalism and, as we
can now see, to those of imperialism. Hybridization or adulteration resist identification both in the sense that they cannot be subordinated
to a narrative of representation and in the sense that they play out
the unevenness of knowledge which, against assimilation, foregrounds
the political and cultural positioning of the audience or reader. To
each recipient, different elements in the work will seem self-evident
or estranging. That this argument does not involve a celebration of the
irreducible singularity of the artistic work, which would merely be to
take the detour of idealist aesthetics, is evident when one consider to
what extent *Ulysses* has been as much the object of refinement and
assimilation in the academy as were the street ballads before. This is,
after all, the function of cultural institutions, metropolitan or postcolonial, which seek to reappropriate hybridization to monology. By
the same token, such works are continually reconstituted as objects in
a persistent struggle over verisimilitude.

It is precisely their hybrid and hybridizing location that makes such

David
Lloyd

works the possible objects of such contestations, contestations that can only be conducted oppositionally by reconnecting them with the political desire of the aesthetic from which they are continually being separated. The same could be said for the multiple locations which constitute the terrain of a postcolonial culture: it is precisely their hybrid formation between the imperial and the national state that constitutes their political significance. If, as postcolonial intellectuals, we are constantly taunted—and haunted—by the potentially disabling question "can the subaltern speak?" it is necessary to recall that to speak politically within present formations one must have a voice and that the burden of the question here cited is to deprive two subjects of voices: the subaltern, who cannot speak for herself, and the intellectual, who, by speaking for him or herself is deprived of the voice that would speak for others. The postcolonial intellectual, by virtue of a cultural and political formation which is for the state, is inevitably formed away from the people which the state claims to constitute and represent and whose malformation is its raison d'être. What this entails, however, is not occasion for despair and self-negation but rather that the intellectual's own hybrid formation become the ground for a continuing critique of the narrative of representation which legitimates the state and the double disenfranchisement of subaltern and citizen alike. Within this project, the critique of nationalism is inseparable from the critique of postcolonial domination.[51]

By way of a coda, and as a move toward formulating possible bridges between the situation of Third World nationalisms on the one hand and that of North American minorities on the other, I would venture to comment that the situation of minorities throws the logic of hybridization into only sharper conflict with the narrative of representation. In the absence of any practicable recourse to territorial nationhood, being minority is defined specifically in becoming a citizen of the state and in strict, even logical, opposition to "being ethnic." The former category is one constructed in the state, the other, no less a construction of domination, determines effective exclusion from state culture. In Norma Alarcón's beautiful formulation, to be chicano/a is to say at once "I am a citizen, I am not a citizen." To adhere to what is called an ethnic culture is to refuse the cultural formation of the citizen; to be formed as a citizen is to undertake the impossible task of negating one's given ethnicity. To occupy this "interstitial" dislocation is, as Cherrie Moraga points out, to be utterly recalcitrant to representation either side of the borderline—to represent or to be represented, to represent one's people or to be the representative citizen.[52] An impossible predicament, this dislocation is nonetheless the irreducible space in which the critique of the political aesthetic of representation must proceed.

Notes

Note: A version of this essay was first published in *Anomalous States: Irish Writing and the Post-Colonial Moment* (Dublin: Lilliput P and Durham: Duke U P, 1993).

1   See Immanuel Kant, *Critique of Judgement*, trans. James Creed Meredith (Oxford: Clarendon P, 1952), 181. I have discussed the ramifications of the concept of exemplarity for politics and pedagogy in "Kant's Examples," *Representations* 28 (Fall 1989), 34–54.

2   D. F. McCarthy, cited in Charles Gavan Duffy, *Four Years of Irish History, 1845–1849* (London: Cassell, Petter, Galpin, 1883), 72.

3   On the concept of *Naturgabe* as grounding the economy of genius, see Jacques Derrida, "Economimesis," trans. Richard Klein, *Diacritics* 11.2 (Summer 1981), 10–11.

4   Jacques Derrida explores the logical paradoxes involved in the founding of the state in the name of the people in "Declarations d'independance," in *Otobiographies: l'enseignement de Nietsche et la politique du nom propre* (Paris: Galilee, 1984), 13–32. The consequences of these logical paradoxes are worked out later in Ireland's own declaration of independence in 1916 as I have tried to show in "The Poetics of Politics: Yeats and the Founding of the State," *Qui Parle*, 3.2 (Fall 1989), 76–114; reprinted in *Anomalous States*.

5   See especially David Lloyd, *Nationalism and Minor Literature: James Clarence Mangan and the Emergence of Irish Cultural Nationalism* (Berkeley: U of California P, 1987), esp. chap. 2, and "Writing in the Shit: Beckett, Nationalism and the Colonial Subject," *Modern Fiction Studies*, special issue on "Narratives of Colonial Resistance," 35.1 (Spring 1989), 71–86; reprinted in *Anomalous States*.

6   See Mikhail Bakhtin, *The Dialogic Imagination: Four Essays*, ed. Michael Holquist, trans. Caryl Emerson and Michael Holquist (Austin: U of Texas P, 1981), 67, 262–63, and passim.

7   To this extent, Bakhtin is still in accord with Erwin Rohde, whose history of the Greek novel he cites critically: both see the condition of emergence of the novel as being the collapse or disintegration of "a unitary and totalizing national myth," 65.

8   See Charles Gavan Duffy, *Young Ireland: A Fragment of Irish History, 1840–1850* (London: Cassell, Petter, Galpin, 1880), 155.

9   As Thomas Flanagan has argued in his *The Irish Novelists, 1800–1850* (New York: Columbia U P, 1959), esp. chap. 3, the problem for Irish novelists was precisely to overcome the polemical heteroglossia of "race, creed, and nationality," 35. In a society in which identity is defined by opposition to others, the conventional form of the novel which concentrates on individual development set over against social conventions, what Lukacs

David
Lloyd

describes as "second nature," is unavailable. I have discussed some of the crises of representation faced by Irish novelists and constitutional thinkers in the early nineteenth century in "Violence and the Constitution of the Novel," in *Anomalous States*. The tendency of Bakhtin's analysis of the novel and its social determinants makes it impossible for him to grasp the normative socializing function of the novel and therefore to explore fully the implications of Hegel's remark, which he cites, that "the novel must educate man for life in bourgeois society," 234. Bakhtin's representation of the novel as a largely progressive and subversive genre stands in need of considerable correction by other theorists who have more fully grasped its ideological and socializing functions. See for example, Franco Moretti, *The Way of the World: The Bildungsroman in European Culture* (London: Verso, 1987), and David Miller, *The Novel and the Police* (Berkeley: U of California P, 1988), as well as Georg Lukacs, *The Theory of the Novel*, trans. Anna Bostock (Cambridge, Mass.: MIT, 1971). Without attention to the socializing ideal of the novel in the nineteenth century, the crisis of representation in the Irish at this period cannot be fully grasped. As Benedict Anderson has argued, nationalism as a political doctrine requires a novelistic representation of social time as well as individual developmental time—the two must progress in a unified field. See Anderson, *Imagined Communities: Reflections on the Origin and Spread of Nationalism* (London: Verso, 1983), 30–40. Without the possibility of a "novelistic" organization of society, Irish nationalism is seriously disabled and turns to the recomposition of literary developments, as it were *ab origine*.

10 See Lloyd, *Nationalism and Minor Literature*, chap. 2. Citation from Duffy, *Four Years*, 153.

11 See Thomas Osborne Davis, "The Ballad Poetry of Ireland," in *Selections from his Prose and Poetry*, intro. T. W. Rolleston (Dublin; Gresham, n.d.), 210.

12 It should be remarked that these categories are constitutive more than analytic, inventing both demographic and aesthetic categories which, as this essay will suggest, subserve distinct political ends. All of them are, in different ways, highly problematic.

13 Daniel Corkery's *The Hidden Ireland: A Study of Gaelic Munster in the Eighteenth Century* (1924; Dublin: M. H. Gill, 1967) is one of the first texts to decipher in Gaelic poetry of the eighteenth century the remnants of the traditions forged in a high or aristocratic tradition rather than the effusions of illiterate peasants.

14 Davis, "The Songs of Ireland," *Prose and Poetry* (Dublin: Gill, 1914), 225.

15 Dennis Florence MacCarthy, *The Book of Irish Ballads*, new edition (Dublin: James Duffy, 1869), 24; hereinafter *BIB*.

16 Samuel Taylor Coleridge, "The Statesman's Manual" (1816), in *Lay Sermons*, ed. R. J. White, Bollingen Edition (Princeton: Princeton U P, 1972), 29. The currently most influential discussion of the Romantic tradition of symbolism as opposed to allegory is Paul de Man's "The Rhetoric of Temporality," in *Blindness and Insight: Essays in the Rhetoric of Contemporary Criticism*, 2d ed. (London: Methuen, 1983), 187–228. I discuss some of the limitations of this account in "Kant's Examples," 46–47. For

the symbolist tradition in Irish nationalism's aesthetic politics, see Lloyd, *Anomalous States*, "Poetics of Politics," 88–95.

17 Charles Gavan Duffy, ed., *The Ballad Poetry of Ireland* (Dublin: James Duffy, 1845), xv.

18 On the anxiety concerning English miscegenation with the Gaels, see David Cairns and Shaun Richards, *Writing Ireland: Colonialism, Nationalism and Culture* (Manchester: Manchester U P, 1988), 5–7. On the economic and social currents in nineteenth-century Ireland which affected the emergence of Irish cultural nationalism, see Lloyd, *Nationalism and Minor Literature*, chap. 2. The question of the decline of the Irish language is more vexed, since recent research gives us reason to doubt the inexorability and rapidity of the decline of the Irish language. Akenson, *Irish Educational Experiment*, 378–80, uses census data to corroborate the notion, current at least since Davis's 1843 essay, "Our National Language," that the language was in use only in the western half of the country and among less than 50 percent of the population. Yet it, may be that such statistics reflect only the predominant language of *literacy*, and that for a far greater proportion of the population than formerly acknowledged oral proficiency in Irish went along with literacy in English. The ballads often seem to assume a considerable degree of passive competence in Irish, at the least, and certainly an awareness of Gaelic cultural referents. Kevin Whelan remarks: "I would argue that in 1841 the *absolute* number speaking Irish was at an all-time high. Remember the population of Ireland in 1600 was ca. 1.5 million. By 1841, it was up to 8.5 million. 100% of 1.5 million is still 1.5 million, 50% of 8.5 million is 4.25 million. Thus, the decline model of eighteenth and nineteenth century Irish is misleading in absolute terms—and remember population was increasing most rapidly in the west and south west—the Irish speaking areas! The vitality and flexibility of pre-famine Gaelic-speaking culture has been severely underestimated" (private correspondence). See also Niall O Ciosain, "Printed Popular Literature in Irish 1750–1850: Presence and Absence," and Garrett FitzGerald, "The Decline of the Irish Language 1771–1871," in Mary O'Dowd and David Dickson, eds. *The Origins of Popular Literacy in Ireland: Language Change and Educational Development 1700–1920* (Dublin, 1990), 45–57 and 59–72, respectively, and Tom Dunne, "Popular Ballads, Revolutionary Rhetoric and Politicisation," in David Dickson and Hugh Gough, eds. *Ireland and the French Revolution* (Dublin: Irish Academic Press, 1990), 142.

19 Colm O Lochlainn, ed., *Irish Street Ballads* (1939: revised ed.; Dublin: Three Candles, 1946).

20 See, for example, Robert Welch, *Irish Poetry from Moore to Yeats*, Irish Literary Studies 5 (Gerrards Cross: Colin Smythe, 1980), 43–45, 71, 131. Carleton famously cites his mother's remark that English words to an Irish air are like man and wife, always quarrelling (cited in Welch).

21 See for "The Barrymore Tithe Victory" and "A New Song," Georges-Denis Zimmermann, *Irish Political Street Ballads and Rebel Songs, 1780–1900*, doctoral thesis presented to University of Geneva (Geneva: La Sirene, 1966), 204–5, 208–9; for "The Kerry Recruit," see O Lochlainn, *Street Bal-*

84

David
Lloyd

lads, 2–3. I am grateful to Brendán O Buachalla for alerting me to the wider significance of such allusions.

22 "Father Murphy," in O Lochlainn, *Street Ballads*, 54–55; "Billy's Downfall" in Zimmermann, *Irish Rebel Songs*, 220–21. Dunne, "Popular Ballads," 149–50, discusses six recorded versions of "Father Murphy," and comments on the extent to which different versions may indicate either popular adaptations of bourgeois songs or, contrarily, bourgeois refinements of popular ballads.

23 An excellent account of the confusion of high and low in popular forms and of its pleasures is Peter Stallybrass and Allon White, *The Politics and Poetics of Transgression* (Ithaca: Cornell U P, 1986). Zozimus's own defense at his trial for causing an obstruction in the Dublin streets is itself a magnificent example of the mixing of genres with exuberant disrespect for the canons:

> Your worship, I love me counthry. She's dear to me heart, an' am I to be prevented from writin' songs in her honour, like Tommy Moore, Walter Scott an' Horace done for theirs, or from singin' them like the an-shent bards, on'y I haven't got me harp like them to accompany me aspirations! . . . An' as a portion ov the poetic janius of me counthry has descended upon me showlders, ragged an' wretched as the garmint that covers them, yet the cloth ov the prophet has not aroused more prophetic sintiments than I entertain, that me country shall *be* a free counthry! . . . Homer sung the praises ov his counthry on the public highways; an' we are informed that dramatic perforformances wor performed in the streets, with nothin' else for a stage but a dust cart. (Laughter.)

Quoted in the Dublin publican and antiquarian P. J. McCall's pamphlet "In the Shadow of St. Patrick's" (1893; Blackrock: Carraig Books, 1976), 32–33, this account is clearly refracted through oral history. Yet even in its own parodic fashion, it stands as an interesting index of the unstable tone of the popular discourse on cultural politics, which reproduces serio-comically all the terms of nationalist aesthetics but with an indeterminacy of address calculated to pull the wool over the authorities' eyes.

24 See John Mitchel, "Our War Deparment," *United Irishman* 1.2 (April 22, 1848), 171.

25 See William Wordsworth, *The Prelude*, in *Poetical Works*, ed. Thomas Hutchinson (Oxford: Oxford U P, 1973), book 7, 701–4, 546.

26 I have developed these arguments in *Nationalism and Minor Literature*, chaps. 2 and 3.

27 MacCarthy, *Irish Ballads*, 26.

28 Paul Ricoeur has noted the relation between the minimal element of metaphor and the maximal element of plot in Aristotle's *Poetics*, both as it were narrating a coming to identity of disparate elements. See Paul Ricoeur, "Metaphor and the Main Problem of Hermeneutics," *New Literary History* 6.1 (Autumn 1974), 108–10. I have argued that the transfer from the metonymic to the metaphoric axis is the fundamental rhetorical structure of cultural assimilation and racist judgments in "Race under Representation," *Oxford Literary Review* 13 (Spring 1991), 71–73. See "Violence and

the Constitution of the Novel" in *Anamalous States* for further reflections on the political meaning of this distinction.

29 MacCarthy, *Irish Ballads*, 127. In his symbol making, MacCarthy ignores recent discoveries by George Petrie who showed that the round towers which are so prominent a feature of Irish landscapes were of relatively recent Christian origin, thus dispelling numerous myths of origin which had gathered around them. See my *Nationalism and Minor Literature*, chap. 3.

30 On the proliferation of kitsch, nationalist and otherwise, see Kevin Rockett, "Disguising Dependence: Separatism and Foreign Mass Culture," *Circa* 49 (Jan./Feb. 1990), 20–25. Nationalist artefacts work precisely, and not without calculated political effect, as kitsch in the sense that Franco Moretti defines it: "Kitsch literally 'domesticates' aesthetic experience. It brings it into the *home*, where most of everyday life takes place." See *The Way of the World*, 36.

31 James Joyce, *Ulysses* (New York: Random House, 1986), 152–53. Cited hereinafter as *U*.

32 Douglas Hyde, "The Necessity for De-Anglicising Ireland," in *Language, Lore and Lyrics: Essays and Lectures*, ed. with preface and introd. by Breandan O Conaire (Blackrock: Irish Academic Press, 1986), 154.

33 Douglas Hyde, "Gaelic Folk Songs," in *Language, Lore and Lyrics*, 107.

34 In both *Anthropology from a Pragmatic Point of View* and the *Critique of Judgement*, Kant describes the enlightened subject as adhering to three precepts: to think for oneself, to think consistently, and to think from the standpoint of all mankind. See *Anthropology from a Pragmatic Point of View*, trans. Mary J. Gregor (The Hague: Nijhoff, 1974), 96–97, and *Critique of Judgement*, 152–53. Though Bakhtin's formulation apparently abandons the final maxim, it is *formally* and therefore universally prescriptive in exactly the same manner as Kant's. Samuel Beckett's terse formulation, "I'm in words, made of words, others' words" is perhaps the most succinct deconstruction of both. See *The Unnamable*, (London: Calder, 1959), 390.

35 I have discussed the complexities, largely resistant to nationalist aesthetics, of the process of translation in chap. 4 of *Nationalism and Minor Literature*. See also, in this volume, Tejaswini Niranjana, "Colonialism and the Politics of Translation."

36 Robert Tracy, in his essay "Loving You All Ways: Vamps, Vampires, Necrophiles and Necrofilles in Nineteenth Century Fiction," in *Sex and Death in Victorian Literature*, ed. Regina Barreca (London: Macmillan, 1990), 32–59, gives an excellent account of the social and political background to the vampire tales of Irish writers like Sheridan Lefanu and Bram Stoker, creator of Dracula.

37 On Joyce's personal obsession with adultery and betrayal, see for example Richard Ellmann, *James Joyce* (Oxford: Oxford U P, 1959), 255, 288–93. This obsession was written out not only in *Ulysses*, but also in "The Dead," the last story of *Dubliners*, and *Exiles*, Joyce's only play.

38 On the question of the hybridization of Irish culture, the most useful study is Cheryl Herr's *Joyce's Anatomy of Culture* (Urbana/Chicago: U of Illinois P, 1986), which analyzes in detail the various institutions which

compose and interact within colonial Ireland. As she remarks, "The distortions of reality which one institution imposes on a semantic field operates endlessly in a culture composed of many competing institutions," 14. The chapter pivots around Leopold Bloom's scapegoating as an alien Jew and opens with the figure of the Jewish moneylender, Moses Herzog, whose name connects directly with the identically named Zionist leader. Since in this chapter Bloom is also given credit for Sinn Fein leader Arthur Griffith's adaptation of Hungarian nationalist strategies, it is clear that Joyce is deliberately playing up the paradox that lies at the heart of nationalism, namely, its dependence on the dislocatory forces of modernization for its "local" appeal. If Leopold Bloom be considered Everyman, that is, in Odysseus's own formulation to the Cyclops, "Noman," then he is so only in the sense that he fulfills Karl Marx's prediction in "On the Jewish Question," that the principle of exchange for which anti-Semitism castigates the Jew will be most fully realized in "Christian" civil society. See especially the second essay, in *Early Writings*, intro. Lucio Colletti, trans. Rodney Livingstone and Gregor Benton (New York: Vintage, 1975). Morton P. Levitt, in "A Hero for Our Time: Leopold Bloom and the Myth of Ulysses," in Thomas F. Staley, ed., *Fifty Years Ulysses* (Bloomington: Indiana U P, 1974), 142, makes a representative claim for the notion that "In the urban world, in which we all live, no man could be more representative." For J. H. Raleigh, "he is modern, secular man, an international phenomenon produced in the Western world at large in fairly sizable numbers by the secular currents of the eighteenth, nineteenth, and twentieth centuries, a type often both homeless in any specific locale and at home in any of the diverse middle-class worlds in the Europe and America of those centuries." See "*Ulysses:* Trinitarian and Catholic" in *Joyce's* Ulysses. *The Larger Perspective*, ed. Robert D. Newman and Weldon Thornton (Newark: U of Delaware P, 1988), 111–12.

39   See Colin MacCabe, *James Joyce and the Revolution of the Word* (London: Macmillan, 1978), 92. See also Karen Lawrence, *The Odyssey of Style in Ulysses* (Princeton: Princeton U P, 1981), whose excellent analysis of the "Cyclops" chapter recognizes its hybrid or uneven character stylistically (esp. 106–7), but confines its implications to a modernist problematic of style and to "Joyce's skepticism about the ordering of experience in language *and* a personal desire to be above the constraints that writing usually imposes" (119). The nature of this chapter has been best described, in terms that would be quite critical of MacCabe's rendering of it, by Eckhard Lobsien, *Der Alltag des* Ulysses: *Die Vermittlung von aesthetischer und lebensweltlicher Erfahrung* (Stuttgart: J.B. Metzler, 1978), 106: "Die zunächst so selbstverständlich anmutende Perspektive des Ich-Erzählers zeigt sich alsbald ebenso verformt und von undurchschauten Spielregeln eingeschränkt wie die Interpolationen" and 110: "Die verschiedenen, in sich geschlossenen Versionen von Alltagswelten werden derart in Interferenz gebracht, daß die Leseraktivität auf die Aufdeckung der geltenden Spielregeln und damit eine Disintegration des Textes abzielt." Lobsien emphasizes throughout the "interference" that takes place at all discursive

levels in "Cyclops" and its effect of relativizing the "Repräsentations-anspruch jeder einzelnen Sprachform," 108. In the present essay, I seek to give back to that "claim to representation" its full political purview.

40 Joyce's fascination with malaproprism is evident from as early as the first story of *Dubliners*, "The Sisters," in which Eliza speaks of the new carriages' "rheumatic wheels" to *Finnegans Wake*, for which it might be held to be a stylistic principle. Unlike the pun, which generally is more likely to be "forced," that is, the product of an eager intention to subvert, malaproprism (as the name nicely implies) evokes a subject not entirely in control of the metonymic productivity of language. If puns condense, malaproprisms displace. *Finnegans Wake* clearly plays on the borderline between the two, generating more displacements than an individual subject can master. The Citizen's pun on "civilisation" and "syphilisation" is especially interesting insofar as it invokes standard nationalist attacks on the corrupting effects of English civilization on a morally pure Irish culture in the form of a verbal corruption. The movements of displacement or dislocation which construct colonized society are grasped in the displaced language of the colonized. Both are at once indices of damage *and* impetuses to the dismantling of the appropriative autonomous speaking subject.

41 See Lloyd, *Nationalism and Minor Literature*, 113–15, for a fuller discussion of the oscillation between antagonism and dependence in parody. An excellent study of the dynamics of parodic forms is Margaret A. Rose, *Parody/Metafiction: An Analysis of Parody as a Critical Mirror to the Writing and Reception of Fiction* (London: Croom Helm, 1979).

42 In the present context, I am forcibly reminded of the figure of La Malinche in Mexican/Chicano culture who, as Cortez's mistress and interpreter, condenses with exceptional clarity the complex of racial betrayal, translation, and adultery which Joyce equally seeks to mobilize in "Cyclops." On La Malinche, see Octavio Paz, "The Sons of La Malinche," in *Labyrinths of Solitude* (New York: Grove, 1961), 65–88; Norma Alarcón, "Chicana's Feminist Literature: Re-vision through Malintzin/ or, Malintzin: Putting Flesh Back on the Object," in *This Bridge Called My Back: Writings by Radical Women of Color*, ed. Cherríe Moraga and Gloria Anzaldúa (New York: Kitchen Table, 1983), 182–90; and Cherríe Moraga, "A Long Line of Vendidas," in *Loving in the War Years: Lo que nunca pasó por sus labios* (Boston: South End, 1983), esp. 113–14, 117. In his essay "Myth and Comparative Cultural Nationalism: The Ideological Uses of Aztlan," in Rudolfo A. Anaya and Francisco Lomelí, eds., *Aztlan: Essays on the Chicano Homeland* (Albuquerque: Academia/El Norte, 1989), Genaro Padilla provides a valuable critical history of such recourses to mythic figures in Chicano cultural politics and indicates the similarities in political tendency and value of such tendencies across several cultural nationalisms, including Ireland's. In the Chicano as in the Irish context, what is politically decisive is the appropriative or malapropristic, displacing effect of the mythic gesture with regard to dominant culture.

43 Colin MacCabe explores all these issues in Joyce's writings throughout *James Joyce and the Revolution of the Word*. See also, among others, Bonnie Kime Scott, *Joyce and Feminism* (Bloomington: Indiana U P, 1984),

esp. chap. 2, "Mythical, Historical and Cultural Contexts for Women in Joyce," 9–28; Dominic Manganiello, *Joyce's Politics* (London: Routledge and Kegan Paul, 1980); Hélène Cixous, *L'exil de James Joyce ou l'art du remplacement* (Paris: Grasset, 1968), esp. 2.1, "Le réseau des dépendances," is a valuable exploration of linkages between family, church, and nation, which perhaps surprisingly takes the father's rather than the mother's part.

44 On the socializing function of the novel, see especially Moretti, *The Way of the World*, 15–16. Even where he lays claim to Irish identity ("I'm Irish; I was born here") or where he seeks to define a nation ("The same people living in the same place"), Bloom appeals to the contingencies of merely contiguous relationships as opposed to the nationalist concern with a lineage of spirit and blood which must be kept pure. Bloom's insistence on contiguity underwrites his own figuration as a locus of contamination or hybridization as against the assimilative principles of nationalist ideology.

45 See respectively: Hyde, "The Necessity for De-Anglicising Ireland," 169; Daniel Corkery, *Synge and Anglo-Irish Literature* (1930; repr. Cork: Mercier, 1966), 14; Paz, "The Pachuco and Other Extremes," *Labyrinths of Solitude*, 16; Roberto Schwarz, "Brazilian Culture: Nationalism by Elimination," *New Left Review* 167 (Jan./Feb., 1988), 77; Roberto Fernandez Retamar, "Caliban," in *Caliban and Other Essays*, trans. Edward Baker, foreword by Fredric Jameson (Minneapolis: U of Minnesota P, 1988), 3; Samuel Beckett, "Dante . . . Bruno. Vico . . . Joyce," in *Disjecta: Miscellaneous Writings and a Dramatic Fragment*, ed. Ruby Cohn (New York: Grove, 1984), 19; Cherríe Moraga, *Loving in the War Years*, vi.

46 Retamar writes in "Caliban," 5, of the singularity of Latin American postcolonial culture in terms of its having always to pass through metropolitan languages, those of the colonizer. In this, as in many other respects, there are evidently close affinities between the Irish and the Latin American experience. But this appeal to specificity may in fact be spurious. As Ngugi Wa Thiong'o has pointed out, African literature has also by and large been written in the colonizers' languages despite the ubiquitous survival of African vernacular languages. See *Decolonising the Mind: The Politics of Language in African Literature* (London: James Currey, 1986), 4–9. What this indicates, as I shall argue in what follows, is that the crucial issue is the space constituted for the citizen-subject in the postcolonial nation not only by the languages but also by the institutional and cultural forms bequeathed by the departing colonizer. As Thiong'o grasps, these are the sites and the subjects in which colonialism continues to reproduce itself.

47 See, for example, Jean-François Lyotard, *The Postmodern Condition: A Report on Knowledge*, trans. Geoff Bennington and Brian Massumi; foreword by Fredric Jameson (Minneapolis: U of Minnesota P, 1984), 76:

> When power is that of capital and not that of a party, the "transavantgardist" or "postmodern" (in Jencks's sense) solution proves to be better adapted than the antimodern solution. Eclecticism is the degree zero of contemporary general culture: one listens to reggae, watches a western, eats McDonald's food for lunch and local cuisine for dinner, wears Paris perfume in Tokyo and "retro" clothes in Hong Kong; knowledge is a matter for TV games. It is easy to find a public for eclectic works. . . . But this

realism of the "anything goes" is in fact that of money; in the absence of aesthetic criteria, it remains possible and useful to assess the value of works of art according to the profits they yield. Such realism accommodates all tendencies, just as capitalism accommodates all "needs," providing that the tendencies and needs have purchasing power. As for taste, there is no need to be delicate when one speculates or entertains oneself.

Perceptive as this critique of a vulgar postmodernism's "cosmopolitanism" is, we might note that the "one" of "general culture" is only restored at a higher level by the invocation of "taste" and "aesthetic criteria," that is, at the level of the cosmopolitan point of view of the Subject. For an excellent critique of the confusion between postcolonial and postmodern forms, see Kumkum Sangari, "The Politics of the Possible," *Cultural Critique* 7 (Fall 1987), 157–86. Both she and Julio Ramos, in his "Uneven Modernities: Literature and Politics in Latin America," forthcoming in *boundary 2*, have pointed out that many of the distinguishing characteristics of Latin American literature, which often appear as postmodern effects, can in fact better be derived from the uneven processes of modernization that have occurred there. This is not, of course, to suggest a single, developmental model for all societies but, on the contrary, to suggest the radical variability of modes as well as "rates" of change. Given the contemporary allure of the "nomadic subject" or of "nomadic theory," it is perhaps cautionary to recall that the legitimating capacity of the imperial subject is his ability to be everywhere (and therefore nowhere) "at home." For some exploration of this notion as it structures imperialist and racist representations, see Satya Mohanty, "Kipling's Children and the Colour Line," in *Race and Class*, special issue, "Literature: Colonial Lines of Descent," 31.1 (July/September 1989), 36–38 especially.

48 Early-twentieth-century nationalist appeals to Celticism are an excellent instance of this process, reversing the value but retaining the terms of stereotypes of the Celt first promulgated systematically by Samuel Ferguson and then extended by Matthew Arnold. I have discussed the formation of this stereotype in Ferguson's writings of the 1830s and Arnold's in the 1860s in "Arnold, Ferguson Schiller: Aesthetic Culture and the Politics of Aesthetics," *Cultural Critique* 2 (Winter 1986), 137–69.

49 Homi Bhabha has explored the hybrid status of the colonized subject in "Of Mimicry and Man: The Ambivalence of Colonial Discourse," *October* 28 (Spring 1984), 125–33. On the foreclosure of the native intellectual's assimilation to the imperial state, see Anderson, *Imagined Communities*, 105. I owe the distinction between the dominant and hegemonic phases of colonialism to Abdul JanMohamed's powerful essay "The Economy of Manichean Allegory: The Economy of Racial Difference in Colonial Literature," in *"Race," Writing, and Difference*, ed. Henry Louis Gates, Jr. (Chicago: Chicago U P, 1986), 78–106. JanMohamed critiques Bhabha in this essay for failing to respect the dissymmetry between the colonizing and the colonized subject in the Manichaean social relations of colonialism. I try to show here that the two positions are intervolved, insofar as any nationalist opposition to colonialism is first articulated through the

transvaluation of forms furnished by the colonial power. The moment of dependence in this relationship in no way diminishes the force of the antagonism in the national struggle for independence, but it does determine the forms taken by the postcolonial state and the necessity for a continuing critique of nationalism as a mimicry of imperial forms. On these aspects of nationalism, see Partha Chatterjee's *Nationalism and the Colonial World. A Derivative Discourse?* (London: Zed Books, 1986), esp. chaps. 1 and 2. With regard to the logic of assimilation and its perpetual production of residues, I am greatly indebted to Zita Nunes's analysis of the formation of Brazilian national identity in literary modernism and anthropology of the 1920s and 1930s. Her work lucidly shows how the Manichaean construction of otherness and the hybrid forms produced by colonialism are logically interdependent moments in the process of assimilation. It thus provides a means to repoliticizing Bhabha's understanding of "hybridization," since that process is shown to be captured in the hierarchic movement of assimilation which necessarily produces a residue which resists. Hybridization must accordingly be seen as an unevenness of incorporation within a developmental structure rather than an oscillation between or among identities. Nunes also demonstrates clearly the necessarily racist constructions implicit in cultural solutions to problems of national identity, thus introducing an invaluable corrective to concepts such as *mestizaje* which continue to be uncritically espoused even by thinkers such as Retamar. See Nunes, "Os Males do Brasil: Antropofagia e Modernismo," Papeis Avulsos do CIEC (Rio de Janeiro), no. 22.

50 My terms here are indebted to Louis Althusser's seminal essay, "Ideology and Ideological State Apparatuses (Notes towards an Investigation)" in *Lenin and Philosophy and Other Essays*, trans. Ben Brewster (New York: Monthly Review Press, 1971), 127–86. Anderson, *Imagined Communities*, 108–9, indicates the extent to which nationalist intellectuals are formed within the colonial state apparatus, a perception borne out in the case of Young Ireland by Jacqueline Hill's analysis of the social composition of the movement in "The Intelligentsia and Irish Nationalism in the 1840s," *Studia Hibernica* 20 (1980), 73–109. See also Frantz Fanon's essays, "The Pitfalls of National Consciousness" and "On National Culture," in *The Wretched of the Earth* (New York: Grove, 1963), 148–205 and 206–48, respectively. These essays, which analyze the dialectical process by which a bourgeois anticolonial nationalism may give way to a popular nationalism in the postindependence state which is not subordinated to a fetishized "national culture." As such, they provide the ground for a critique of intellectual tendencies such as Irish revisionist history which criticize the antimodernist and Manichaean tendencies of nationalism only to valorize British imperialism as an essentially modernizing force.

51 I allude of course to Gayatri Chakravorty Spivak's seminal essay, "Can the Subaltern Speak?" in *Marxism and the Interpretation of Culture*, ed. Cary Nelson and Lawrence Grossberg (Urbana: U of Illinois P, 1988), 271–313. I make no attempt to paraphrase this essay here, wishing only to suggest that the opposition it establishes at one point between *Darstellung* and *Vertreten* requires to be transformed dialectically through the concept of

the state in which both are subsumed into a unity of being and being capable of being represented. That the subaltern cannot speak in our voice is only a problem insofar as the postcolonial intellectual retains the nostalgia for the universal position occupied by the intellectual in the narrative of representation. Similarly, the inevitability of employing Western modes of knowledge is a critical condition of the intellectual's formation and inseparable from her/his occupation of a *national* space. The logical inverse of these propositions is that the contradictory existence of the postcolonial intellectual equally affects the coherence of Western modes of knowledge which are necessarily reformed and hybridized in other locations. The most interesting discussion of these issues is Homi Bhabha's "The Commitment to Theory," *New Formations* 5 (1988), 5–24. In all this, as in the composition of this essay as a whole, I am indebted to conversations with Dipesh Chakrabarty.

52 See Norma Alarcón, *T(r)opics of Hunger*, forthcoming, and Cherríe Moraga, *Loving in the War Years*. Moraga's work is one of the most compelling current explorations of the crisis of representation brought about by the cultural struggles of ethnic and sexual minorities. I have entered these arguments somewhat in "Ethnic Cultures, Minority Discourse, and the State," forthcoming in *Colonial Discourse / Post-colonial Theory*, eds., Peter Hulme, Francis Barker, and Margaret Iveson, forthcoming, Manchester U P.

92

David
Lloyd

Seeing

with

Another I:

Our Search

for Other

Worlds

Eugene C.

Eoyang

In the major intellectual movements in this century, it is now clear —as we enter its concluding decade—that a recurrent theme runs throughout the various discoveries and insights in different fields, from relativity theory to quantum mechanics to the Heisenberg principle to phenomenology to semiotics to deconstructionism to chaos theory. Different as these paradigms are, they all highlight the relationship between the object and subject, between the knower and what is known. In each of these mind-sets, the traditional opposition of bipolar thinking is undermined, and a dialectic model of knowledge has been posited. To put it simplistically, we are what we know, and what we know defines who we are. A corollary would be: *how* we know affects *what* we know. Our modes of knowing have become as much a subject for our research as the objects we strain to discover.

One accessible approach to uncovering what we take for granted— which is one way of saying: to make a discovery—is to examine some of our most familiar reference points. Certainly the most familiar are the four cardinal directions: north, south, east, or west. One cannot imagine a culture that does not have these basic concepts. Now, while there are commonalities in the etymology of these markers in different languages—in most languages, for example, east is associated with the sun rising and west is associated with the sun setting, still, the four directions assume different valuations in different languages. If, for example, one is asked to name the four directions in order, there are twenty-four possible permutations in the sequence in which they can be named: in English, the most common is "north, south, east, west" or "north, east, south, west"; English inherits its order from German, where it is "north, east, south, west," and from French, where it is "north, south, east, west." However, in Chinese, one cites the four cardinal directions is this order: "east, south, west, north," whereas in Japanese, which uses the same Chinese characters to mark the directions, the order is "east, west, south, north." Nor can one assume that the order of citation is totally random. When I asked a German colleague in what order he would cite the four cardinal directions, he said, "Of course, it has to be clockwise: north, east, south, west." That "of course" is not all that obvious. "Clockwise" need not have been "clockwise" but its opposite if clocks had been invented in the southern rather than the northern hemispheres, for we are told that the directions in which the hands move followed the motion of the shadow on a sundial. In the southern hemispheres, the shadow would have moved in the opposite direction.[1] Of the four directions, north is privileged in Chinese, because it was associated with the emperor, who generically occupied the northernmost residence in the capital and faced south. Japan, as the land of the rising sun, seems to have given a special place to east. West, as a direction, has been associated, at least since the age of exploration, with discovery and adventure, with sailing off into the unknown, with new opportunities and new perspectives. East has been associated with origins, west with destinations: "Go West, young man," Horace Greeley said. While its opposite corollary, "Go East, old man," is not as familiar, the east has been often characterized as the direction one turns to for wisdom rather than discovery, for the origin of things, for insight and transcendental knowledge rather than new experiences and new worlds: *ex occidente lex; ex oriente lux* the medieval aphorism went, "out of the west, law; out of the east, light."

Another pseudo-universal might be left- and right-handedness. The preponderance of right-handedness among world civilizations has occasioned heightened interest by the brain research of the the Russian physiologist, A. R. Luria, in the forties and now familiar in the

Eugene C.
Eoyang

concept of the so-called "bicameral" brain. This concern with left- and right-handedness in the universe became especially interesting, since the discoveries of Tsung-tao Lee and Chen-ning Yang, for which they won the Nobel Prize in 1957. Those discoveries posited parity in the subnuclear universe and left-handedness and right-handedness in the elementary particles in nature. The arbitrariness of right-handed bias in our civilization—indeed most civilizations—can be illustrated by a paradoxically apposite, and opposite example, taken from the history of American technology.

Some arbitrary conventions that seem so familiar are at bottom not arbitrary "the "qwerty" typewriter keyboard, for example, which was presumably based on the frequency of the letters and the relative dexterity of each of the ten fingers. English-speakers are often not aware of the fact that the keyboard is different for other—even cognate—languages. Some of you may be old enough to remember that, before word processors and electric typewriters, the carriage return lever was on the *left* side. Indeed, almost all typewriters manufactured after 1910 had left-hand carriage returns. Now, this seems a trivial enough detail, until one stops to think that pulling the carriage return lever with the left hand—in some cases, with the left pinky, perhaps the least dexterous of the ten digits— doesn't make very much sense for the 83 percent of the population that is right-handed. Indeed, ergonomics would suggest that instead of requiring the operator to use his left pinky at the periphery of one's vision to pull a heavy carriage and return it to the right does not make as much sense as having the carriage return lever move toward the center, just above the keyboard, where it might be pulled with the strongest digit for most people, the right thumb. Yet, despite these considerations, the preponderant majority of typewriters were manufactured for half a century with a left-hand carriage return. How did this come about? Well, the company that dominated the office typewriter market in those years, particularly in the early stages, was the Underwood Office Machines Corporation. Underwood's corporate president was, as it turns out, left-handed. So, for more than a generation, millions of right-handers used an instrument that favored a left-hander—one of the few times that left-handedness has been privileged in our society. You may wonder why no one ever thought of this and considered a carriage return that would be more convenient for right-handers to use. Well, they did. Some of the early typewriters, including one invented for the L. C. Smith company by Carl Gabrielson in 1904 does have a right-hand carriage return, which is much easier for right-handers to use than conventional manual typewriters. At the end of a line the carriage return lever ends up just above the keyboard, at the center of the typists field of vision, rather than far out to the periphery of one's vision at the left; the thumb-grasp extends downward so that the right thumb has no difficulty finding it. This configuration is much easier to use for someone who is right-handed. I know, because I own—and use—a 1907 L. C. Smith.

Let me consider another set of directional biases that may not be obvious. In the West, and in this country in particular, forward is favored over backward; what is ahead is favored over what is behind. Implicit in this is a preference for the future, which lies ahead, than for the past, which lies behind. We trust what is before our eyes and are made anxious by what is in back of us. We distrust those who work behind our back, and we tend to trust those with whom we see eye-to-eye. Yet, we may be as deceived by what we see as comforted by what we do not see. The most deceptive salesmen have trained themselves to make "eye contact" in order to complete a sale. And those who are truly trustworthy do not need to be monitored and don't need to work before our very eyes.

The bias in forward and backward may be reflected in the biblical injunction —"Satan! Get thee behind me!"—which expresses a determination to mend one's ways, to avoid henceforth the temptations of sin. The suggestion is that one yielded to sin in the past, but that in the present and in the future, Satan will have no sway over the faithful. Yet, when this passage was translated into the Bolivian Quechua language, the translator encountered a difficulty, because in that language, the logic underlying the orientation of past and future to what is in front and what is behind was the reverse of what we are accustomed to. The logic of this Indian tribe went as follows: one knows the past, because one has lived it; hence, one can see the past; it is, therefore, before your eyes. Who among us can see clearly into the future? Except for seers and prophets, no one. Hence, the future, being unknown, is not before one's eyes; it can't be seen and hence can be plausibly assumed to be behind and eternally elusive to view. Hence, the past is in front or before one's eyes; the future cannot be seen and is, therefore, behind. So, in order to preserve the directional biases of each language, as well as to capture the original sense of the passage, our "Get thee behind me, Satan!" must be translated in Bolivian Quechua, as "Get thee in front of me, Satan!"[2]

The reckoning of time and age is another example of pseudo-universals. A person's age in the West does not correspond to a person's age in China, for example. Time is computed on an absolute scale in the West, so that a person's age is determined by the exact amount of time he has lived. But, in China, the question about a person's age asks—more literally—in how many calendar years have you lived, which is not entirely the same thing. Farmers are familiar with calculating how many springs they've lived through. In other words, a one-month-old baby is considered by the Chinese as having lived in one calendar year: the Chinese, and their language, consider him one *sui* until the next year. On New Year's Day, everyone adds a year to his or her *sui*. New Year's Day is, in a sense, everyone's birthday. So, in point of fact, a baby born a month before the New Year can be in his second year by his second month: he is one *sui* at birth, and then a month later, because of New Year's Day, he is two *sui*. If one assumes that there is an inclination to "age" persons faster than one might prefer to be aged in the West—that impression would be, I think, fairly accurate. For in China, it is a compliment to be thought older than one really is. There is a saying in Chinese: "Zhong lao, qing xiao" which means to prefer age to youth—which seems to be the reverse of what it is in America, where old age is a negative, youth is a positive. The forces one admires here are energy, vitality, dynamism, freshness, daring, innocence—all attributes of youth. Senility, fuddy-duddyness, cautiousness, decrepitude—these are all attributes of old age. Yet, the obverse is conveniently ignored: thoughtlessness, immaturity, self-centeredness—these not so attractive tendencies are also commonly encountered in youth; just as steadfastness, consistency, constancy, loyalty, perseverance, and wisdom are often identified with the old. If we appreciate this point, we can understand why, in China, age is positive, youth is negative.

There is also a telescoping of generation as a marker of time. In biblical times, a generation meant a thirty-year period, but in this computer age, a generation has diminished to a third of that. The first electronic computer can be dated to 1939, and we are already into our "fifth generation" of computers. Technological generations advance faster than human generations, and they are becoming shorter and shorter.

Perhaps the most dramatic contrast to be found in conceptual ethnocentricities concerns the notion of the self. American society since Freud has been preoccupied with the self in its various guises. I checked the number of books in print with the word "self" in the title: there are 4,189—which reflects the pervasiveness of the concept. The stress on the self seems particularly prominent in this country: I believe there is even a periodical out now with the title: "Self"! Is it coincidental that English is the only language in the world that superannuates the self punctuationally by capitalizing its first person nominative singular reference: "I"? All other Indo-European languages using the Roman alphabet and Western orthography cite the first-person nominative in lowercase letters: French "je," German "ich," Spanish "yo," Italian "io."

It's an article of faith—particularly among the young—that a meaningful activity is to search for the self. No one seems to question that there is a self to be found. Yet, there are certain illogicalities that elude notice: how is it, I'm prone to ask, that if one hasn't found oneself, one is so sure that the self exists? And if one is constantly in search of one self, who or what is doing the searching? Does it make sense for the self to search for itself? Yet, inherent in these irrationalities is a cherished premise: that everyone has an individual self, however ill defined, however unformed or wayward, however indeterminate. Our entire liberal, democratic tradition, our belief in freedom and liberty, depends on the reality of this self.

Yet, the concept of the individual self, as a separate, privileged entity set apart from the community, is a fairly recent development, even in the West. Its pervasiveness blinds us to other notions of existence which stress the contiguity of humanity rather than the atomistic autonomy of each individual. For anyone who has dealt with adolescent children or teenage students, the supreme expression of the independence of the self, which too often goes unchallenged, is: "It's my life, and I can do anything I want with it!" Over the years, my retort has been to ask: "Were you immaculately conceived?" Even if they say yes (and no one has, so far), I still insist that there is at least another human being involved in our coming into this life. For the rest of us, there are at least two parents who contributed to our being. If we go back two generations, there are four other human beings involved in who and what we are: with each generation we go back the numbers double. If we assume, as most intelligent humans believe, that we are descended from hundreds if not thousands or millions of generations since the first humans evolved, then it isn't hard to imagine that there are whole populations in us, represented by our ancestors and reflected in our genes. To reverse the issue, and perhaps to satisfy our most egoistic urges, one could cite the thousands and millions of offspring of whom we are potentially the progenitors. We can be, we may be, fathers and mothers to entire populations! When viewed in this context, it is hard to understand just what it means to say: "It's my life, and I can do anything I want with it!" This claim is based on no factual premise, and it recognizes no plausible prospect for the future. When one decides, for example, not to have children, not to continue the family

Eugene C.
Eoyang

line, one is discontinuing a tradition that has existed since the beginning of human civilization. For our very lives are testimony to at least one unbroken line of procreation from generation to generation since the dawn of humanity to the present. Indeed, without this unbroken chain, each of us would not have seen the light of day; none of us would be alive today. We owe our very existence to a continuous line that we threaten to cut off when we decide we will no longer have children. At a very basic level of human feeling, that seems—at the least—an ungrateful and uncharitable thing to do. Where would we be if just one of our ancestors were equally selfish and also decided not to have children?

There are many societies that have no concept of self apart from one's community. The Dinka in Africa, according to Godfrey Lienhardt, "have no conception which at all closely corresponds to our popular modern conception of the 'mind,' as mediating and, as it were, storing up experiences of the self."[3] The Chinese have perhaps the most elaborate reinforcement of this "fact of life" in their family structure. Here is a "table of consanguinity" in which each family relation has a special name, depending on three factors, whether the relative is: (1) male or female, (2) older or younger, (3) on the mother or the father's side. In other words, your cousin who is the daughter of your mother's sister and younger than you has a different label, a different term of address, than a cousin who is the daughter of your father's sister and older than you. There are, in fact, names for virtually every possible relation extending over five generations. Each time one refers to a relative, in citing or addressing a relative, one invokes an entire onomastic network that reminds one of one's place in a multigenerational family. In this welter of relations, it would be hard to conceive of the self as separate. (Is it any wonder that some Western observers have noticed the significance of the fact that in China, there is no word for "privacy"?)

In some of my comparative studies,[4] I have analyzed various contrasts between Western (specifically American) and Eastern (specifically Chinese) ways of conceiving of the world. One of these examples relates to the mind/heart question. It is axiomatic to believe, in the West, that the mind thinks and the heart feels. Subject to the test of ordinary language, the obverses of these formulations seem awkward, farfetched, if not meaningless: "the heart thinks," "the mind feels." In this premise, there are two possibly factitious assumptions: (1) that emotion and mentation are separate or separable and (2) that each can be assigned to either the head or the heart. This dichotomy is so strong that common parlance enshrines the difference, when, for example, one is warned against "thinking with one's emotions," or when one is being asked, rhetorically, "Is that your head or your heart talking?"— as if to suggest that the "heart talking" is a supererogation of authority. These distinctions are left meaningfully vague in Chinese, which regards "*hsin*" as the seat both of emotion and of thought. The very earliest dicta on Chinese poetry—*shih yen chih*—will be affected by this disjunction between Western and Chinese notions of what might be "psychological physiology," for this phrase can be tenably translated either as: "Poetry expresses intention" (which is its usual rendering) or "Poetry expresses emotions." The word "*chih*" is comprised of the ideographs for "scholar or soldier," *shih*, and the ideograph for "heart-mind," *hsin*. But neither translation of "shih yen chih" really does justice to the original, for poetry in Chinese can express both thought, unalloyed with emotion, as well as emotion devoid of thought. Most commonly, however, and there is in this an implicit value judgment, good poetry expresses a fusion of both feeling and thinking. There is, in Chinese aesthetics as well as in Chinese ethical teaching, a distrust of both pure mentation and pure emotion. In Western terms, the heart is a check to the coldness of the mind; the mind is a check on the fervency of the heart. But, this formulation also reflects a bias, for it assumes that two prior entities must somehow be brought together in a symbiosis, when in the Chinese view, the situation is quite the opposite. The two faculties are not two, but one, and it is their separation, either in abstract or concrete terms, that violates the wholeness of things and creates distortions that disrupt the natural order.[5] We need not pause to consider which view of things is correct: indeed, there are adherents for both points of view, and it may turn out that they are not contradictory.[6]

Another cross-cultural anomaly concerns Ruskin's notion of the "pathetic fallacy," which he characterizes as "a falseness in all our impressions of external things," a morbidity in which life is attributed to the lifeless and feeling to the unfeeling. Literary critics since have tended to identify instances of pathetic fallacies with disdain, recalling Ruskin's own dictum on its use: "I believe, if we look well into the matter, that we shall find the greatest poets do not often admit this kind of falseness,—that it is only the second order of poets who much delight in it."

These considerations will illuminate certain anomalies in the history of taste and provide important insights into aesthetics. Certainly, most moderns would agree with Ruskin's censure of the dull tropes in

Pope and his almost guilt-ridden enjoyment of Coleridge's "morbid" images. Yet, when we apply these criteria to one of the most famous lines in Chinese poetry, we find them curiously unavailing. Tu Fu's "Spring Prospect" begins with the oft-quoted lines:

> Country ruined, mountains and rivers remain;
> City in spring, grass and trees are thick.
> Moved by the times, flowers spill tears;
> Hate being apart, birds startle the heart.

The attribution of sorrow to flowers is an instance of what Ruskin would have a called a "morbid" pathetic fallacy. Yet it is precisely what one encounters in one of the most admired lines in Chinese poetry.[7] Implicit in the line is an assumption, which Ruskin would characterize as "false," that flowers are capable of shedding tears.[8]

One is left with a dilemma: either Ruskin is wrong in his characterization of meretricious rhetoric, or Tu Fu must be demoted, at least in this instance, from the "first order of poets," for his lapse into the pathetically fallacious. But, is this Manichaean dichotomy really necessary, or has a "middle" possibility not been excluded? One need not discard the poetry to vindicate a critical insight, nor need one undermine the critical insight to maintain one's admiration of a precious line. The underlying assumption in Ruskin is the superiority of the mental faculty over the emotional: truth is conceived of as only intellectual. Emotions can only distort the truth or cloud the truth or suppress the truth, but it cannot itself be an instrument for the discovery of truth. And if truth is to be preferred to passion, then, clearly, thinking must be superior to feeling. Yet, we must acknowledge the existence of "false feelings" and "true feelings" even if we cannot entertain the converse, which yields either the contradiction or the redundancy of "false truths" or "true truths." Tu Fu comes from a tradition where such bifurcations and discriminations would have been, in any event, inhospitable.

Two adjustments in premise interpretation are available to resolve the dilemma. First, there might be no division between heart and mind, and hence no hierarchy necessary between the faculty of thought and the faculty of feeling: there can, therefore, be no qualitative difference between an assertion of the mind and an assertion of the heart (both would be represented by the word *chih*, which denotes both intention and conation). Second, there is no real exclusivity in the human capacity for feeling: it doesn't take a rampant animism to entertain the prospect of sentience being variously attributed to all creation.

There is a certain intellectual onanism in Ruskin's analysis of the "pathetic fallacy": it assumes the prior existence of human emotions on their own terms, then suggests the impropriety of attributing those emotions to nonhuman objects. But Chinese, language and people, do not conceive of emotions in quite the same way. The terms for feeling are themselves metaphors borrowed from nature: it is nature that has provided the vocabulary of feeling. The word for "sorrow" is etymologically the word for "autumn" over the word for "mind-heart": *ch'ou.* Our modern sense of sophistication should not blind us to the admission that emotional terms are conventional abstractions, the existence and identity of which are notoriously difficult to establish (consider the meaning of "love" and "hate," the existence of which no one would deny, but they are also words that no one can define with absolute precision). It may be that a sense of "autumn in the heart" is the most concrete, the most precise, and the most comprehensive definition of sorrow that there is. For the Chinese word *ch'ou* encompasses the sense of the sadness of time passing, the lamentation for things dying, the dread of inhospitable winter, the intimation of one's own mortality—all easily recognizable as autumn feelings.

To "attribute" human emotion to inanimate objects of nature is, far from being fallacious, merely a restitution of the sources of feeling, a return of semantic capital to the resources of meaning. In Tu Fu's poem, of course, it is all the more powerful, because the contrast of human dishevelment with the steadfastness of nature is superseded by the confluence and congruence of change and stability in the word "tear." The sense of the poem is precisely that human culture has strayed too far from nature, which is why the one atrophies and the other abides.

In the West, the dominance of corresponding abstract-concrete pairs, whether Ideal-Real, or abstract-concrete, or noumenon-phenomenon, reflect a conception of validation posited on separable categorical worlds, whose very plausibility depends on their being autonomous realms of existence. Conflations of the ideal with the real, the abstract with the concrete, the noumenal with the phenomenal are difficult, if not impossible, to grasp. In any event, they would erode the clarity, hence the usefulness, of these concepts if their very conceptual purity is sullied. Furthermore, the logic of Western validation, and of Western epistemology, stresses the persuasiveness of correspondence as a factor in truth functions. One is more inclined toward accepting validity in the presence than in the absence of correspondence, although no prior proof has been given as to the role of correspondence as a warrant

Eugene C.
Eoyang

of validity. It may be that correspondence is a heuristic, rather than a validating factor, that is, that it inspires the human brain with confidence because it is easier to understand (because it reinforces prior knowledge) than because it is inherently valid. Departures from correspondence schemes are viewed with suspicion, are seen *as* deviations, rather than as data in their own right. The character of knowledge gained by positing a correspondence between an other-worldly and a this-worldly realm is powerfully familiar, of course, with the Platonic vision of the cosmos, where the immutable realm of Ideas exist concurrently with the mutable realm of diurnal reality. This notion of separateness of the permanent and the impermanent, of the universal and the particular, the perdurable and the ephemeral, pervades much of Western philosophy and poetics.

But these familiar contrasts are not as persuasive in an ontology or epistemology which sees wholeness and change, oneness and immanence, as the warrants of reality. We might posit Chinese forms of validations as those that identify a "resonant immanence." The suasions of Chinese philosophy do not develop out of abstract reason, or by a logic of correspondences, but by an appeal to the experiential corroboration of the reader. Consider, for example, the following text from the *Mencius:*

> Therefore, what is relished in the mouth is the same in everybody; the sounds perceived by the ear are heard alike by everybody; the colors of the eye are alike, beautiful to all. When one reaches the mind, is it alone without agreement on such things as "principle" or "righteousness"? The sages arrive at earlier what my mind already confirms, and therefore "principle" and "righteousness" gratify my mind, just as the meats of the table gratify my mouth.[9]

There is more than analogy here, more than correspondence: the suasion depends not on the recognition of the "facts" of tasting, hearing, or seeing for anyone who has a mouth or ears or eyes. Note how the citation skips neatly over the deviations of apperception in tasting, hearing, or seeing (*De gustibus non est disputandem;* "Beauty is in the eye of the beholder"); it seems verification in the mind of the reader is sought for "principle" and "righteousness," in terms as natural (hence as real) as tasting, hearing, and seeing. The argument is: If you can taste, hear, and see, then you must acknowledge the reality of "principle" and "righteousness." The reality of these experiences, their immanence in our experience, compels us to acknowledge the reality of the abstractions proposed: there is no "proof" beyond the heightening of experience, for if we can, each of us, experience "the meats of the table" gratifying our mouths, we cannot then deny the existence of "principle" and "righteousness." The appeal in this discourse is to the immediacy of our own experience, not to an abstract principle beyond our own experience.

The tendency in some Chinese texts to derive mysteries from actual experience may be contrasted with the Platonic practice of imagining an abstract realm that corresponds to concrete experience, or of Aristotle analyzing concrete particulars to discover the abstract universals. For a number of significant Chinese philosophers, the division of the abstract and the concrete is untenable: truths derive from the actuality of experience, not in spite of it. There is a resolute insistence that diurnal experience, actuality, is the only reality, and there is an inherent skepticism of that which can be abstracted as never really existing. Ancient Chinese philosophical texts, whether Confucian or Taoist, share with Aristotelians, empiricists, and logical positivists the notion that no truth is to be credited that is not grounded on actual experience. Where Chinese philosophy departs from Western notions, however, is in the tendency of ancient Chinese discourse to require an assertion to be felt in human terms, not merely abstractly and intellectually recognized. An example from Liu Hsieh's *Wen-hsin tiao-lung* will illustrate the point: "Natural excellence may be compared to the splendors of flowers in the woods; their vivid beauty is like the silk-dyed vermilion and green. Silks dyed vermilion and green are deep, rich and vibrant; the blossoms and the sun-drenched trees, blaze forth in glory. Brilliant writing radiates in the garden of literature in much the same way."[10]

It would be a serious misreading of this text to see Liu Hsieh as merely intending a metaphor between "the blossoms of nature" and the "flowers of literature," though the translation easily accommodates such an interpretation. The aptness of the comparison lies in no correspondence between the characteristics in nature and in literature: the force lies in the similarity of experience in one's reaction, on the one hand, to nature and, on the other, to literature. One accepts the validity of the comparison, not by seeing it as a metaphor, equating subjunctively two disparate entities, but only by identifying indicatively the response to nature and to literature as one and the same. The homology borders on identity: "Brilliant writing radiates in the garden of literature in much the same way."

One might posit, by way of contrast, a poetics of correspondence (which one finds in Plato) alongside a poetics of resonance. In the first

Eugene C.
Eoyang

case, poetry establishes a truth through the sometimes allegorical, sometimes symbolic, sometimes metaphoric description of concrete details: the experience described and preserved in the poem always points to something else—whether moral truth or aesthetic beauty or romantic sentiment. The Western reader of Chinese poetry often searches in vain for the "point"—especially if he is reading in translation, because the poem is not mimesis either in the Platonic or the Aristotelian sense, that is, it is not an imitation of ideal reality twice removed, nor is it the creation of the imagination. It is both the recording and the reenactment of an indicative moment, its realization in words.

For Chinese philosophers, truths are always contingent: one's knowledge is always compromised. There is little or no desire to extrapolate human truths beyond human experiences, even if the cosmic experiences are explained in terms of familiar human realities. We might posit on the one hand the Tao of existence, and on the other hand, the truth of life, and we might see a model of mimesis contrasted with a model of immanence. In the first instance, the model of mimesis, the unknown is conceived of as corresponding to the known and is real and valid the more that correspondence can be established and reiterated. In the second instance, the model of immanence, the only reality is whatever is immanent, whatever is, at the moment, now, thus. In the first instance, the Truth is adducible and achievable, if elusive; in the second instance, the Tao is ever-present and yet not adducible. The Truth is replicable, accessible, and powerful: "Know the Truth and it will set you free." But the Tao is inimitable and fugitive and evanescent: "The Tao that can be said is not the commonplace and universal Tao."

The purpose in positing such polarities is to extend the basis for discussion, not from one vantage point or another but from both. Our "horizon of expectations" must include more than one perspective, seen from more than one reference point. The result will not be, as some indolent intellects too readily assume, a relativity of values, but a more rigorous, indeed, a more open recognition of values with due acknowledgment of tacit premises. Each set of premises, what Stephen Pepper calls "world hypotheses," highlights another aspect of reality. As heirs to the traditions in both East and West, we are the beneficiaries of a multiple perspective, but along with the panoptic perspective is the challenge to check our own myopia. The bigot with perfect eyesight should not be preferred to the blind man with perfect vision.

The virtues and the limitations of both traditions should become more apparent in any comparison. Our task is not to disown our own heritage, but rather by comparing it with another heritage, to truly discover it, to see it in relief against the background of a different context. Too often what is accepted as universal is only customary and commonplace within the province one inhabits. But commonplaces are not the same everywhere, and what is common to one may be uncommon to another. We can continue to pursue the mysteries, and we may even call our speculations the truth. What we discover may, in fact, be true with the facts on which we have based our theories. But, in the construction of any lasting theory, in the development of any durable understanding, analysis and intuition must proceed as one: the paradigms of mimesis must be alloyed with the paradigms of resonance.

I now proceed to "self-discoveries"—that is, reflections on the self that emerge from an exploration of the other. Because this discussion may be very abstract, I'd like to begin with an unexpected example, involving the translation into Chinese of an English nursery rhyme. I was once asked to check the Chinese version of: "Jack be nimble, Jack be quick, Jack jump over the candlestick."

A simple enough assignment, to be sure. But when I saw the translation into Chinese, with "candlestick" correctly translated as "zhutai," I noticed an anomaly that had never troubled me before in English. My immediate response was that jutai was literally correct, but it was, somehow, also wrong. In Chinese, the nursery rhyme became absurd— more absurd than would be appropriate even for a nursery rhyme: who would be so foolish as to jump over a candle *holder?* Yet that is what the rhyme said. In remonstrating with the Chinese translator, I indicated that the word "candlestick" in the rhyme is implicitly interpreted by every speaker of English as a "candlestick" *with* a lighted candle. Contemporary speakers of English will, in reading "candlestick" unwittingly supply the candle and the flame;[11] traditional interpretations place an even greater emphasis on the flame, if the following etymology can be credited: "For centuries, jumping over a candle has been both a sport and a way of telling fortunes in England. A candlestick with a lighted candle in it was placed on the floor. The person who could jump over it without putting out the flame was assured of having good luck for a full year."[12] The use of the "candlestick" was, of course, dictated by the exigencies of rhyme, but the meaning in the rhyme is unmistakable, even if implicit. Yet, what interests me about the example is that only an outside perspective forced me to see what an insider sees *through* and, seeing through, fails to notice.

Earlier, I mentioned that the phrase "Satan, get thee behind me,"

Eugene C.
Eoyang

when translated into Quechua, required the equivalent of "Satan, get thee in front of me"—deriving from the unimpeachable logic that the past is known: it is spread out, as it were, before one's eyes, whereas the future is unknown: it can't be seen and therefore is not before one's eyes. The logic of this made me think of Western preconceptions as illogical if we proceed from the same premises. However, they may be logical if we proceed from different premises. In what way does it make sense, I asked, to conceive of a future that is unknown to us as being in front of us, before our very eyes, and of the past, though known, as out of sight. I realized that the implicit paradigm in the Quechua was of someone standing *at rest*, whereas the implicit paradigm of Western preconceptions was of someone *moving forward*. Only by such an implicit paradigm—of someone walking ahead—does it make sense to see the future as in front of us, even when we don't know what it is, and to see the past as behind us, even though we can look at it anytime we want. Does it seem significant that we more often and more naturally speak of facing the future, rather than facing the past? Might it say something about the biases in our civilization that we value the future more than we value the past? We would rather speculate (subject to ocular inspection as well as to intellectual scrutiny) on the future than give due recognition of the past. Is the model of someone stationary necessarily inferior to the model of someone moving forward? Ordinary language preconceptions in English would suggest that it is. We believe it is better to move forward than to stand still or to move backward. We believe it is better to contemplate the future than to dwell on the past. We believe that—to paraphrase Scarlett O'Hara in *Gone With the Wind*—"Tomorrow is another (and presumably better) day!"

Perhaps the most unexpected self-discovery to be made is the perspective on modern physics. For one would think that, physics is emblematic of the most objective, least subjective intellectual pursuits: the study of material things, which traditionally does not admit of abstractions that cannot be scientifically measured. One would hardly go to physics for discoveries about the self. However, these days, physicists talk more like poets: in his celebrated popular exegesis of quantum mechanics, Gary Zukav writes: "the philosophical implication of quantum mechanics is that all of the things in our universe (including us) that appear to exist independently are actually parts of one all-encompassing organic pattern, and that no parts of that pattern are ever really separate from it or from each other."[13]

This formulation would seem to reinforce the Chinese or Confucian of the self as a nexus of human relationships that connects each of us with thousands, perhaps millions of ancestors and progenitors and with potentially a vast number of offspring. The description by Zukav and others of the physical world interpreted through quantum mechanics is strikingly filial in its orientation: "the physical world . . . is not a structure built out of independently existing unanalyzable entitites, but rather a web of relationships between elements whose meanings arise wholly from their relationships to the whole" (72). Among the many "weird" postulations of the new science, Zukav cites the "Many Worlds Interpretation of Quantum Mechanics," which "says that different editions of us live in many worlds simultaneously, an uncountable number of them, and all of them are real" (87). The new science has adopted some of the stances of the Chinese, and we hear echoes of the linguistic conflation of "heart" and "mind" in Chinese when Zukav writes: "religion has become a matter of the heart and science has become a matter of the mind. This regrettable state of affairs does not reflect the fact that, physiologically, one cannot exist without the other. Everybody needs both. Mind and heart are wholly different aspects of *us*" (88).

Even the teaching of writing as self-expression has undergone a sea change in recent years. For years the process of writing was—erroneously, in my opinion—presented as a "feel-good" scam toward self-fulfillment. This slant on writing seemed to suggest that the greatest writers were the most self-centered, the most self-indulgent. It left out writing as a discipline, writing as a rigorous dialectical activity which, far from being a solipsistic verbal display, is a rigorously analytical heuristic activity of the mind. Writing is, if it's anything, disciplined self-discovery. This point was emphasized in a piece some years ago in *College English* by Joseph Harris, which considered Roland Barthes, a French deconstructionist critic, and William Coles, a teacher of writing, who published a book called *The Plural I* in 1978. Harris's comments are directly relevant to our effort to discover ourselves through the study of others and provides yet another reinforcement of our theme, that the discovery of our selves is crucially dependent on our ability to understand and to recognize the other. Again the divisions between subject and object are dissolved in the process of semantic if not nuclear fusion. "The task of the teacher of writing," Harris reminds us, "is not to train students to make their prose ever more Clear and Efficient. Neither is it to simply encourage them to be Expressive and Sincere. Rather it is to set up a situation that dramatizes the forces at work in writing. . . . It is to suggest that to reduce the complexities of writing to a single demand to be personal or to be clear is to trivial-

108

Eugene C.
Eoyang

ize it, that good writing is not simply writer-based or reader-based, but something of both."[14] The discovery of the self in the singular turns out to be an illusion, and the question we asked facetiously at the outset can now be answered seriously: "if one is constantly in search of one self, who or what is doing the searching? Does it make sense for the self to search for itself?" The answer, however, requires a reformulation of the question. If one takes what is called the self as multiple and plural rather than single and singular, the answer becomes clear, even if language makes it hard to formulate. For one can say that the selves of which we are conscious set out in pursuit of other selves as yet undiscovered. We are, each of us, comprised of a virtual infinity of selves, perhaps as numerous as the number of our progenitors since the beginning of our evolution. Harris tells us that for both Coles, the teacher of writing, and for Barthes, the literary aesthete, "the voice of a writer is always a weaving of other voices, the self is seen not as an isolated whole but as an amalgam of other selves, voices, experiences." Our discussion of the Confucian notion of self as an interstice in an elaborate network of human relationships, finds an echo in Harris's citation of Barthes: "The image of the text Barthes continually returns to is that of a network, 'woven entirely with citations, references, echoes, cultural languages . . . which cut across it through and through in a vast stereophony.' . . . As Barthes writes in *S/Z*: 'This "I" which approaches the text is itself a plurality of other texts'" (161).

Harris's conclusion resonates with the strategy of "seeing with another I": in our search for other worlds, we must start by realizing that, as Harris insists, "We are what our languages make of us and what we can make of our languages" (169). The use of languages in the plural is the key to a proper understanding of the complexity of the self, which we now must view as a complexity of selves subsumed in that unitary concept, the self.

As a final exercise in "seeing with another I," I offer a puzzle, which will serve as a parable for ways in which we can expand our vision even as we multiply the individual selves which comprise the "I" which each of us uses to designate a self. The puzzle goes as follows:

> There are three men in a room, each with a hat on his head. Each is allowed to see the hats on the other two, but he is not allowed to take off his own hat. The three are all told that there are altogether five hats available, three blue, two red. The first person is asked if he knows the color of his own hat. He looks at the other two, then says he doesn't know. The second person is asked

the same question: he doesn't know either. The third person is blind. He is asked what is the color of the hat on his own head. He knows. The question is: "what color is the hat on the blind man, and how does he know?"

The solution is a matter of deduction: it is, of course, crucial that the blind man is asked last. The first person—let's call him A—doesn't know, which eliminates the possibility that the second person—let's call him B—and the blind man both have red hats, since that would mean that only blue hats would be left, and he could thereby deduce that the hat on his own head must be blue. So A's not knowing suggests that between B and the blind man, three possibilities remain: both hats are blue; B's hat is red and the blind man's blue; or B's hat is blue and the blind man's is red. Each of these possibilities allows for the color of the hat on A to be either red or blue—which is why he doesn't know. Let's turn to B: B cannot be seeing both A and the blind man with red hats, or he would know, just as A would have, that his own hat must be blue. When B indicates in turn that he doesn't know, this reduces these remaining possibilities even further: Now we can assume that since B also knew the remaining possibilities determined by A's answer, that he, B, and the blind man cannot both have red hats, B would figure out that if the blind man had a red hat, he, B, must have a blue hat. But B doesn't know, so this possibility—that the blind man has a red hat when B has a blue hat—is eliminated. Of the three remaining possibilities that remained after A indicated he didn't know—(1) that B and the blind man both had blue hats; (2) that B had a red hat and the blind man had a blue hat; and (3) that B had a blue hat and the blind man had a red hat, we can eliminate the third option, since we have already deduced that, if the blind man had a red hat, B would know that the hat on his head was blue (it couldn't have been red as well or else A would have been able to answer the question in the first place). You will note that in the remaining options "(1) that B and the blind man both have blue hats, and (2) B has the red hat and the blind man has the blue hat—B could, depending on the option, have a blue or a red hat—which is why he doesn't know. But the blind man has a blue hat in either option, whatever the color of B's hat. Therefore, the blind man concludes, the hat on his own head is blue.

The point of this puzzle is that the blind man is able to "see" what his two sighted colleagues cannot know: the color of his own hat. One could speculate on the irony of a blind man "seeing" more than those with sight, but that would miss the point. The point is that the

Eugene C.
Eoyang

blind man "sees" what the eyes of his two companions see, and that insight allows him to know more than they do. It is also important to notice that merely borrowing their sight is not enough to solve the puzzle: the blind man also puts himself in the minds of the other two in order to arrive at his conclusion. He not only figures out what his colleagues see and don't see, he also puts himself in their place, he "envisions" himself in their positions, he imagines himself as the other two, putting his "I-as-self" into their "I-as-self," imagining what their experience as the subjective first-person I would be. He borrows not only their eyes to see what they see; he also borrows their subjective first-person I to determine what it is they know or don't know. The blind man, in this puzzle, cannot see through his own eyes, but he sees very accurately through the "eyes" and the "I's" of the others.

If a blind man can do this, how much more can we see through another I? How many other worlds might we discover in our search for the multiple selves in that consciousness we refer to routinely as "I"? And, how many "I's" might each of us find in our individual selves, if we can project our view past our own provincial horizons to a larger perspective. We who have sight must not miss the chance to develop vision. For the blind man in the puzzle tells us the difference between sight and vision. The Bible has identified those who have eyes, and yet who do not see: the blind man reminds us that vision is seeing through another I.

Notes

Presented at the second statewide conference on Multicultural Scholarship: Towards a Broad-based Implementation Across the Curriculum," Jersey City State College, April 5, 1990.

1   David Feldman, *Why Do Clocks Run Clockwise? and Other Imponderables* (New York: Harper and Row, 1987), 150.

2   Cf. Eugene Nida, "On Bible Translating," in *On Translation*, ed. Reuben Brower (Cambridge, Mass.: Harvard U P, 1959; Oxford U P, 1966), 12.

3   *Divinity and Experience: The Religion of the Dinka* (Oxford: Clarendon Press, 1961), 149–51; quoted by Yi-fu Tuan, *Segmented Worlds and Self: Group Life and Individual Consciousness* (Minneapolis: University of Minnesota Press, 1982), 142.

4   Cf. my "Polar Paradigms in Poetics: Chinese and Western Literary Premises," in *Comparative Literature East and West: Traditions and Trends* (East-West Center: Honolulu, 1989), 11–21.

5   Two passages in the *Mencius*, fairly close to each other, illustrate the latitude of the word *hsin*. Book 2, A, chap. 2, verse 1 refers to the "unperturbed mind." When asked if his mind were perturbed or not, Mencius replies:

"No. At forty, my mind was unperturbed." Yet, several verses later (2A:6), Mencius says: "All men have a mind which cannot bear to see the sufferings of others."

6   Recent developments in Western medicine have revived previously discarded notions of mind-body influences, although "holistic medicine" is still greeted with skepticism from the majority of doctors trained in Western medicine; see Daniel Goleman, "The Mind over the Body," *New York Times Magazine* (September 27, 1987), 36ff.

7   Indeed, Ruskin adds a footnote to his initial essay on the "pathetic fallacy" and quotes lines almost identical to these, but from Tennyson's *Maud:* "There has fallen a splendid tear / From the passion-flower at the gate."

8   Interpretations that suggest that the tears can only be human, and that these tears have been shed by humans onto the flowers (as if the poet were "crying over flowers" instead of "spilt milk"), strike me as grotesque.

9   *Ssu-pu pei yao* (SPPY) edition, *chüan* 11, 8b.

10 *Wen-hsin tiao-lung* (Hong Kong, 1960), 1.

11 The following sample of illustrated nursery rhymes all included a lighted candle: *The Tall Book of Mother Goose* (New York, 1943), 35; *The Real Mother Goose* (Chicago, 1916, 1944), 16; *The Sesame Street Players Present Mother Goose* (New York, 1980), 82, unpaginated. Richard Scarry's *Best Mother Goose Ever* (New York, 1964, 1970), 3, shows the candle in the candlestick, but with no flame.

12 *The Annotated Mother Goose*, eds. William S. and Ceil Baring-Gould (New York: Bramhall House, 1962), 194.

13 *The Dancing Wu-li Masters: An Overview of the New Physics* (New York: William Morris, 1979; Bantam edition, 1980), 47–48.

14 Joseph Harris, "The Plural Text/The Plural Self: Roland Barthes and William Coles," *College English* 49:2 (February 1987), 168.

Eugene C.
Eoyang

Cut

Throat

Sun

———————————

Jean-Luc

Nancy

Translated
by Lydie
Moudileno

You are called *Chicanos*. This name shortens your name, *Mexicanos*, in the language that was once yours but has not remained the language of each one of you. Your name was given back to you, cut. In what language? What language is this word, your name? It is the idiom of a single name as well as your way to cut and shuffle languages: babel without confusion, that you *do* speak, that your poets *do* write. You were given back your name, cut, and your language, also cut. (By whom? The others, us, and you too, your other selves within yourselves.) It was a very old name, much older than this Castilian language in which it was first transcribed, copied, and cut; it was an Indian name and much older than the name "Indian," by which Mexicans were forcibly baptized before Mexico was called Mexico. Born in the mistake of the Occident thinking it had found the Orient, this name cut off from themselves a land, a history, several territories and several histories, cut off cultures of the sun, suns of culture, of fire, feathers, obsidian, and gold. Iron was cutting into gold. But this iron was itself gold: the gold turning from *takin*, excrement of the sun, into *silver*, wealth and power, and it was that gold that severed the sun itself. The Occident brought forth only the Occident, *aggravating* it, and the same sun just had to set in another ocean. These are your ancestors, all these people, Indians and cutters of Indian. Cut races, mixed bloods.

Cut throat sun: May I return to you, as if it were your emblem, this line by a French poet with so Greek a name, Apollinaire? As if it were your emblem, and almost as your idiom and your music? I don't speak your language, your languages; I only appropriate them through these words of my own language—*soleil cou coupé*—and I give them back to you. Could it be that the state of language when it no longer belongs to anyone in particular, when it no longer belongs to itself and surrenders itself to all, is poetry?

Your throat: the throat of the rednecks, poor field-workers of California, Arizona, and New Mexico (is there a *new* Mexico?). But you are not the *white* rednecks. Your red is not overcooked white skin. It is a red gold replacing the white trash, its burns and its cuts. Cut throat: the Mexican sun has been cut from your head, with your head.

Throat slashed red, like a coagulating sun, like a dry and burning source of paint. It was to spurt, later in the thirties, on to the Chicago walls. At the time, you didn't have that identity—that had been yours for centuries, anyway—that *chicano* cut of identity to which you refer us today, but they were yours, these *murals* that Pollock or De Kooning would go to see.

This throat has been cut several times. Indian, by a Spanish cut, Spanish, by a yankee cut. Emigrants from the interior of Mexico, migrating through Spanish states like California, Arizona and *others*, you also became the migrants who cross the border in order to form another frontier, moving in long lines across the fields, penetrating into cities of *barrios* whose colors contrast so sharply (and the sounds, and the thoughts). Broadway in Los Angeles, its buildings ornamented like those in Manhattan, with solemn and businesslike guilloche: how it has become your frontier and your fair and your fever!

Perhaps you barbecue sausages on Sundays in the *heights of Griffith Park*, and it makes me think of the way Turks barbecue sausages on Sundays in Berlin near the Reichstag. It's almost the same smell.

In order to get there, you had to cross the border, often the law, and the militia, and the police (one arrest every thirteen minutes), and also the Mexican smugglers who sometimes rob you. Sun cut down, one then has to spend the night, to swim across the Rio Grande on one's back with a bundle kept dry on the chest. You were these *wetbacks*.

By this wet mark they recognized that you could be gunned down or exploited. That water is not the water streaming down the sides of the Mayflower, and you do not celebrate Thanksgiving by which America commemorates the gift of America to the Americans, with all its Indians and turkeys. Or, you are in need of water under the sun of that desert you illegally cross, and you are dead, with whitened bones, somewhere around Yuma. Or else, on the freeway that goes North from Tijuana to San Diego, cars, pickups, and *Aztec* buses have to stop: U.S. officials in their large hats with stiff brims can tell your Chicano faces at a glance. The place is a little above Camp Pendelton, where the Marines are stationed. They have a big board announcing that their camp is dedicated to protecting nature.

Cut throat Americans, you are Mexican-Americans. What is this name, American? Another name that has been cut, transplanted, displaced, stolen. It was not this Italian man called Amerigo, Spain's *Piloto Mayor* after Columbus had fallen into disgrace, who discovered America, no more than the ones called Americans (U.S. citizens) account for the peoples of the three Americas. You are more American (Native American and proud of it, as is sometimes declared on bumper stickers of old Oldsmobiles that belong to a Zuni, a Hopi, an Apache). More American: but what does American mean?

Language keeps social cohesion, but it keeps it to a limit, to the limit of its own looseness. Language itself is always borderline; it is always at odds with language. But moreover, being loose and invasive, it passes and trespasses the limits; it underlines them and passes them. "American," "Chicano," one can merely understand, too well and not enough, at the same time.

All of this doesn't mean very much. It can only open on the undefined, multiple, radiating, reticulated, and broken track of *mestizaje*, of *métissage*, of the cutting, of the uncountable cuttings. Couplings and cuttings: what each "people" is made of—made of/cut of. Which people can claim it is not? You are Visigoths, Jews, Mandingos, Manchurians, Vikings, Francs, Arabs, as well as people from Aztlán, the legendary land that the Aztecs had already emigrated from, immigrating to central Mexico.

> Tell me when you are ready
>   for the rebirth
>   the dream of AZTLAN! (Mora)

But the birth of your people is an incessant birth and rebirth, continuing to today—when you come into this *world*, into this whole world into which we are all coming. But your rebirth will not mean the return to myth. It will be, and it is already, the foundation of that which has neither pure foundation nor identifiable origin: of that Aztlan that you *are* coming in from yourselves, cut throat suns. It is a foundation in the cutting. You are, you will be—and who, of us, will be with you?—like the founders of Los Angeles, the list of whom can be found in the rare-document section of the Berkeley Library: nine Mexican Indians, eight mulattos, two blacks, two Spaniards, one *mestizo*, and one Chinese named Antonio Rodríguez. (Not only is this list a *mestizaje* of people: it is also a linguistic *mestizaje:* "mulatto" and "Spaniard" are not of the same register; we mix ideas of "blood" and "nation," and with what has each of these ideas already been mixed?) They founded *El Pueblo de Nuestra Señora de Los Angeles de Porciúncula;* name that was cut down to *LA;* L.A. that is always your first city, and a city that is itself cut, made of cuttings. Your first city, but not your capital: decapitated capital, throat cut.

What is your foundation? What will it be? It is, will be, more than America's foundation or opening—cleavage, wound, open mouth—to its own absence of foundation. You make a Founding Fathers *mestizaje*, showing that all foundation is itself unfounded, and it is well founded to be unfounded. You aren't the only ones to do that. Here and elsewhere, and otherwise, it is the blacks, the Filipinos, the Jamaicans, the Koreans, the Thais, the Syrians and however many others, who found in this way, who cut the cities, the languages, the *marks.* You will not melt into another identity; you will not accomplish the *American Dream*, no more than the *dream of Aztlan.* You are, on the contrary, actors of, and witnesses to, an immense and extraordinary novelty, and yet it is not a dream: it is a different, completely different "identification," a different rift, a different sectioning of America. And it is not enough to talk about America only: in Europe, blacks, Arabs, Chinese, Turks, and Vietnamese people also drive us toward our foundation in the absence of all foundation, toward this cross-current that cuts and covers territories, faces, languages and makes histories happen. A history is happening to us, yours or ours, inalienable like all histories. No one is its subject, and we cannot pin it down beforehand in order to know it. Yet, we know the flash signals its presence, but we cannot look at it head-on: the brightness from all those cut throat suns.

The brightness of a sun which is no longer the sacrificer but the sacrificed. It is a different brightness. Or, a brightness even more differ-

ent: neither sacrificer nor sacrificed. The brightness of an existence—
without justification, but not unjustified.

You use the word, and you claim to be, *La Raza*, the race, the people,
nuestra gente.

Therefore you want us to hear this word "race" completely differently, for there is nothing of racism that you are unaware of: it also
marks your cut. But you do not know to what extent the thought of
"race," and its systematic implementation, extermination that is, prevents us from reeducating our perception of the word, despite everything, despite you. (You also come from an extermination that numbers in the tens of thousands of lives. But it had not imposed itself
as "thought"; it had not brandished a "concept" or an "idea" of race.)
And yet what we will hear in your word, as well as besides the word,
is that the *gente chicana* does not propose the purity of a bloodline
nor a superiority. It gets its identity from the cut, in the cuttings. It is
no less an identity for it, but it is not an identity in terms of blood or
essence.

Your identity is obtained through cuts. Through *mestizajes*, but also
through those cuts that irretrievably separate West Hollywood from
East L.A., and those, in the heart of L.A., that slice through Santa
Monica Boulevard leaving on one side the memories of the big studios,
and on the other, the pawn shops where you hock all the watches,
boots, and miserable bits and pieces you've had to forsake.

In naming *la raza*, you are naming a division of labor, class, and role.
La raza was not simply born in Aztlán or in the barrios, it was born in
the revolts, strikes, and riots, of the *Crusada para la justicia* and many
other movements. It is not simply a class, but made of the cuttings of
classes, as of languages and peoples.

> La raza hurt,
> bent back—sacrificed
> to gringoismo—(Omar Salinas)

Gringo, the name you use for the white American (who claims to
be white), derived from *Griego*, the Greek, who was in the past, the
typical foreigner. The same foreigner that made you foreigners on your
own land, on the land that everybody and nobody owns. Gringoismo:
egoismo.

But I have no intention of celebrating the difference in *la raza:* that
would be celebrating its poverty and mere estrangement. I will not

glorify the cutting. The cutting, in its two senses—cutting themselves and mixing—is not to be glorified. There are no words, there is no rejoicing or mourning for its dark radiance. But there is your language and your languages, your poems, your paintings, your plays, and your movies. And let us also make sure we don't, just for the sake of another dream of integration and assimilation, for the sake of an easy accommodation of our questions and expectations, assign them to the idea of a "transculture" with its multiple and enriching facets. Your difference, your differences, arrive in a world that pretends to be reclaiming differences in general (is there difference "in general"?), but that can always trap those differences into its indifference. It is always possible for the postromantic celebration of the "spirit of the people" to be made to serve the interests of some overall exploitation of all people.

In such a scheme, you and the blacks, the white trash, and all the rednecks of the earth are alike. Today an unjustifiable, intolerable identity that is forced on us today by the callous monster of technoeconomic necessity and the management or administration of this necessity. How to cut loose from it, what sort of revolution that would not be already outdated? Maybe that of mestizaje. . . . But that would assume that the fate of misery is linked to the fate of identity: yet if they are linked de facto, must it be a single slice that severs one from the other? This unprecedented question concerns all of us.

Our *naked* existences: Who wants them? How do we want to want them? *Naked:* interwoven (*métissées*), ill-woven (*mal tissées*), but woven (*tissées*) one into the other. Sharing and crossing and bordering.

This unprecedented question concerns all of us. But it does not return to us as the question of "another world" being born. If a *world* is a totality of presence where each existence is inscribed, it is no longer certain that we have to reproduce, even if this figure or configuration were transformed. "People of the world!": it is doubtful that such a call could still reach us. "People without a world"?

Chicanos, it may also be something you tell us. With you, with all the cuts similar to yours "but singularly yours, large, multiple, less "identifiable" if that is possible—it is not merely change that is shaping up for the world. It is something else (how easy it is to say "something else" when a world is stamping and stamping on itself on the edge of what once was the *world*). It is a way to be on the border of every possible world: on the edge of what all our possibilities gauge as impossible (let's say: man without a world), that is, however, what happens to us, what is offered to us, exactly what we must confront.

Instead of a "world," its order, its *ordinance*, its presence, something else, another configuration of space, of time, of community, of history.

Something is happening to us, the same way Aztlan was born one day, the way the Americas were born, the way Chicanos were born, and always in the process of arriving. And, the same way, empires waver and identities split. "America" can no longer have the absolute self-knowledge. It too is throat cut, a civilization falling to pieces, while "Europe" wonders what its own name might mean: a breathless discourse, breath cut short. A whole history is coming upon us: as always, we cannot see it coming. We only see that it cuts but without being able to tell who is cutting and who is being cut. From the depths of the cut, from its depths or its surface, from its slice, a dark sun blinds us: our own event is neither "one" nor "distinctive" (and is it even an event? How should we take that word?). It comes upon us as you do, clandestine, illegal, scattered. The freedom of history which is "ours," always surprises us.

It is no longer a question of what was called the meeting, or the confrontation, "of the Other." You are more other than the others, you are simultaneously the same as we are and cut from yourselves and from us, as we are also cut.

You say: not even the same where it most resembles, where it most assembles—and still the same, all the same, where it is different, where it disassembles the most. Each one encamped in his camp, and every-one displaced.

> What if the U.S. was Mexico?
> What if 200,000 Anglo-Saxicans
> Were to cross the border each month
> to work as gardeners, waiters
> 3rd chair musicians, movie extras
> bouncers, babysitters, chauffeurs
> syndicated cartoons, feather-weight boxers, fruit-pickers
> and anonymous poets?
> What if they were called Waspanos
> Waspitos, Wasperos or Waspbacks?
> What if literature was life, eh?

What if yo were you
& tu fueras I, Mister? (Guillermo Gómez-Peña)

I say: "you say." By what right? By virtue of whose authority? Or in what sign language? I cannot, I must not say "you say." Cut throat speech. But this speech can also cut: It can cut me /from you/from myself/ from the same/ and from the other. It is the cut that ties me and joins me—to what? to something, to some*one* that you and I don't know.

I cannot set myself free from this unknown, from this variable. Everything has yet to be done: everything has yet to be learned, the ways, the art, and the strength needed to make the cut tie together. But I am already at a point where I can no longer detach myself.

It is no longer possible is to do nothing but look at you (and at myself at the same time). There is nothing left in the spectacle any more. It is no longer possible to take part in the representation of a New World, from the standpoint of another world.

There is sun and there is sun. Once there was Verlaine's sun:

> Je suis l'Empire à la fin de la décadence,
> Qui regarde passer les grands Barbares blancs
> En composant des acrostiches indolents
> D'un style d'or où la langueur du soleil danse.

There is the one I am giving back to you, Apollinaire's:

> A la fin tu es las de ce monde ancien
> (. . .)
> Tu en as assez de vivre dans l'antiquité grecque et romaine
> (. . .)
> Adieu Adieu
> Soleil cou coupé

There is also, passing in front of the sun, other voices close to you, all from far away, from California and elsewhere at the same time:

> or growing crystalling
> passing in front of the sun
> brilliant diffusion speaking in scale
> the trivial requiring time to speak of it
> direction unvocalized clicks in succession. (Norma Cole)

Still others, farther, closer: the German writer from San Diego:

Als ich den Schalter erreichte, antwortete ich auf die Frage nach meiner Augenfarbe mit den Worten: "Brown, Sir!" Aber vor mir war ein junger Mexikaner an der Reihe, der wie aus einer Märchen aussan. Einem herbeigewunkenen Kollegen gegenüber bezeichnete ihn der Sheriff flüsternd als "real cunt." (Reinhard Lettau)

Closer, farther, the Calabrian woman from Strasbourg:

Era nuovo il paese in cui abivata; gli amici non giudivacano le sue debolezze. (Dora Mauro)

We need to relearn everything from "peoples" and "people." We need to relearn everything about identities and cuts, relearn everything about the infinite of the finitudes that are our discrete existence: how they never cease not totalizing themselves, neither in each individual nor in each "people" nor in each "language" nor in "humanity," and how in truth that would be our chance. Our chance for truth. One cannot *know* that, one cannot seize it like an object of knowledge, or like a philosophical view of the "world." Nonetheless, we have to know, even in an impossible way.

Our science should be the cosmography of a universe of cut-throat suns. Or the anthropology of *"l'humanité métissée"* ("mestizo human ness," as Ricardo Sánchez puts it). But this *mestizaje* would not be one of races, that would only suggest a trope. It would be, in people, peoples, histories, events of existence, the *mestizaje* of their multiplicities that cannot be assigned to places of pure origins. It would be less a question of mixed identity *d'identité métissée* than of the *mestizaje* of identity itself, of any identity.

Singular existences, points of *mestizaje*, identities are made/cut of singularities (places, moments, languages, passions, skins, accents, laws, prayers, cries, steps, bursts). They are in turn the singular events of these compositions and cuts. Like any proper name, *Chicano* does not appropriate any meaning: it exposes an event, a singular sense. As soon as such a name arises—cut—it exposes all of us to it, to the cut of sense that it is, that it makes, far beyond all signifying. "Chicano" breaks into my identity as a "gringo." It cuts into and re-composes it. It makes us all *mestizo*.

Increasingly, the "mestizos" in South Africa refuse to use this word: *métis* is only another term of exclusion, imposed on them by a racist legislation. What if it were possible, somewhere else, to change this word into a word that excludes exclusion (not through inclusion and fusion, but through the inscription of cuts)?

The community: as if it were no longer the closure that excludes, but the multiple, cut network from which exclusion only is excluded? Neither the integration of nations nor the disintegration of the masses nor a "*milieu*" between the two, and always threatened by both: how is this conceivable?

Has there been *a* world so far? Has there been *a* History, one single destination for so many singular existences? Has there been a singular for so many singularities? Nothing is less certain. But a multitude of arriving and leaving, of mixing and sharing. A multitude of presentations and exhibitions. This multitude gives us day after day, a little more to consider than we know how to consider.

Exposed existences: suspended, fragile, offered, like paintings exposed on walls. Cut throat suns. And we, all of us, you and us, who do not gaze at any spectacle, who do not contemplate any vision. Rather, the walls are holding us and tying us to the exposed fragility.

I can still see the stretched out rows of your people in the fields, bending down over rows of strawberry plants. And the scarlet tram that goes from San Diego to San Ysidro, on the border. And of that border, toward Chula Vista, the wire fence, breached and cut. And the unemployed lying on the sidewalks, in downtown L.A. But I have seen nothing, nothing but cuttings, and the red, and the brown.

Strasbourg, February 1989

Jean-Luc
Nancy

Postscriptum

Reservation: Isn't it already going too far to talk about *mestizaje*? As if *mestizaje* were "some thing," a substance, an object, an identity (an identity!) that could be grasped and "processed."

Mestizaje is always a very long, vast and obscure story. It is such a slow process that no one can see it happening. A single *mestizo* does not make for *mestizaje*. It takes generations—and more, an imperceptible drift toward infinity.

When this story is completed, there is no point in retracing it. The end result cannot be explained in terms of cause and effect, encounters and influences.

For the end result is as new and as different as if another "raza," another people had been produced out of thin air. The mix gets lost in the act of mixing. The mixing itself is no longer "mixed," it is an other, no more, no less.

As a twentieth-century Frenchman, I am a *mestizo* of Spanish and Viking, of Celt and Roman, and more importantly: of *je-ne-sais-quoi*.

So in the end, what we call *"mestizaje"* is the advent of the other. The other is always arriving, and always arriving from elsewhere. There is no point in waiting for, predicting, nor programming the other.

Everything, everyone—male, female—who alters me, subjects me to *mestizaje*. This has nothing to do with mixed blood or mixed cultures. Even the process of "mixing" in general, long celebrated by a certain theoretical literary and artistic tradition—even this kind of "mixing" must remain suspect: it should not be turned into a new substance, a new identity.

A *mestizo* is someone who is on the border, on the very border of *meaning*. And we are all out there, exposed. As the century ends, our world has become a tissue, a *métissage* of ends and fringes of meaning.

At each point, at each border where my humanity is itself exposed, cut throat, suns aflame with meaning.

123
—————

Cut Throat
Sun

Conjugating

Subjects:

The Hetero-

glossia of

Essence &

Resistance

———————————

Norma

Alarcón

T his essay is necessarily layered as I attempt to write and connect circuits of signification arising in specific historical locations on the one hand, while also attempting to bring into view their relationality through processes of appropriation, translation, and recodification. Terms such as subject(ivity) *différance*/difference, identity, experience, history, resistance, *negritude*, and *mestizaje* are implicated in such processes. These, however, will be threaded through the term *essential(ism)* to bring into relief the politics of "identity" on the one hand and the cultural politics of "difference" on the other as well as the consideration of the complex possibilities of "identity-in-difference" as a privileged nexus of analysis. Moreover, following, implicitly or explicitly, the diverse uses or charge of the vexed term essentialism may aid the reader to weave the layered text. (May my "instructions" be simpler to follow than those for assembling a bicycle.)

In the preface to her book *Between Past and Future: Eight Exercises in Political Thought,*[1] Hannah Arendt meditates on the "lost treasure" of the generation that came of age during and after World War II. That "lost treasure," I suggest to you, is the loss of a *grand recit*, or a coherent metanarrative, or exhausted versions of some metaphysics. (As an aside conquest, displacement, migration, and colonization have had similar effects for non-Europeans. Thus, it may be argued that global war had the effect of putting in question, both in the "center" and the "periphery," the value of modernity, reason, and enlightenment. That is highlighting its dark side. Moreover the unique historical role of the United States in this potential binarization gives its entry into the debates of modernity and postmodernity peculiar twists.)

Arendt points out that the loss is beset by a "namelessness." It is an unwilled situation. It was without testament. It had no story. She resolves the metaphors by suggesting that the "lost treasure" be named "tradition—which selects and names, which hands down and preserves, which indicates where the treasures are and what their worth is." However, because there no longer seems to be a "willed continuity in time and hence, humanly speaking neither past nor future" which she suggests is a situation totally unforeseen by any tradition because no "testament had willed it for the future" (6).

Through that moment of virtually total social and political breakdown, Arendt suggests, there set in a recognition of the existential experience of the rupture between "thought and reality." That is "thought and reality [had] parted company" (6). Arendt locates the moment of recognition in the aftermath of World War II, "when it began to dawn

upon modern man that he had come to live in a world in which his mind and his tradition of thought were not even capable of asking adequate, meaningful questions, let alone of giving answers to its own perplexities" (9). In a sense that West European experience, which promotes the growth of existentialism with its inversion of the "essence-existence" binary,[2] and which is followed by poststructuralism, attempts to reverse through these theoretical trends the assertion that "Modern[ist] philosophy began with a loss of the world . . . [indeed] the autonomous bourgeois subject . . . began with the withdrawal from the world."[3]

The most recent challenges to that subject have emerged with a larger degree of simultaneity than we have recognized. Though Arendt was writing in the 1950s, that same decade promotes the proliferation of the "new" social movements on a global scale and their concomitant "poetics of identity in difference." Thus, for example, even as Arendt is rewriting the epistemological politics of western philosophy, Simone de Beauvoir is rewriting the ontological and epistemological sexual politics in *The Second Sex*. Moreover, in the United

States even as Jacques Derrida was addressing the French Philosophical Society in January 27, 1968, with his ground-breaking theorization of "Différance," people of Mexican descent, under the recodified name Chicano, signaling *différance*, mobilized in Los Angeles for the school walkouts of March 1968.[4] In brief with broad strokes, I am attempting to convey the convergence of discourses of identity-in-difference as linked to the "essence-experience" binary which has taken so long to recognize as the patriarchal "west" engages in resistances of its own. The potential of the discourse of identity-in-difference and its nuances was derailed by the oversimplified hegemonization of a universalized concept of woman aided and abetted by the media, for example.[5] The hegemonization of feminism as woman brought on an attack by a patriarchal media commodification of feminism on the assumption that feminism entailed strictly a recodified appropriation of the autonomous, self-determining, bourgeois, unified, subject presumed to be male-owned, as if that kind of subject was essential to maleness. That is, if women claimed that facet of the subject as well, what is man to do? In other words feminism was read by the Reaganomic media as a mimetic inversion of an essential aspect of maleness, thus, producing anxiety. These processes of identification and counter-identification barely permitted the articulations (in both senses of the word—enunciation and linkage) of a politics of identity-in-difference by "women of color" to be heard in the United States. Historically racialized women were not heard until postmodernism in the 1980s invaded the hegemonic 1970s liberal agenda of feminism. That is, post-structuralist theory made it possible to (mis)manage a variety of other feminist discourses, that is, socialist, radical, Marxist, "of color," etc.[6]

By working through the "identity-in-difference" paradox, many racialized women theorists have implicitly worked in the interstice/interface of (existentialist) "identity politics" and "postmodernism" without a clearcut postmodern agenda. Neither Audre Lorde's nor Chela Sandoval's notion of difference/differential consciously subsumes a Derridean theorization—though resonance cannot be denied and must be explored—so much as represent a process of "determinate negation" a naysaying of the variety of the "not yet," that's not it. The drive behind the "not yet/ that's not it" position in Sandoval's work is termed "differential consciousness," in Lorde's terms "difference" and in Derrida's work "*différance.*" Yet each invokes dissimilarly located circuits of signification codified by the context of the site of emergence which nevertheless does not obviate their agreement on the "not yet," which points toward a future. The difficulties of articulating these

Conjugating
Subjects

sites across languages, cultures, races, genders, and social positions are painfully hard but yield a space for debate beyond "ethnocentrisms" without denying them.

Arendt herself, in an effort to theorize the critical interstitial intervention of the existential and historical subject who has lost the testamental "treasure," turns to Kafka to provide her with the poetics for a theorization of the gap. It is there, in the interstice, that Arendt thinks the simultaneity of time-and-space, thought-and-event will henceforth take place. Kafka's valuable parable is as follows:

> [S]he has two antagonists: the first presses her from behind, from the origin. The second blocks the road ahead. She gives battle to both. To be sure, the first supports her in her fight with the second, for it wants to push her forward, and in the same way the second supports her in her fight with the first, since it drives her back. But it is only theoretically so. For it is not only the two antagonists who are there, but she herself as well, and who really knows her intentions? Her dream, though, is that some time in an unguarded moment—and this would require a night darker than any night has ever been yet—she will jump out of the fighting line and be promoted, on account of her experience in fighting, to the position of umpire over her antagonists in their fight with each other. (Arendt 7)

Arendt translates Kafka's forces into past and future. The fact that there is a fight at all is due to the presence of the [wo]man. Her insertion, her inscription break up the motion of the forces, their linearity. It causes the forces to deflect, however lightly, from their original direction. The gap where she stands is an interstice or interval.[7] It is a time-space from which she can simultaneously survey what is most her own and that "which has come into being" through her "self-inserting appearance." Arendt falters, as does every theorist including Derrida, as to what precisely drives one to that differential self insertion which through "a double gesture, a double science, a double writing, practice an *overturning* of the classical opposition *and* a general displacement of the system" (*Margins of Philosophy* 329). (Psychoanalysis and its theory of the unconscious provides a venue for understanding such impulses *within* the subject, for others it is the experience of "otherization" *between* subjects. See below for further discussions.) However, anyone outside of contexts that entail "classical oppositions" proper to the West's systematizing reasoning processes is likely to practice more than "double" gestures and writings. Thus

Anzaldúa through the textual production, self-insertion, and speaking position of a "*mestiza* consciousness" disrupts the possibility of such tidiness.[8] A different tactic with similar effects is that of Luce Irigaray who disrupts the tidiness of deconstruction's use of the feminine[9] by introducing the contingent woman outside of metaphysical circuits of representation and meaning.[10] The one who engages the essentialization of Woman renegotiates symbolization.

Both Anzaldúa and Irigaray have been suspected of essentializing: the first on the basis of race, that is, *mestizaje,* and the second on the basis of the female body. While the charges against Anzaldúa are made at conferences, or muttered in classrooms and academic hallways, those against Irigaray are subject to extensive debates with a healthy bibliography.[11] (In the United States the debate on race and [anti]essentialism has been largely left to African American theorists and Diana Fuss;[12] while the debate with respect to Chicanas and Latin Americans and other groups is largely obscured as the discourses of race continue to binarize into black and white.)

Taking up the question of essentialism and race from another angle, in this volume, for example, Jean Luc Nancy resists the possibility of turning *mestizaje* into "a substance, an object, an identity . . . that could be grasped and "processed." The notion that one could *be a mestiza* or a *mestizo* is deplored. He continues, "Everything, everyone--male, female--who alters me, subjects me to *mestizaje.* This has nothing to do with mixed blood or mixed cultures. Even the process of 'mixing' in general, long celebrated by a certain theoretical literary and artistic tradition—even this kind of 'mixing' must remain suspect: it should not be turned into a new substance, a new identity."

Even as he wants to valorize the notion of *mestizaje,* indeed claim the terms *mestizo* for himself, he cautions against "biologisms," or even cultural mixing, and cautions against ultimate *meaning* by having us place ourselves "on the border, on the very border of *meaning.*" To be pinned down by meaning and intentionality to mean is to essentialize. The pursuit of identity as a quest for meaning closes off possibility, thus in postmodernist terms the drive to privilege our constructedness through the deconstruction of our essential(izing) quest for identity meaning. Jean-Luc Nancy speaks of the constructed subject who is traversed by the world and by others in such ways that he is never pure. The subject is unbounded and open to the other through whom "mestizaje," [s/he who] "alters me, subjects me to *mestizaje.*" Significance cannot come to rest, cannot stop; intersubjectivity as well as interaction with the world is always at play. However, we are indeed in the face of a paradox/contradiction. For Nancy does not want us to mistake his meaning of the term. In wanting to set it free and open to the future in specific ways, we are cautioned that this does not mean "mixed blood" or "mixed cultures," one of the modes in which Anzaldúa, for example, employs the term. With that prohibition he closes up the time and space of *mestizaje;* it is now under control, yet of course open to the future "towards infinity." Thus is Jean-Luc Nancy subjected to the politics of his own location, "a 20th century Frenchman, of Spanish and Viking, of Celt and Roman." What I mean to say is that the politics of his own location, his own time and space, lead him to appropriate and recodify the notion such that now it refers to the specificity of his own history, the "melting pot" that is France. Though he too is a *mestizo,* it is a kind open to the drift of the future, "on the border, on the very border of *meaning.*" Indeed, one may view Anzaldúa's work as doubly located on the "border of meaning." That is the U.S. Mexican geopolitical border as juridical sociopolitical division, which simultaneously opens up the past and the future as unfolding "borders of meaning" wherein Kafka's (wo)man struggles, and insofar as there is meaning, it emanates from the prohibition itself. The historical discussion of "mixed blood" in the Americas including its juridical normalizations, further problematizes Nancy's prohibition since it might silence the legal history of the racialization of the pre-Columbian subject, that of postslavery African Americans, and of others such as Chicanos.

Another example of a different kind of prohibition, yet with similar silencing effects is Fanon's protestation of Sartre's translation of *negritude* into class on the basis that the former is too particularistic/concrete and the latter abstract and universal, whereas Fanon suggests that the former is a "psychobiological syncretism," a methodical construction based on experience (Fanon 120).[13] Fanon notes that in Sartre's system *negritude* "appears as the minor term of a dialectical progression: the theoretical and practical assertion of the supremacy of the whiteman is its thesis; the position of negritude as an antithetical value is the moment of negativity. Proof was presented that my effort was only a term in the dialectic" (Fanon 120). "I defined myself as an absolute beginning. . . . I put its machinery together again. What had been broken to pieces was rebuilt, reconstructed by the intuitive lianas of my hands" (Fanon 124). The very inflected force of the selected theoretical frameworks from a universalizing center expel the narratives and textualization of difference and resistance. However, the expulsion itself is a resistance; that is, resistance becomes the site of the emergence of meaning itself and the concomitant practices should there be no resistance to deflect the projected course of meaning. In a sense the coexistence of prohibitions and resistances forecloses conditions of possibility for the renegotiation of relations and structures. The very emergences of syncretic new subjects, recodified on their own terms and rehistoricized anew are dismissed without taking up the task of inquiring as to the changing structures and relations inherent in conditions of the possibility for the new subject appearing as it does. The maneuver to avoid the probing is done through a reobjectification of the "new subject," a reification or a denial of the historical meaning posited by the differential signifier. As a result the difference is not fully engaged as a resistance to the monologizing demands of the West. The desire to translate as totalizing metaphorical substitution without acknowledging the "identity-in difference," so that one's own system of signification is not disrupted through a historical concept whose site of emergence is implicated in our own history, may be viewed as a desire to dominate, constrain, and contain— the "center's" own resistance to renegotiate meaning and structure.

The possibility that racial difference may be ontologized in the process of exploring *mestizaje* or *negritude* as "psychobiological syncretism" leads to a prohibition rather than a careful evaluation of how the drive to decolonize, free up the subject from subjection, has embattled her inscription as represented by Kafka's allegorical parable. If to "ontologize difference" in the pursuit of identity and meaning as modes of resistance to domination entails essentializing by relying on the concept of an authentic core that remains hidden to one's consciousness and that requires the elimination of all that is considered foreign or not true to the self, than neither Anzaldúa nor Fanon are essentialists at all. Both are quite clear that the pursuit of identity through "psychobiological syncretism" is one engaged through the racial difference imputed upon them as a stigma that is now revalorized through reconstruction in historical terms. In fact both acknowledge the impossibility of regaining a pure origin. Where does the terror of the "ontologization of difference" come from if not from the possibility that the result will continue to be inequality in the face of a liberal legal subject which has been naturalized on masculine terms?[14] This particular fear is more pronounced in feminist theory than in anti-essentialist theories of race because as I have stated earlier the latter is dominated by men who do not bother to remark gender.

The possibilities that the combination of gender with race may transform our mode of speaking about the constructedness of the subject from both the outside *and* the inside are virtually unexplored by men.

Derrida's considerations on the two interpretations of interpretation as irreconcilable yet lived "simultaneously and reconcile[ed] . . . in an "obscure economy' " (*Writing and Difference* 292–93)[15] have not been explored precisely as simultaneous and irreconcilable in conjunction with the "obscure economies" that emerge, such as Kafka's parable for example. The two interpretations noted by Derrida are (1) the one that seeks to decipher . . . a truth or an origin, which escapes play and the order of the sign, and which lives the necessity of interpretation as an exile; and (2) the one that no longer turned toward the origin, affirms play, and tries to pass beyond man and humanism. Further, it is not a question of choosing one or the other since both are irreducible and to choose is to trivialize, thus, Derrida continues, "we must conceive of a common ground, and the difference of this irreducible difference" (*Writing and Difference* 293). The fact that the resistant texts of minoritized populations in the United States are often read as interpretation and charged with essentializing (as is the case in Fuss's treatment of African American women critics and the debate on Irigaray, for example) is a misreading in light of the theorists' own resistance to conjugating interpretations of interpretation and conjugating significance for the present. It is often the case as well that no one claims an "immutable origin," however, the anxiety of pursuing the *"différance* of this irreducible difference"* continues to surface as a charge of essentialism on the one hand, and a fear of losing ground on the equality battlefront given patriarchal resistance to equality via a naturalized liberal subject whose criteria we all must be. That is, while identity labors under a charge of essentialism, difference is now checked by the charge of unequal. The double bind of *différance* emerges in the struggle between the old age metaphysics of *being* and the liberally inspired politics of *becoming*—dare I say the past and the future?

Fuss struggles with this double bind, justifying "the stronger lesbian endorsement of identity and identity politics" on the basis that it may indicate that "lesbians inhabit a more precarious and less secure subject position than gay men (Fuss 98). Interestingly she argues for the progressiveness (i.e., anti-essentialism) of lesbian scholarship by arguing via Heidegger for the metaphysical unity of identity as a fictional coherence which "theories of 'multiple identities' fail to challenge effectively" (Fuss 103). The unity of identity even as fictional coherence can be maintained and thereby make "identity politics" theoretically acceptable if one does away with the claim of "multiple identities." That is, "*différance*" must be relocated to the "space *within* identity" and withdrawn from the "spaces *between* identities" (Fuss 103). A theory of the fictional unity of identity via the Freudian-Lacanian unconscious is selected by Fuss, in my view, in order to salvage, through complementariness, the autonomous, self-determining, liberal bourgeois subject which is important to the kind of struggle made necessary by current hegemonic views of juridical equality.[16] In the process, however, she discards "the spaces *between* identities" which are paramount to cross-cultural exploration and analysis of "women of color." Thus, one of the major questions that arises in these theoretical debates is what is behind the anti-essentialist position? Certainly it is one that too readily assumes that the other is, of course, being essentialist. What are the stakes in such oppositional arguments wherein one is implicated in Derrida's interpretations (no. 1 or no. 2) but not shall we say engaged in a struggle such as that of Kafka's [wo]man?

In Anzaldúa's terms "*mestiza* consciousness" reveals a "tolerance for contradictions," paradox, and ambiguity because the term *mestiza* projects a confluence of conflicting subject positions which keep "breaking down the unitary aspect of each new paradigm" (Anzaldúa 79–80). Mudimbe designates an "intermediate space between the so-called . . . tradition and the projected modernity of colonialism." It is apparently an urbanized space in which "vestiges of the past, especially the survival of structures that are still living realities (tribal ties, for example), often continue to hide the new structures (ties based on class or on groups defined by their position in the capitalist system)." At any rate this intermediary space "could be viewed as the major signifier of underdevelopment. It reveals the strong tension between a modernity that often is an illusion of development, and a tradition that sometimes reflects a poor image of a mythical past."[17] These in-between/interstitial zones of instability presents us with paradigms of "obscure economies." In these zones theoretical frameworks are both affirmed and resisted, especially when experiential and historical meanings are erased and differences go unengaged, their irreducibility unnamed despite the risk of misnaming.

In resonance with Anzaldúa, Chela Sandoval[18] claims that "U.S. Third World feminism represents a central locus of possibility, an insurgent movement which shatters the construction of any one of the collective ideologies as the single most correct site where truth can be represented." She adds, what "U.S. Third World feminism demands is a new subjectivity, a political revision that denies any one ideology as the final answer, while instead positing a *tactical subjectivity* (sic) with the capacity to recenter depending upon the kinds of oppression to be confronted. This is what the shift from hegemonic oppositional theory and practice to a U.S. Third World theory and method of oppositional consciousness requires" (Sandoval 14). Sandoval calls attention to the many "women of color" who have pointed the way toward the development of a "new subject of history" and as such a "new political subject." Hurtado has claimed that "women of color" develop political skills "like urban guerrillas trained through everyday battle with the state apparatus" (Sandoval 14–15). For Moraga feminist "guerrilla warfare" is a way of life: "Our strategy is how we cope" on an everyday basis, "how we measure and weigh what is to be said and when, what is to be done and how, and to whom . . . daily deciding/risking who it is we can call an ally, call a friend." [19]

Citing Audre Lorde's remarks of 1979 at a conference commemorating the thirtieth anniversary of the publication of *The Second Sex (1949)*, Sandoval points to the fact that "ideological differences" must be seen as "a fund of necessary polarities between which our creativities spark like a dialectic. Only within that interdependency" of historical and ideologically positioned differences "can the power to seek new ways of being in the world generate the courage and sustenance to act where there are no charters" (Sandoval 15). In a sense, if as Moraga, also claimed feminists of color are "women without a line," coalescing with Sandoval, then the "new subject of history" is the one who struggles "to insure our survival" (Moraga 127), who is always "challenging women to go further" (Moraga 127), who in my view engages a politics of the "not yet," in the interstice between past and future. And as Sandoval herself states the "politics of the not yet" waged by U.S. Third World feminists is that of "differential conciousness" that posits no "ultimate answers, no terminal utopia . . . no predictable final outcomes. . . . Entrance into this new order requires an emotional commitment within which one experiences the violent shattering of the unitary sense of self, as the skill which allows a mobile identity to form. . . . Citizenship in this political realm is comprised of strategy and risk" (Sandoval 23).

Who is this "new subject of history" whose "identity-in-difference" politics were so dramatically documented in *This Bridge Called My Back* and given form in the context of second wave, that is contemporary, feminism? Whose existential writings foreshadowed *avant-la-lettre*, the poststructuralist subject, yet emerged as a paradoxical, contradictory subject whose own pursuit of "identity politics" was fissured by every other sentence through an affirmation of difference which questioned every category of import to the formation of a new society. Categories such as nation, class, race, gender, sexualities, and ethnicities were intermittently questioned and disrupted. In brief her very constitution as a "speaking subject" called attention to contradiction and difference as her constitutive ground by way of discursive political and intersubjective practices. When Sandoval publishes her essay ten years later, she calls it differential consciousness. She gives it a name that at its core signals a situated (located in the interval/gap/interstice/time-space) subject whose practice "cannot be thought *together*" (Derrida, *Margins of Philosophy*, 19). It cannot be thought simultaneously because the reinscription is thought out from the site of displacement which is subject to misnaming, misrecognition, misalliance, as well as hitting the mark. It cannot be thought together because it aims to situate that which has no place and through naming may fall short of the mark. The name may never be quite "it" because names are "relatively unitary . . . structures" whose oppositional status one may not intend yet take over. When Sandoval claims that the differential consciousness that calls for entering the "between and amongst" demands a mode of consciousness once relegated to the province of intuition and psychic phenomena, but which now must be recognized as a specific practice," she is in effect moving us toward and/or finding the relationality between the inside as affirmed by Fuss, per the earlier discussion, and the outside as the cross-cultural, intersubjective site. That is she poses the challenge of resistance to oppositional hegemonies through a *différance* that works inside/outside on multiple planes. A factor that works itself out through a "speaking subject" conscious that she can be "constituted by discourse and yet not be completely determined by it" (Benhabib 218). Benhabib asks, "What psychic, intellectual or other sources of creativity and resistance must we attribute to subjects for such [agential variation to discursive subject determination] to be possible?" (Benhabib 218). Hannah Arendt called it "spirit." Some called it "aesthetics," while others called it a "project." Lorde called it a "sparking dialectic." Anzaldúa called it the "Shadow Beast." All grope for the name of the impulse. As stated above some have settled for the "unconscious." Metaphors for the drives and impulses toward structural and symbolic change in the name of feminism.

The critical desire to undercut subject determination through structures and discourses, in my view, presupposes a subject-in-process who construct *provisional* identities, or Sandoval's *tactical subjectivity*, which subsume a network of signifying practices and structural experiences imbricated in historical *and* imaginary shifting national borders of Mexico and the United States for Chicanas (other "borders" that mediate (im)migration might be invoked). A subject-insertion into such a geographical economy and politics may presuppose not only specific historical sociosymbolic texts but a situated contemporaneous horizon of meanings and intentions that swerve away from those produced and enunciated by Euroamericans and Europeans especially when the latter produce structures and discourses of containment that resist change. Identity formations through differentially theorized experience and history—in this instance through the term Chicana, thus signaling a historically raced/gendered/class position forged through the interstices of two nation-states—proposes a subject in process, desirous of self-determination yet is "traversed through and through by the world and by others. . . . It is the active and lucid agency that constantly reorganizes its contents, through the help of these same contents, that produces by means of a material and in relation to needs and ideas, all of which are themselves mixtures of what it has already found there before it and what it has produced itself" (Castoriadis 17).[20] Through the speaking critical subject-in-process cultural production reintroduces what was there before in new and dynamic combinatory transculturations. A bi- or multi-ethnicized, raced, and gendered subject-in-process may be called upon to take up diverse subject positions which cannot be unified without double binds and contradictions. Indeed what binds the subject positions together may be precisely the difference from the perceived hegemony and the identity with a specific auto-history. The paradoxes and contradictions between subject positions move the subject to recognize, reorganize, reconstruct, and exploit difference through political resistance and cultural productions in order to reflect the subject-in-process. It is not a matter of doing away with the discourse of the other "because the other is in each case present in the activity that eliminates [it]" (Castoriadis 106). The traces of a process of elimination may construct the subject as much as the efforts to incorporate. A critical subject-in-process who reorganizes "contents" upon the demands of the contingent moment and context may discover that it is in the inaugural transitional moment from being traversed to reconfiguration that the political intention as well as the combinatory transculturating takes place. Through such time-spaces one can discover diverse cultural narrative formations, translations, appropriations, and recodifications which generate texts which are "hybrid" or "syncretic" and far from wanting to re-

Norma
Alarcón

main at rest in that taxonomy make a bid for new discourse formations bringing into view new subjects-in-process. In Gloria Anzaldúa's terms these are the "borderlands" through which the "theory circuits" of geopolitics and critical allegories find resonance but the zones of figurations and conceptualizations remain nonequivalent. That is, the very contingent currents through which the geopolitical subject-in-process is dislocated and forced into (im)migration will retain an irreducible difference that refuses to neatly correspond to the subject's account of herself and the theory we produce to account for her appearance.

Notes

1 Hannah Arendt, *Between Past and Future: Eight Exercises in Political Thought* (New York: Penguin, 1978).

2 Jean-Paul Sartre, *Search for a Method*, trans. Hazel E. Barnes (New York: Vintage, 1968).

3 Seyla Benhabib, *Situating the Self: Gender, Community and Postmodernism in Contemporary Ethics* (New York: Routledge, 1992), 205–7.

4 Carlos Múñoz, *Youth, Identity, Power: The Chicano Movement* (London: Verso, 1989).

5 Susan Faludi, *Backlash: The Undeclared War Against American Women* (New York: Crown, 1991).

6 Alison M. Jaggar, *Feminist Politics and Human Nature* (Totowa: Rowan & Allanheld, 1983).

7 Jacques Derrida, *Margins of Philosophy*, trans. Alan Bass (Chicago: U of Chicago P, 1982).

8 Gloria Anzaldúa, *Borderlands/La Frontera: The New Mestiza* (San Francisco: Spinsters/Aunt Lute, 1987).

9 Gayatri C. Spivak, "Displacement and the Discourse of Woman," *Displacement: Derrida and After*, ed. Mark Krupnick (Bloomington: Indiana U P, 1983), 169–96; and Rosi Braidotti, *Patterns of Dissonance: A Study of Women in Contemporary Philosophy*, trans. by Elizabeth Guil (New York: Routledge, 1991).

10 Luce Irigaray, *Speculum of the Other Woman*, trans. Gillian C. Gill (Ithaca: Cornell U P, 1985).

11 Toril Moi, *Sexual/Textual Politics* (London: Methuen, 1985); Judith Butler, *Gender Trouble: Feminism and the Subversion of Identity* (New York: Routledge, 1990); and Nancy Fraser and Sandra Lee Bartky, *Revaluing French Feminism: Critical Essays on Difference, Agency & Culture* (Bloomington: Indiana U P, 1992).

12 Diana Fuss, *Essentially Speaking: Feminism, Nature and Difference* (New York: Routledge, 1989).

13 Frantz Fanon, "The Fact of Blackness," *Anatomy of Racism*, ed. David Theo Goldberg (Minneapolis: U of Minnesota P, 1990), 108–26.

14 Michèle Barrett and Anne Phillips, *DestabilizingTheory: Contemporary Feminist Debates* (Stanford: Stanford U P, 1992).

15 Jacques Derrida, *Writing and Difference,* trans. Alan Bass (Chicago: University of Chicago P, 1978).

16 Kimberlé Crenshaw, "Demarginalizing the Intersection of Race and Gender in Antidiscrimination Law, Feminist Theory, and Antiracist Politics," *Chicago Legal Forum* (1989).

17 M. Y. Mudimbe, *The Invention of Africa* (Bloomington: Indiana U P, 1988).

18 Chela Sandoval, "U.S. Third World Feminism: The Theory and Method of Oppositional Consciousness in the Postmodern World," *Genders* 10 (Spring 1991), 1–24.

19 Cherríe Moraga and Gloria Anzalúa, *This Bridge Called My Back: Writings by Radical Women of Color,* 1st ed. (Waterton: Persephone Press, 1981), xix.

20 Cornelius Castoriadis, *The Imaginary Institution of Society,* trans. Kathleen Blamey (Cambridge: MIT P, 1987).

138

Norma
Alarcón

The Ruins

of Representa-

tion: Shadow

Survivance

and the

Literature

of Dominance

_____

Gerald Vizenor

T he postmodern turn in literature and cultural studies is an invitation to the ruins of representation; the invitation uncovers traces of tribal survivance, trickster discourse, and the remanence of intransitive shadows.

The traces are shadows, shadows, shadows, the natural coherence of archshadows, visions, and memories in heard stories. The postmodern shadows counter paracolonial histories, dickered testimonies, simulations, and the banal essence of consumerism; at the same time, trickster pronouns, transformations, and the shimmers of tribal consciousness are heard in literature.

"The representation of history becomes the history of representation," Linda Hutcheon wrote in *The Politics of Postmodernism*. She pointed out that the "issue of representation in both fiction and history has usually been dealt with in epistemological terms, in terms of how we know the past."

The representations of the tribal past are more than mere human mimesis and more than the aesthetic remains of reason in the literature of dominance. The posers, of course, must concentrate on the sources of incoherence that trace causation in transitive histories. The cold simulations of tribal cultures, or the paracolonial pretensions that precede a tribal referent, are the most common representations in histories. Simulations are new burdens in the absence of the real and the imposture of presence.

The archshadow is the consciousness of natural reason, the silence and animate shadows over presence. The shadow is that sense of intransitive motion to the referent; the silence in memories. Shadows are neither the absence of entities nor the burden of conceptual references. The shadow is the silence that inherits the words; shadows are the motions that mean the silence, but not the presence or absence of entities. Archshadows are honored in memories and the silence of tribal stones. Shadows and the postmodern are the natural trace of liberation in the ruins of representation.

There are at least four postmodern conditions in the critical responses to Native American Indian literatures: the first is heard in aural performances; the second condition is unbodied in translations; the third is trickster liberation, the uncertain humor of survivance that denies the obscure maneuvers of manifest manners, tragic transvaluations, and the incoherence of cultural representations; the fourth postmodern condition is narrative chance, the cross causes in language games, consumer simulations, and the histories of postexclave publications.

These four conditions turn a diverse discourse on tribal literatures: the uncertain testimonies, the remanence of shadows, and tribal transvaluations; the enigmatic nature of memories, imagination, and autobiographies; the translation of nicknames, picture fictions, or memorial expressionism, and shamanic visions; the tragic flaws and denials of tribal wisdom in the literature of dominance, and the morass of social science theories; the enervation of modernism; the rise of simulations and manifest manners, that vernacular of racialism and continuous elaborations on the rights, responsibilities, and the dubious duties of dominance.

These postmodern conditions are both oppositional and noetic mediations on narrative chance; these conditions are an invitation to tribal survivance. The traces of natural reason and the shadows of coherence have endured over science in the humor of cotribal stories.

"Science has always been in conflict with narratives," wrote Jean-François Lyotard. "I define postmodern as incredulity toward metanarratives." Science, translation, and the discoveries of otherness in tribal cultures, are the histories of racialism and the metanarratives of dominance. The foundational theories of the social sciences have denied natural reason, tribal memories, and the coherence of heard stories. Lyotard argued that "knowledge has become the principle force of production over the last few decades."[1] The literature of dominance maintains the scientific models and tragic simulations of a consumer culture.

"Scientific knowledge has lost its objective privilege and its epistemology has collapsed into incoherence," wrote Will Wright in *Wild Knowledge*. He argued that science is "conceptually wrong, wrong about nature and wrong about knowledge." Coherent knowledge "must begin to articulate its inherent reference to language as a formal structure, rather than to some particular form of language as magical access."[2]

Linda Hutcheon pointed out that accession to the past in fiction and histories is through the traces of "documents, the testimony of witnesses, and other archival materials. In other words, we only have representations of the past from which to construct our narratives or explanations. In a very real sense, postmodernism reveals a desire to understand present culture as the product of previous representations."[3] This narrow accession would burden the narratives of chance and the shadows of tribal survivance.

The ironies and humor in the postmodern are heard in tribal narratives; the natural reason of tribal creation has never been without a postmodern turn or counterpoise, a common mode that enlivened the performance and memories of those who heard the best of their own experiences in stories. The shadows of the heard and that touch of coherence in natural reason persists in the postexclave literature of resistance, and in the stories that are told after federal exclaves and reservations.

Native American Indian literatures could be read as the eternal shadows of the heard, rather than as mere evidence, and as the serious wisps of natural reason in postmodern tribal narratives. These narrative wisps are the "stories that one tells, that one hears, that one acts out," wrote Lyotard. "[T]he people does not exist as a subject but as a mass of millions of insignificant and serious little stories that sometimes let themselves be collected together to constitute big stories and sometimes disperse into digressive elements."[4]

Social science narratives, those unsure reins of incoherent paracolonialism, overscore the tribal heard as cultural representations. David Carroll argued that any "narrative that predetermines all responses or prohibits any counter-narratives puts an end to narrative itself, by making itself its own end and the end of all other narratives."[5]

Johannes Fabian, the anthropologist, conceded in the introduction to *Language and Colonial Power* that he lost his faith in the assumption that language is a representation of a real world. That assumption has been one of the foundations of the social sciences and colonial dominance. Concessions and antitheses are an invitation to a discourse on racialism, but at the same time the "assumptions" of foundational representations have become the simulations of the real and serve a consumer paradise in the literature of dominance.

The wild unities of heard stories and the pleasures of performance are unbodied in translations. The shadows and tribal experiences that are *heard* in stories, and variations on natural reason, are transformed in publications that are *seen* as cultural representations. The conditions of postmodern identities must sue for more than revisions in the new historicism.

Native American Indian literatures have endured the manifest manners of translation for more than three centuries. The sudden closures of the oral in favor of the scriptural are unheard, and the eternal sorrow of lost sounds haunts the remains of tribal stories in translation. Brian Swann, in an edited collection of essays on translation, explained that given "the history of this hemisphere, to settle for the dignity of mystery is far preferable to any claim of definitiveness."[6]

Modernism is a persuasive disguise of pretentious individualism and the tragic flaws of historicism; the postmodern condition is a counterpoise in wild knowledge and language games, an invitation that would undermine the power of translation, representation, and simulations. What is published and seen is not what is heard or remembered in oral stories. Postmodern narratives are poses, and the poses are neither representations nor the terminal sources of aesthetic modernism. The printed word has no natural evolution in tribal literatures. The heard words are traced in silence, the archshadows of tribal memories, and the printed words reach over presence and absence to the shadows of trees, water, air, and hear stone, hide, and paper, as words have been heard forever in tribal stories.

The representations of the heard are simulations, no more than nuances in the best translations. Representation and the obscure maneuvers of translation "produces strategies of containment." These strategies are "deployed across a wide range of discourses, allowing us to name translation as a significant technology of colonial domination," argued Tejaswini Niranjana. "Paradoxically, translation also provides a place in 'history' for the colonized." The histories are texts in the literature of dominance, and the shadows of the heard emerge from the *différance* and traces of the texts.[7]

Jacques Derrida turns his *différance* to overread the dash, variance, and indeterminate traces that misconstrue the past representations of presence and absence in written literature. The causal compromises of objectivization in transitive actions are the terminal poses of presence and past. The archshadows arise in tribal silence and are heard in that aural distance to the chance concept, the reach of lonesome silence between the signifier, signified, and their signs; the traces and *différance* of meaning are dashed and deferred to the silence of other texts in the literature of dominance. Shadows are that silence and sense motion of memories over the sign; shadows are not the burdens of conceptual references. Shadows and *différance* in other texts threaten the representations of presence and the run on simulations.

Not even the tease of trace and *différance* is answerable to the tone and dissemblance of scriptural, hermeneutical, and representational translations of the heard stories. The shadows are heard in names and stories but not as mere representations. The shadows of tribal memories are the active silence, trace, and *différance* in the literature of dominance.

The "charge of 'linguistic idealism' has probably been the accusation most frequently leveled against deconstruction over the years," wrote Richard Wolin in *The Terms of Cultural Criticism*. "Derrida's approach to criticism, argues Foucault, remains exclusively *textual*. As an interpreter and critic, he leads us into the text from which, in turn, *we never emerge*."[8]

"Not only is there no kingdom of *différance*, but *différance* instigates the subversion of every kingdom. Which makes it obviously threatening and infallibly dreaded by everything within us that desires a kingdom," Derrida wrote in "Différance."[9] Jacques Derrida is an indirect reflexive trace to his own *différance* and absence in deconstruction. Shadows are over the sounds, words, and traces. The shadows and traces are silence, but shadows and silence are not the trace. Shadows are motion not presence, shadows touch no presence or absence over sound and sentences.

"Presence is reduced to signs of itself—to traces," wrote Raymond Tallis in *Not Saussure*. "We never touch presence unmediated by signs —immediate presence, presence itself. Mediation is primary; immediacy but an impossible, elusive dream."[10]

The trace is a nickname that leaves a presence in literature. The shadows are the silence in heard stories, the silence that bears a referent of tribal memories and experience. The shadows are active memories and the memories of heard stories. The shadows are intransitive, an animate action in the silence of stories. The word *agawaatese* is heard in the oral stories of the *anishinaabe*, the tribal people of the northern woodland lakes. The word hears silence and shadows and could mean a shadow or casts a shadow. The sense of *agawaatese* is that the shadows are animate entities. The shadow is the unsaid sense in names, the memories in silence, and the imagination of tribal experiences.

Luther Standing Bear, for instance, wrote in *My Indian Boyhood* that the "Indian very seldom bothers a bear and the bear, being a very self-respecting and peaceful animal, seldom bothers a human being."[11] The bear is an archshadow in tribal memories and heard stories. The sound, silence, and shadows of the bear are animate and intransitive. The shadows, silence, and unsaid essence of bears end in signification; shadows and silence have no representations, presence or absence.

The bear is "so much like a human that he is interesting to watch. He has a large amount of human vanity and likes to look at himself," wrote Standing Bear. "Before we had looking-glasses, we would look at ourselves in a clear pool of water. This the bear does, too, and I suppose he thinks, 'Well, I'm not such a bad-looking fellow,' for he walks away after an inspection of himself as if quite satisfied, and as for myself I do not see why he should not be. He is wise and clever and probably knows it."

The bear is an archshadow in the silence of tribal stories, the memories and sense that are unsaid in the name. Luther Standing Bear hears the shadow of the bear in his memories; the bear is a shadow and has no presence in heard stories or in the silence of the written name. The bear he hears, reads, and writes is a shadow of the bear, not the real bear, not a mere concept of the bear, but the shadow memories of the bear. The shadow, not the bear, is the referent and the trace to other stories.

"The bear is not only a powerful animal in body, but powerful in will also. He will stand and fight to the last. Though wounded, he will not run, but will die fighting. Because my father shared this spirit with the bear, he earned his name," wrote Standing Bear. The shadows in the name are the memories in the shadow of the bear and the silence in translation. The name is heard and read, and there are traces and *différance* that defer the meaning, but without the stories of the bear and the name the shadow has no memories in the silence of translation.

N. Scott Momaday, in *The Way to Rainy Mountain*, wrote that his tribal grandmother "lived out her long life in the shadow of Rainy Mountain, the immense landscape of the continental interior lay like memory in her blood. She could tell of the Crows, whom she had never seen, and of the Black Hills, where she had never been. I wanted to see in reality what she had seen more perfectly in the mind's eye, and traveled fifteen hundred miles to begin my pilgrimage."[12] Aho, his grandmother, heard stories of the long migration of the tribe, and these stories became her memories in imagination, so that she could hear the shadows of a landscape that she had never seen. The archshadows are the creations of the tribe, and shadows are memories that are heard in stories. Shadows, memories, and imagination endure in the silence of translation.

Momaday honors the memories of his grandmother and touches shadows in his imagination; shadows that trace the stories in three scriptural themes. The stories in *The Way to Rainy Mountain* are not representations of a tribal culture or the presence of sacred traditions; the stories uncover the intransitive shadows of tribal survivance.

Native American Indian literatures have been overburdened with critical interpretations based on structuralism and other social science theories that value incoherent foundational representations of tribal experiences. Brian Swann and Arnold Krupat pointed out in *Recovering the Word* that structuralism, a "concern for principles of organization and function" dominated their edited collection of critical essays on Native American literatures. The "Indian as an individual is not much examined in these essays."[13]

Claude Lévi-Strauss and Alan Dundas have been cited more than Mikhail Bakhtin, Jean-François Lyotard, or Jacques Derrida in the historical and critical studies of tribal literature; the theoretical persuasions have been more structural and representational than postmodern in the past few decades of translation and interpretation.

Foundational theories have overburdened tribal imagination, memories, and the coherence of natural reason with simulations and the cruelties of paracolonial historicism. Anthropologists, in particular, were not the best listeners or interpreters of tribal imagination, liberation, or literatures.

The elusive and clever trickster characters in tribal imagination are seldom heard or understood in translation. Missionaries and anthropologists were the first to misconstrue silence, transformation, and figuration in tribal stories; they were not trained to hear stories as creative literature and translated many stories as mere cultural represen-

Ruins of
Representation

tations. Victor Barnouw, for example, wrote that from trickster stories "we can learn something about the belief systems of the people." He misconstrued the trickster as "a real person whom they respected although they also laughed at his antics."

Barnouw reduced the oral trickster stories that he heard to unreasonable social science evidence and cultural representations; moreover, an analysis of the storyteller concluded that "there was evidence of emotional dependency and also some confusion about sex." This outrageous interpretation was based on a Rorschach record.[14]

Karl Kroeber pointed out that anthropologists and "folklorists, whose disciplines are not directed toward appreciation of superior artistry, usually play down, or ignore, the individual distinction of creative accomplishment in ethnographic material."[15]

Moreover, anthropologists have used the inventions of ethnic cultures and the representations of the tribes as tropes to academic power in institutions. "The critical issue, so far as concerns the anthropologist as author, works and lives, text-building, and so on, is the highly distinctive representation of "being there" that *Tristes Tropiques* develops, and the equally distinctive representation, invertive actually, of the relationship between referring text and referred-to world that follows from it," wrote Clifford Geertz. "To put it brutally, but not inaccurately, Lévi-Strauss argues that the sort of immediate, in-person "being there" one associates with the bulk of recent American and British anthropology is essentially impossible: it is either outright fraud or fatuous self-deception. The notion of a continuity between experience and reality, he says early on in *Tristes Tropiques*, is false: 'there is no continuity in the passage between the two.' "[16]

Native American Indian imagination and the pleasures of language games are disheartened in the manifest manners of documentation and the imposition of cultural representation; tribal testimonies are unheard, and tricksters, the wild ironies of survivance, transformation, natural reason, and liberation in stories are marooned as obscure moral simulations in translations.

Andrew Wiget, for instance, declared that the behavior of the trickster is "always scandalous. His actions were openly acknowledged as madness by the elders who performed the stories with obvious relish on many winter evenings. Yet these same respected voices would solemnly assert the sacredness of these very tales, which always involved the most cavalier treatment of conventionally unassailable material like sexuality or religion." Wiget, a literary scholar, bears the worst of colonial historicism in his interpretations of trickster figuration in tribal literature. "To many Westerners reading these stories for the first time, it seemed at best a puzzling inconsistency and at worst a barbaric mystery that in many tribal mythologies this idiot and miscreant was in some unaccountable way also the culture hero."[17]

Wiget, in turn, could be read as a modern moral censor, an overman of occidental binaries and the tropes to academic power. The tone of his critical review, and the use of the words *scandalous* and *barbaric*, would prescribe a righteous paracolonial presence in tribal stories. The trickster is a language game, a wild cross-causal neotic liberation, not a measure or representation of invented cultural values.

Wiget is a sincere exponent, to be sure, but he has undermined the natural reason and creative power of tribal literatures with his use of structuralism and other social science theories; he has that, and much more, in common with other scholars who have translated and interpreted tribal literatures.

Wiget comes closer to modernism and the social sciences than to other critical theories in his interpretations of tribal literature; he separates tribal stories with morphologies and genre representations. In *Native American Literature* he covers the tribal world from oral narratives to the novel in six short chapters. Alas, he announced that "trying to find some clear and universal criteria for distinguishing different types of narrative has been the ever-elusive goal of folklorists and anthropologists." He asserted that oral cultures were not static but at the same time he explained that "there has been no single effort to order and assess that literature."[18]

The Native American Indian "implicitly acknowledged he could continue living only in the white man's representation of him," wrote the historian Larzer Ziff. "The process of literary annihilation would be checked only when Indian writers began representing their own culture."[19] However, even then most readers and critics influenced by structuralism, modernism, and the dualism of subject, object, or otherness, have more confidence in the paracolonial discoveries and representations of tribal literatures. Familiar simulations have more in common with the philosophies of grammar and translations than with shadows and the silence of heard stories in the unbearable fields of tribal consciousness.

Translation, in another sense, is a monothematic representation of silence and distance. Published stories move in silence over time, and that silence is never secure. Clock time is dominance, and those who research the unsaid in time are marooned in the ruins of representation. The shadows of heard stories are not bound by the measures of time and space. The first "hermeneutical motion" of translation is "initiative trust, an investment of belief, underwritten by previous experience," George Steiner wrote in *After Babel*. "If culture depends on the transmission of meaning across time, it depends also on the transfer of meaning in space."[20]

The "power of language is one of N. Scott Momaday's most enduring themes" Wiget wrote about *House Made of Dawn*. "Momaday is breaking new ground with his intensely personal, poetic narratives, which essay the principal dilemma of an urbanized, thoroughly acculturated Indian: how to retain continuity with one's cultural heritage though displaced from the community that sustains it. The very structures of these works express the dynamic by which the psyche internalizes the mythic, historical, and cultural components of identity."[21]

Winter in the Blood by James Welch is "a hopeful book," wrote Wiget. "In the mock-epic struggle to rescue the mired cow, there are signs of a recovery of commitment to life to replace the internalized distance."[22] The consumer notion of a "hopeful book" is a denial of tragic wisdom and seems to be a social science paradise of tribal victims.

"She was lying on her side, up to her chest in mud," said the unnamed narrator in *Winter in the Blood*. The cow "had earned this fate by being stupid, and now no one could help her. . . . As she stared at me, I saw beyond the immediate panic that hatred, that crazy hatred that made me aware of a quick hatred in my own heart. Her horns seemed tipped with blood, the dark blood of catastrophe."[23] She turned her head in the mud, one eye to the clouds. That laconic sense of chance and death bears tribal ironies and tragic wisdom; the characters and scenes are more than victims and mock separations.

Charles Larson studied three generations of fiction writers in *American Indian Fiction*. He started with a review of *Queen of the Woods* by Simon Pokagon, one of the first Native American Indian novels published at the turn of the last century, and ended with *Ceremony* by Leslie Marmon Silko. His book was the first serious critical interpretation of fiction by more than sixty authors identified as Native American Indians. Larson inherited the language games of racialism that determined tribal identities; the intricate blood quantum theories were uncertain and dubious measures of identities; so, in the end, he decided that the known "acceptance by one's peers" was a "more meaningful test of Indianness."[24]

Larson invented four categories to describe tribal novelists and their creative publications: assimilationists, reactionaries, revisionists, and qualified separatists. His inventions have more in common with the colonial dominace of political theories in the literature of dominance than with the wild memories and rich diversities of tribal literature.

The novelists Pokagon, John Oskison, the author of *Wild Harvest, Black Davy,* and *Brothers Three,* and John Mathews, the author of *Sundown,* are classified as assimilationists because, it seems, some of the characters in their novels lean toward the literature of dominance. "Taken together," Larson wrote, these and other assimilationist novels are "conventional in form, traditional in subject, anything but innovative," and "indistinguishable from hundreds of other fictional works of the time. . . . If we did not know that these men were Native Americans we might conclude from their novels that they were white."[25]

Larson must search for racial purities in tribal literature because his four categories are denials of cross-blood identities and tribal survivance; he assumed, based on the novels he considered, that he would discover and understand the essential tribal experience. However, he dedicated more attention to the colonial conditions of determining tribal identities and enrollment documents on federal reservations than to criticism of racialism, the cruelties of relocation, the burdens of postexclave assimilation policies, and elitism in publishing.

"Suddenly he was dreaming," Mathews wrote in *Sundown.* Challenge Windzer "was riding at the end of a party of warriors, and the Pawnees were fleeing over the hill before them, calling in Pawnee, 'Here comes Chal and his Osage Wolves.' He could see a white girl standing there on the prairie in long blue mantle like the mantle of the Virgin Mary, and she turned toward him as a savior. The reasons for her predicament were absent, but the dream was delightful. When she tried to thank him he frowned and walked away, but his dream-heart was full."[26]

Larson represented education as assimilation rather than survivance; his arrogance would humor the tragic flaws of savagism and slander tribal imagination. "Paradoxically," he asserted, "Pokagon, Oskison, and Mathews would not have written and published novels if they had not received the schooling they did and been assimilated (in their varying degrees) into the white man's world. And that, of course, is the crux of their dilemma. Their education took something away from them, yet their writing became a way of reconciling or exploring the problems of assimilation that each man met in his own distinct way."[27]

Larson reviewed *Seven Arrows* by Hyemeyohsts Storm as a historical revisionist novel, because it depicted survival and "aggressive confrontations" between tribal people and the dominant culture. He insisted that the issue of how representative a tribal author might be "to his people" is a question "best left to cultural anthropologists." Storm was denounced by some tribal elders for his personal interpretations of cultural traditions and for his pose as a member of the Northern Cheyenne. The paperbound edition of the novel was released over the objections of traditional tribal elders on the reservation. Such serious tribal matters are not the missions of anthropologists.

Larson pointed out that in "theory I believe that asking such questions is a futile exercise. In practice, however, some benefit may be derived from the answer simply because by and large we are dealing with ethnic materials that depict some aspect of the Indian-white confrontation. No doubt we would expect these writers to be true to the cultures they write about, though, reading fiction solely to learn about another culture may be misleading. A novel must be something more than an anthropological document if it is to engage our aesthetic sensitivities."[28]

Not to fault social science theories and the literature of dominance in the ruins of representation is to believe that the causes of racialism are the same as the cures. Larson noted that the tribal novelists he studied were educated, and their education, he assumed, was the end of tribal cultures. He seemed to bear the tragic flaw of racial nihilism; otherwise, he must mourn over the ruins of mock innocence, the nostalgia for paradise, or over the simulations of tribal cultures.

D'Arcy McNickle and N. Scott Momaday are categorized as reactionaries because their novels are about "individuals, isolated Indians trapped in the present world, unable to return to the ways of the past."[29]

McNickle and Momaday are recognized as distinguished scholars in two worlds, and their publications, though separated by one generation, are related in theme. The central characters in their novels, Archilde in *The Surrounded* by McNickle, first published in 1936, and Abel in *House Made of Dawn* by Momaday, published in 1968, are postexclave crossbloods who returned to reservations; these characters return to a memorable landscape and the ruins of their families. "Although their present existence is individualistic, the past from which they have been severed is collective," wrote Larson. He asserted that Momaday, who won the Pulitzer Prize for *House Made of Dawn*, "has become trapped in a literary holding pattern. . . . With a vision as bleak as his, one wonders whether Momaday can write another novel about the Native American without making a complete reversal and thereby undermining the validity of his earlier work."[30]

Larson was a hard-hearted reader, to be sure, and his captious criticism was unwarranted then and now. "That night Grey dreamed of sleeping with a bear," Momaday wrote in *The Ancient Child*, his outstanding second novel.

> The bear drew her into its massive arms and licked her body and her hair. It hunched over her, curving its spine like a cat, until its huge body seemed to have absorbed her own. Its breath, which bore a deep, guttural rhythm like language, touched her skin with low, persistent heat. The bear's tongue kneaded her—her feet, her belly and her breasts, her throat. Her own breathing became exaggerated, and there were long, orgasmic surges within her; she felt that her body was flooding with blood. The dream was full of wonder. . . .
>
> Set took the medicine bundle in his hands and opened it. The smell of it permeated the whole interior. When he drew on the great paw, there grew up in him a terrible restlessness, wholly urgent, and his heart began to race. He felt the power of the bear pervade his being, and the awful compulsion to release it. Grey, sitting away in the invisible dark, heard the grandmother's voice in her mouth. When Set raised the paw, as if to bring it down like a club, she saw it against the window, huge and phallic on the stars, each great yellow claw like the horn of the moon.[31]

Larson praised *Winter in the Blood* by James Welch as an "almost flawless novel . . . one of the most significant pieces of fiction by an American Indian." Welch and Leslie Marmon Silko, the author of *Ceremony*, are named qualified separatists, the last category invented by Larson. The characters in these novels lived in urban areas and "survived because they adapted themselves to the dual world that surrounded them."[32]

Silko and the characters in *Ceremony* are not separatists, no matter how clever the critical reviews and interpretations might sound in *American Indian Fiction*. LaVonne Ruoff is closer to the heart of *Ceremony*. She observed that Silko "demonstrates the healing power of tribal ritual and storytelling by reuniting her mixed-blood hero with his tribe at the end of the novel. More overtly than Momaday, she evokes myth and ritual."[33]

"I have made changes in the rituals. The people mistrust this greatly, but only this growth keeps the ceremonies strong," said the crossblood healer Betonie in *Ceremony*. "They are things the witchery people want. Witchery works to scare people, to make them fear growth. But it has always been necessary, and more then ever now, it is. Otherwise we won't make it. We won't survive. That's what the witchery is counting on: that we will cling to the ceremonies the way they were, and then their power will triumph, and the people will be no more."[34]

Several Native American Indian novelists have published, in the past decade, their own studies of tribal consciousness, culture, and literatures. Paula Gunn Allen, in *The Sacred Hoop*, overturned androcentric structuralism, praised spiritualism, and celebrated a renaissance of the feminine in cotribal literatures. She boosted social and familial responsibilities and pointed out that one of the "major distinguishing characteristics of gynocratic cultures is the absence of punitiveness as a means of social control. Another is the inevitable presence of meaningful concourse with supernatural beings. . . . Among gynocratic or gynocentric tribal people the welfare of the young is paramount, the complementary nature of all life forms is stressed, and the centrality of powerful women to social well-being is unquestioned."[35]

Allen avowed lesbian spiritualism as a new tribal essentialism, and she maintained that tribal "thought is essentially mystical and psychic in nature." She considered the ethics of essentialist tribal literature, or "using the tradition," in a conversation published in the *Headlands Journal:* "I have specialized in teaching contemporary literature to avoid as many ethical violations as I could, believing that I might teach it and evade or avoid queries about arcane matters." Moreover, "I have gone so far as to learn as little ritual or myth as possible in any particular detail to further buttress my defense against ethical violations. . . . I begin to understand some of the reasons for my extreme ambivalence in doing what I do, some of the reasons I find teaching in Native American Studies so painful, and some of the reasons why some of the poems and fiction I've been working on for years is stymied," she said in a discussion on the problems of teaching the novel *Ceremony* by Leslie Marmon Silko. On the other hand she pointed out that the preservation of tradition "with the sacrifice of its living bearers seems at best reasonless, at worst blasphemous. If people die as a result of preserving tradition in the white way of preservation, for whom will the tradition be preserved?"[36]

Allen considered the contradictions of essentialism and crossblood tribal identities in a personal and indicative comment: "For although I am a somewhat nontraditional Indian, I grew up in the homes of Indians and have spent my adult life in the company of traditionals, urbanites, and all the shades of Indian in between. . . . Whatever I read about Indians I check out with my inner self. Most of what I have read—and some things I have said based on that reading—is upside-down and backward. But my inner self, the self who knows what is true of American Indians because it *is* one, always warns me when something deceptive is going on. And with that warning, I am moved to do a great deal of reflecting, some more reading, and a lot of questioning and observing of real live human beings who are Indian in order to discover the source of my unease. Sometimes that confirmation comes about in miraculous ways; that's when I know guidance from the nonphysicals and the supernaturals, and that the Grandmothers have taken pity on me in my dilemma."[37]

Elizabeth Cook-Lynn is the founder and editor of the *Wicazo Sa Review*. She has published interpretations, critical studies, and reviews that sustain tribal values and governments. Her recent novel, *From the River's Edge*, celebrates the honorable conditions of tribal sovereignty and survivance.

Cook-Lynn, in a critical commentary on *Sending My Heart Back Across the Years* by Hertha Dawn Wong, wrote that the "wannabee sentiment which clutters an otherwise tolerable piece of redundant scholarship is a reflection of a growing phenomenon which precedes and influences the intellectual discourse now emerging from universities all over the place in the name of Native American Studies." Moreover, she argued, the "unnecessary claim of this scholar to be 'part Native American' is so absurd as to cast ridicule on the work itself. But, more seriously, the 'blood quantum' debate, the '*ethnic* identity' issue, has finally obscured or dismissed one of the important sovereign rights of Indian nations, and neither Congress nor the Supreme Court had to act in its usual dubious ways." She pointed out with a sense of ironic humor that curriculum development at universities "has been reduced to offerings which might be called 'What If I'm a Little Bit Indian?' "[38]

Gerald Vizenor edited *Narrative Chance: Postmodern Discourse on Native American Literatures*, the first collection of essays on the postmodern condition in tribal literatures and poststructural interpretations of tribal cultures and consciousness. Alan Velie pointed out in his essay that since "the trickster is the most important mythic figure in most tribes it is not surprising that he would be a major archetype in contemporary Indian fiction. Quite a few protagonists in recent Indian novels bear a resemblance to the trickster." I argued in my essay that the "trickster is androgynous, a comic healer and liberator in literature; the *whole figuration* that ties the unconscious to social experience. The trickster sign is communal, an erotic shimmer in oral traditions; the narrative voices are holotropes in a discourse."[39]

Louis Owens has published the most recent critical studies of Native American Indian novelists. *Other Destinies: Understanding the American Indian Novel* is the third title in the new American Indian Literature and Critical Studies series at the University of Oklahoma Press. Owens considered the themes of cultural survival, the interpretations and recoveries of tribal identities in the characters and scenes created by mixed-bloods novelists. His second novel, *The Sharpest Sight*, is the first title in the new literature series.

"What it boils down to is respecting your world, every little piece of it. When I poach does at night, it's against the law," said Hoey in *The Sharpest Sight*. "But what I'm doing ain't wrong if you look at it in an Indian way. I pick out old does past their prime. . . . And I leave the best breeding bucks and does alone. That ain't like the poison that chicken plant dumps into the creek, the stuff that kills the fish, or all the rest of things people are doing to the earth."[40]

A. LaVonne Brown Ruoff is the undeniable leader of serious research and education in tribal literatures, and she is the most admired historical interpreter of contemporary novels and poetry. "The history of American Indian literature reflects not only tribal cultures and the experience of imagination of its authors but Indian-white relations as well," she wrote in *American Indian Literatures*. "Although individual Indians today vary in the extent to which they follow tribal traditions, their worldviews and values continue to reflect those of their ancestors."[41]

A Son of the Forest by William Apess, published in 1829, could be the first autobiography by a tribal person, and distinct from those "autobiographies" of Indians written by others. LaVonne Ruoff pointed out that Apess was an orphan and that the "whites" Apess lived with "as a child taught him to be terrified of his own people. If he disobeyed, they threatened to punish him by sending him to the forest."[42]

Apess was crossblood Pequot, a Methodist minister, and an activist for tribal rights. "His own birth and death are not documented," Barry O'Connell pointed out in *On Our Own Ground*. "Born to a nation despised and outcast and perhaps, to add to the stigma, not only part white, a 'mulatto' or 'mixed breed,' but also part African American, a child with William Apess's history who simply made it to adulthood would be doing well." The once-despised other learned how to write his name and stories over the racial borders in a crossblood remembrance.

"I cannot perhaps give a better idea of the dread which pervaded my mind on seeing any of my brethren of the forest than by relating the following occurrence," Apess wrote in his autobiography. "One day several of the family went into the woods to gather berries, taking me with them. We had not been out long before we fell in with a company of white females, on the same errand—their complexion was, to say the least, as *dark* as that of the natives. The circumstance filled my mind with terror, and I broke from the party with my utmost speed, and I could not muster courage enough to look behind until I had reached home," wrote Apess. "It may be proper for me here to remark that the great fear I entertained of my brethren was occasioned by the many stories I had heard of their cruelty toward the whites. . . . If the whites had told me how cruel they had been to the 'poor Indian,' I should have apprehended as much harm from them."[43]

Tribal autobiographical narratives and personal life stories have been popular for more than a century. George Copway and Sarah Winnemucca both published autobiographies in the nineteenth century. Charles Eastman, Francis La Flesche, Luther Standing Bear, and John Joseph Mathews published their autobiographies and personal narratives in the early twentieth century.

Standing Bear was raised a century ago to be a hunter and warrior, but the federal government had terminated the buffalo, and he was removed to be educated at the Carlisle School in Pennsylvania. He wrote that when "the train stopped at the station" in Sioux City "we raised the windows to look out" and "there was a great crowd of white people there." The white people "started to throw money at us. We little fellows began to gather up the money, but the larger boys told us not to take it, but to throw it back at them. They told us if we took the money the white people would put our names in a big book. We did not have sense enough then to understand that those white people had no way of discovering what our names were. However, we threw the money all back at them. At this, the white people laughed and threw more money at us."[44]

The Names: A Memoir by N. Scott Momaday and my own *Interior Landscapes: Autobiographical Myths and Metaphors* are recent publications. "My spirit was quiet there," Momaday wrote about his childhood at Jemez, New Mexico. "The silence was old, immediate, and pervasive, and there was great good in it. The wind of the canyons drew it out; the voices of the village carried and were lost in it. Much was made of the silence; much of the summer and winter was made of it."[45]

I Tell You Now: Autobiographical Essays by Native American Writers, edited by Brian Swann and Arnold Krupat, includes literary autobiographies by Maurice Kenny, Elizabeth Cook-Lynn, Carter

Revard, Jack Forbes, Paula Gunn Allen, Diane Glancy, Simon Ortiz, Linda Hogan, Joy Harjo, and nine other writers.

"I tell parts of my stories here because I have often searched out other lives similar to my own," wrote Linda Hogan. "They would have sustained me. Telling our lives is important, for those who come after us, for those who will see our experience as part of their own historical struggle."[46]

"Facts: May 7, 1948. Oakland. Catholic hospital. Midwife nun, no doctor. Citation won the Kentucky Derby. Israel was born. The United Nations met for the first time," wrote Wendy Rose. "I have heard Indians joke about those who act as if they had no relatives. I wince, because I have no relatives. They live, but they threw me away. . . . I am without relations. I have always swung back and forth between alienation and relatedness."[47]

"I was raised by an English-German mother. My father, one-quarter Cherokee, was there also, but it was my mother who presented her white part of my heritage as whole," wrote Diane Glancy. "I knew I was different, then as much as now. But I didn't know until later that it was because I am part heir to the Indian culture, and even that small part has leavened the whole lump."[48]

"When I was about nine my family moved into a northern section of Los Angeles, and there I would have psychologically perished had it not been for a range of hills that came up to our back yard," wrote Jack Forbes. "The hills were full of animals—deer, snakes, coyotes, birds— and I spent much of my spare time crawling along deer trails through brush and exploring draws and canyons. In one nearby canyon was a giant oak tree, and under its branches, where they brushed against the top of a sharp rise in the canyon wall, I had one of my favorite hiding places. Like an animal of the earth, I loved to rest in such secret places, where I could see but not be seen, and where I could dream."[49]

Native American Indian authors have secured the rich memories of tribal generations on his continent; the diverse narratives of these crossblood authors would uncover the creative humor of survivance and tribal counterpoise to the literature of dominance. These autobiographical essays would overcome the racialism of discoveries and the romancism of tribal cultures.

"This conscious awareness of the singularity of each individual life is the late product of a specific civilization," wrote Georges Gusdorf in *Autobiography.* "Throughout most of human history, the individual does not oppose himself to all others; he does not feel himself to exist outside of others, and still less against others, but very much *with* others in an independent existence that asserts its rhythms everywhere in the community. No one is rightful possessor of his life or his death; lives are so thoroughly entangled that each of them has its center everywhere and its circumference nowhere."[50]

These theories and critical notions, with certain conditions, are the most common interpretations of literary autobiographies by tribal writers. In other words, the common conceit is that an autobiographer must "oppose himself to all others" or oppose tribal cultures and postexclave communities. Such notions are romantic at least, and nurture the whimsies of primitivism and otherness at best. The suspicion seems to be that there are essential communal, but not universal, memories that cannot be heard in certain pronouns; the translations of unheard pronouns have never been the sources of tribal consciousness.

The favors of certain pronouns, however, are not the same in translation or tribal autobiographies: pronouns are neither the sources, causes, nor tribal intentions; autobiographies, memories, and personal stories are not the authentic representations of either pronouns, cultures, or the environment.

The stories that are heard are the coherent memories of natural reason; the stories that are read are silent landscapes. Pronouns, then, are the pitch hitters in the silence and distance of translation, and at the same time pronouns are the *différance* that would be unheard in translations. The archshadows of tribal consciousness and the shadows of names and natural reason are overheard in tribal stories and autobiographies; in this sense, stories are shadows, shimmers of coincidence, and tribal traceries in translation. The shadows are unsure scenes in dreams with bears, birds, and demons, and the *différance*, or temporization of pronouns, in tribal nicknames, memories, dance moves, and shamanic visions.[51]

Swann and Krupat, for instance, pointed out in *I Tell You Now* that the "notion of telling the whole of any one individual's life or taking merely personal experience as of particular significance was, in the most literal way, foreign to them, if not also repugnant."[52]

The concerted inventions of tribal cultures are in continuous translations, and the situation of hermeneutics remains the same in simulations; the silence of translation and the absence of the heard antecedes a presence and the shadows of stories. Has the absence of the heard in tribal memories and stories become the literature of dominance? What are the real names, nouns, and pronouns heard in the unbearable fields of tribal consciousness? How can a pronoun be a source of tribal identities in translation? How can a pronoun be essential, an inscription of absence that represents the presence of sound and a person in translation?

The first person pronoun has never been the original absence of the heard, not even as the absence or transvaluation in the silence of a reader. The unheard presence of pronouns, and the temporization of nouns, is the *différance* heard in tribal nicknames and in the absence of the heard in translations. Certain tribal nicknames are stories, and the stories are distinctions that would counter the notions of communal memories. The survivance of tribal nicknames, shadows, and memories, in the absence of the heard, is the *différance* that misconstrues the representations of presence, simulations, and the gender burdens of pronouns. The personal, possessive, demonstrative, relative, and interrogative pronouns are translations and transvaluations, the absence of names, presence, and consciousness heard in tribal stories.

The pronoun endures as twice the absence of the heard, and more than the mere surrogate signifier or simulation in tribal stories. There is a sense of the heard in the absence of the heard; the pronoun is the *différance* that would pronounce and misconstrue memories in postexclave literature. We must represent our own pronoun poses in autobiographies, in our personal invitations to silence and shadows of the heard; first person pronouns have no referent. The other is a continuous pronoun with no shadows. The demonstrative pronouns are the transactions of others, the elusive invitations to a presence in the absence of cotribal entities.

We must need new pronouns that would misconstrue gender binaries, that would combine the want of a presence in the absence of the heard, a shadow pronoun to pronounce memories in silence, in the absence of cotribal names and nouns. The *pronounance* combines the sense of the words *pronoun* and *pronounce* with the actions and conditions of survivance in tribal memories and stories. The *trickster pronounance* has a shadow with no numbered person; in the absence of the heard the trickster is the shadow of the name, the sound, the noun, the person, the *pronounance*.

The tribal healers, shamanic visionaries, and those who hear stories in the blood are not bound to measure their memories as the mere hurrah for nature. Tribal landscapes are heard, read, and the scenes and shadows are remembered in stories. The coherence of natural reason is created in personal stories, and in the elusive unions of shamans with birds, animals, and ancestors. These natural unions are heard in the archshadows that outlast translations. The shamans hear their memories in birds, animals, and shadows in our stories.

The theories of structuralism, the myths of unexpected harmonies, and objective dissociations of natural tribal reason are dubious tropes to power in the literature of dominance. The transitive evidence of objectivism and simulations has no referent, no sense of experience or shadows in the silence in the coherence of natural reason. The tribal referent is in the shadows of heard stories; shadows are their own referent, and shadows are the silence and memories of survivance.

Those lonesome souls who read their identities in metanarratives and trace the distance of their tribal ancestors to an environment of otherness in the literature of dominance are the new missionaries of simulations. The identities that arise from environmental simulations have no referent or shadow in tribal consciousness. "Since the environment cannot be authentically engaged the self becomes its own environment and sole source of authenticity," John Aldridge wrote in *The American Novel and the Way We Live Now*, "while all else becomes abstract and alien."[53]

Hertha Dawn Wong, for instance, declared in the preface to *Sending My Heart Back Across the Years* that she is "not a member of a native community, but much of what my mother taught me reflects traditional values long associated with Native American cultures." No doubt she heard the memorable simulations of a tribal environment. She wrote that "according to the Oklahoma Historical Society, my great-grandfather may have been Creek or Chickasaw or Choctaw or perhaps Cherokee." That whimsical sense of possibilities, "may have been" one of four or more distinct tribes, is not an answerable source of credible identities; moreover, she must be held to her own high academic standards of historical and theoretical research at the University of California, Berkeley.

Wong has received several generous research grants to support her studies of Native American autobiographies; at the same time, she seems to praise panoramic tribal identities and a romantic narrative environment. "Over the years," she wrote, "the unfolding narrative of my family history and the narrative of this book on autobiography have taken on striking parallels."[54]

The narratives she studied in *Sending My Heart Back Across the Years* could be considered the elusive sources of her own sense of tribal identities; otherwise, the overture to the "fundamental activities of autobiography" would be insincere invitations to these associations. The rights and duties of tribal consciousness have never been established in tribal communities or the literature of dominance; imagination is an honorable performance, but autobiographies must arise from memories and the shadows of heard stories. Neither the first person nor the indirect reflexive pronoun are reasonable sources of identities; notions of tribal romanticism and metaphorical parallelism are earnest but without assurance. The subject of her research has become the object of her tribal identities; alas, tribal memories are not heard in objectivism.

"When I began writing this book," she wrote in the preface, "I had little idea that I was part Native American, one of the unidentified mixed-bloods whose forebears wandered away from their fractured communities, leaving little cultural trace in their adopted world." The racialism of these romantic notions would bear minimal honor in tribal memories and literature.

Wong musters the innocence of a wanderer to simulate tribal cross-bloods, and she poses in a transitive narrative on tribal cultures; the metaphor of adoption serves the literature of dominance. "I found a new insight into the meaning of irony," she wrote, "I had believed that I was a non-Indian writing as an outsider about Native American autobiographical traditions."

The conceit of innocuous environmental identities must be ironic, because the panoramic other is a romantic transvaluation and simulation, a consumer precedence over the coherence of natural reason. *Sending My Heart Back Across the Years* could be read as ironic and impressionistic criticism in the literature of dominance.

"My purpose is to expand the Eurocentric definitions of autobiography to include nonwritten forms of personal narratives," she wrote in the introduction. "This study, then, considers Native American autobiography from the context of autobiographical theory, delineates distinctly Native American oral and pictographic traditions of personal narrative and their interaction with Euro-American autobiographical modes." Moreover, she argues that both "female and Native American autobiographical narratives focus on a communal or relational identity and tend to be cyclical rather than linear." How, then, could she have overlooked the significant studies of *pictomyths*, or picture stories, and tribal music at the turn of the last century by Frances Densmore?

Wong widens the serious textual discourse on autobiographies, to be sure, but her earnest search for communalism is closer to an absolute literature than to the nuances of tribal identities. The pictures she construes as autobiographies are picture myths, stories, or memorial expressionism, not historical representations. Tribal narratives are heard and remembered in *pictofiction* and *pictomyths* without closure.

Wong declared that there "is no generic Indian sense of self." Indeed, and that assertion could be read as the closure of her own panoramic sense of tribal identities in literature. "If a Native American sense of self is associated with tribal identity, to realize fully a sense of Indian identity is to realize one's link to the tribe."[55]

True, the "concept of 'race' or 'ethnic origins' means different things in different contexts,"[56] but when the tropes to academic power are tied to nativism and tribal identities, then the context of racialism is prescribed as both essentialist and political in institutions.

Anthony Kerby argued in *Narrative and the Self* that the loss of the "ability to narrate one's past is tantamount to a form of amnesia, with a resultant diminishing of one's sense of self. Why should this be so? The answer, broadly stated, is that our history constitutes a drama in which we are a leading character, and the meaning of this role is to be found only through the recollective and imaginative configuring of that history in autobiographical acts. In other words," he continued, "in narrating the past we understand ourselves to be the implied subject generated by the narrative."[57]

The narrative selves that have no referent, memories, or shadows are the transitive selves overheard in language and the literature; tribal shadows are intransitive and wait to be heard in stories. "Life does not speak; it listens and waits," wrote Gilles Deleuze and Félix Guattari in *A Thousand Plateaus*. "Language is not life; it gives life orders." Literature is the overheard other in the search for selves. Mikhail Bakhtin created the idea of heteroglossia, or the diversities of language, to consider the utterances of selves in the interaction of the other. "Words belong to nobody, and in themselves they evaluate nothing," he wrote in *Speech Genres and Other Late Essays*. "The *I* hides in the other and in others[;] it wants to be only an other for others, to enter completely into the word of others as an other, and to cast from itself the burden of being the only *I* (*I-for-myself*) in the world."[58]

On the other hand, the confessions, simulations of transitive selves, and panoramic identities could be an ironic liberation of pronouns in the literature of dominance. Francis Jacques points out that the first person singular pronoun "is not knowable because it knows. No objectivization, no representation of the subjective in this sense is possible, since any representation is objective. . . . But even if I cannot know this *I*, I can still be conscious of it."[59]

The pleasure of nicknames in tribal memories is an unmistakable sign and celebration of personal identities; nicknames are personal stories that would, to be sure, trace the individual in tribal families and communities rather than cause separations by personal recognition.

There is nothing foreign or repugnant in personal names and the stories that arise from nicknames. Sacred names and nicknames were heard as stories, and there were relatives and others responsible for giving names in most tribal communities. The signatures and traces of tribal names are heard in stories. The risks, natural reason, shadows, and pleasures of dreams and visions are sources of personal power in tribal consciousness; personal stories are coherent and name individual identities within tribal communities and are not an obvious opposition to communal values.

Personal visions, for instance, were heard alone, but not in cultural isolation or separation from tribal communities. Those who chose to hear visions were aware that their creative encounters with the unknown were dangerous and would be sanctioned by the tribe; personal visions could be of service to tribal families and communities. Some personal visions and stories have the power to liberate and heal, and there are similar encounters that liberate readers in the novels and poems by contemporary tribal authors.

Nicknames, dreams, and shamanic visions are tribal stories that are heard and remembered as survivance. These personal stories are not the same as the literature of silence and dominance; these stories are not the same as translation and representational autobiographies. However, the awareness of coincidence in stories is much more sophisticated in tribal memories than in the tragic flaws of a consumer culture, and even wiser are the tribal memories that endured colonial discoveries and the cruelties of a chemical civilization.

Wovoka, at once the inspiration of the Ghost Dance religion, received many letters from tribal people who had heard about his vision in the very language of the treacherous colonial government. Luther Standing Bear, for instance, and thousands of other tribal men and women learned the language and literature of dominance; their memories and survivance were heard and read in more than one language.

Cloud Man Horse wrote to Wovoka, "Now I am going to send you a pair of mocissions but if they are not long enough for you when you write again please send me you foot measure from this day on—I will try to get the money to send to you. I wish I had it just at present I would sent it wright away."[60]

The English language has been the linear tongue of colonial discoveries, racial cruelties, invented names, simulated tribal cultures, and the unheard literature of dominance in tribal communities; at the same time, this mother tongue of paracolonialism has been a language of liberation for many tribal people. English, a language of paradoxes, learned under duress by tribal people at mission and federal schools, was one of the languages that carried the vision and shadows of the Ghost Dance, the religion of renewal, from tribal to tribe on the vast plains at the end of the nineteenth century. "The great underlying principle of the Ghost Dance doctrine is that the time will come when the whole Indian race, living and dead, will be reunited upon a regenerated earth, to live a life of aboriginal happiness, forever free from death, disease, and misery," wrote James Mooney in *The Ghost-Dance Religion*.[61]

Captain Dick, a Paiute, said that "Indians who don't dance, who don't believe in this word," of the Ghost Dance, "will grow little, just about a foot high, and stay that way. Some of them will be turned into wood and be burned in the fire."[62]

English, that coercive language of federal boarding schools, has carried some of the best stories of endurance, the shadows of tribal survivance, and now that same language of dominance bears the creative literature of distinguished crossblood authors in the cities. The tribal characters dance with tricksters, birds, and animals, a stature that would trace the natural reason, coherent memories, transformations, and shadows in traditional stories. The shadows and language of tribal poets and novelists could be the new ghost dance literature, the shadow literature of liberation that enlivens tribal survivance.

Notes

1   Jean-François Lyotard, *The Postmodern Condition: A Report on Knowledge* (Minneapolis: U of Minnesota P, 1984), xxiii, xxiv, 5.
2   Will Wright, *Wild Knowledge: Science, Language, and Social Life in a Fragile Environment* (Minneapolis: U of Minnesota P, 1992), 3, 41, 113.
3   Linda Hutcheon, *The Politics of Postmodernism* (London: Routledge, 1989), 58. "Telling Stories. Fiction and History," essay in *Modernism/Postmodernism*, ed. Peter Brooker (London: Longman, 1992), 239. "Abstraction today is no longer that of the map, the double, the mirror or the concept," wrote Jean Baudrillard in *Simulations*. "Simulation is no longer that of a territory, a referential being or a substance. It is the generation by models of a real without origin or reality: a hyperreal." The real endures in nostalgia, and chance is ironic, but ideologies correspond to a "betrayal of reality by signs." Gilles Deleuze and Félix Guattari wrote in *A Thousand Plateaus* that language "is a map, not a tracing."
4   Jean-François Lyotard, *Instructions païnnes*, quot. David Carroll, "Narrative, Heterogeneity, and the Question of the Political: Bakhtin and Lyotard," *The Aims of Representation*, ed. Murray Kreiger (New York: Columbia U P, 1987), 85.
5   David Carroll, *The Subject in Question* (Chicago: U of Chicago P, 1982),

117. "Hundreds, thousands of little dissident narratives of all sorts are produced in spite of all attempts to repress them, and they circulate inside and eventually, or even initially, outside the boundaries of the totalitarian state," he wrote. "The importance of these little narratives is not only that they challenge the dominant metanarrative and the state apparatus that would prohibit or discredit them, but that they also indicate the possibility of another kind of society, or another form of social relations."

6 Brian Swann, ed., *On the Translation of Native American Literatures* (Washington, D.C.: Smithsonian Institution Press, 1992), xvii. He wrote, "The appropriation can lead to many undesirable results, even to the invention, or reinvention, of Native American tradition, a tradition which is fed back to the native community, and then out again, thus inflicting multiple damage."

7 Tejaswini Niranjana, *Siting Translation* (Berkeley: U of California P, 1992) 3, 21.

8 Richard Wolin, *The Terms of Cultural Criticism* (New York: Columbia U P, 1992), 199, 200.

9 Peggy Kamuf, ed., *Derrida Reader* (New York: Columbia U P, 1991), 64, 70.

10 Raymond Tallis, *Not Saussure* (London: Macmillan Press, 1988), 92.

11 Luther Standing Bear, *My Indian Boyhood* (Lincoln: U of Nebraska P, 1931), 48, 51.

12 N. Scott Momaday, *The Way to Rainy Mountain* (Albuquerque: U of New Mexico P, 1969), 7.

13 Brian Swann and Arnold Krupat, *Recovering the Word* (Berkeley: U of California P, 1987), 8.

14 Victor Barnouw, *Wisconsin Chippewa Myths & Tales* (Madison: U of Wisconsin P, 1977), 4, 61. Barnouw concluded that the "two interpretations suggest the existence of repression, which is also suggested by the origin myth, with its avoidance of women and sex and its recurrent oral and anal themes."

15 Karl Kroeber, "The Art of Traditional American Indian Narration," *Traditional American Indian Literatures* (Lincoln: U of Nebraska P, 1981), 17.

16 Clifford Geertz, *Words and Lives: The Anthropologist as Author* (Stanford: Stanford U P, 1988), 46.

17 Andrew Wiget, *Native American Literature* (Boston: Twayne, 1985), 16.

18 Wiget, 3.

19 Larzer Ziff, *Writing in the New Nation* (New Haven: Yale U P, 1991), 155, 173.

20 George Steiner, *After Babel* (New York: Oxford U P, 1975), 31, 296.

21 Wiget, 85, 121.

22 Wiget, 92.

23 James Welch, *Winter in the Blood* (New York: Penquin Books, 1986), 166.

24 Charles Larson, *American Indian Fiction* (Albuquerque: U of New Mexico P, 1978), 8.

25 Larson, 34, 35.

26 John Joseph Mathews, *Sundown* (Norman: U of Oklahoma P, 1988), 31, 32.

27 Larson, 65.

28 Larson, 14, 15. "Even N. Scott Momaday," Larson argued, "has chosen to

write not about his own people but about the Navahos. As one critic of Momaday noted when *House Made of Dawn* appeared, 'This first novel, as subtly wrought as a piece of Navajo silverware, is the work of a young Kiowa Indian who teaches English and writes poetry at the University of California in Santa Barbara. That creates a difficulty for a reviewer right away."

29 Larson, 14, 15.

30 Larson, 95, 167, 168. Larson pointed out that *The Surrounded* and *House Made of Dawn* "are concerned with central characters who have left their places of birth, gone off for a time and lived in the white man's world, and then returned. That journey Archilde and Abel share with the characters in Pokagon and Mathews's assimilationist novels, but there the resemblance ends." Larson argued that the "two works illustrate a new ideological stance: repudiation of the white man's world coupled with a symbolic turn toward the life-sustaining roots of traditional Indian belief."

31 N. Scott Momaday, *The Ancient Child* (New York: Doubleday, 1989), 29, 303.

32 Larson, 135, 140. "No doubt this is true of the writers themselves, who often appear to be infused with a sense of urgency to proclaim the quality of contemporary Indian life," wrote Larson.

33 A. LaVonne Brown Ruoff, *American Indian Literatures* (New York: Modern Language Association of America, 1990), 78.

34 Leslie Marmon Silko, *Ceremony* (New York: Penguin Books, 1986), 126.

35 Paula Gunn Allen, *The Sacred Hoop* (Boston: Beacon Press, 1986), 2, 3.

36 Paula Gunn Allen, "Special Problems in Teaching Leslie Marmon Silko's *Ceremony*," in *Headlands Journal* (Sausalito: Headlands Center for the Arts, 1991), 43, 44.

37 Allen, *The Sacred Hoop*, 6, 7.

38 Elizabeth Cook-Lynn, "Commentary" in *Wicazo Sa Review*, Spring 1992.

39 Gerald Vizenor, ed. *Narrative Chance: Postmodern Discourse on Native American Literatures* (Albuquerque: U of New Mexico P, 1989), 121, 188.

40 Louis Owens, *The Sharpest Sight* (Norman: U of Oklahoma P, 1992), 57.

41 Ruoff, 2.

42 Ruoff, 53.

43 William Apess, *A Son of the Forest*, in *On Our Own Ground*, ed. Barry O'Connell (Amherst: U of Massachusetts P, 1992), xxiv, xxxix, 10, 11. Ruoff cited the 1831 edition of *A Son of the Forest* by William Apess.

44 Luther Standing Bear, *My People the Sioux* (Lincoln: U of Nebraska P, 1975), 129, 130.

45 N. Scott Momaday, *The Names* (New York: Harper & Row, 1976), 154.

46 Linda Hogan, "The Two Lives," in *I Tell You Now*, ed. Brian Swann and Arnold Krupat (Lincoln: U of Nebraska P, 1987), 233.

47 Wendy Rose, "Neon Scars," in *I Tell You Now*, 254, 255.

48 Diane Glancy, "Two Dresses," in *I Tell You Now*, 169.

49 Jack Forbes, "Shouting Back to the Geese," in *I Tell You Now*, 115.

50 Georges Gusdorf, "Conditions and Limits of Autobiography" in *Autobiography: Essays Theoretical and Critical*, ed. James Olney (Princeton: Princeton U P, 1980), 29, 30. Olney does not mention tribal literature, but

he pointed out that courses in American Studies and Black Studies "have been organized around autobiography . . . black history was preserved in autobiographies rather than in standard histories and because black writers entered into the house of literature through the door of autobiography."

51 Jacques Derrida coined the word *différance* to mean termporization, the spaces and traces of meaning between signifiers and signs. The classical structure "presupposes that the sign, which defers presence, is conceivable only on the basis of the presence that it defers and *moving toward* the deferred presence that it aims to reappropriate," Derrida wrote in his essay "Différance." "*Différance* is the nonfull, nonsimple, structured and differentiating origin of differences. . . . Thus, *différance* is the name we might give to the 'active,' moving discord of different forces, that Nietzsche sets up against the entire system of metaphysical grammar, wherever this system governs culture, philosophy, and science. . . . Rather, *différance* maintains our relationship with that which we necessarily misconstrue, and which exceeds the alternative of presence and absence." *Derrida Reader* (New York: Columbia U P, 1991), 64, 70.

52 Brian Swann and Arnold Krupat, *I Tell You Now* (Lincoln: U of Nebraska P, 1987), ix.

53 John Aldridge, *The American Novel and the Way We Live Now* (New York: Oxford U P, 1983), 157. Charles Taylor points out in *The Ethics of Authenticity* that the "ethic of authenticity is something relatively new and peculiar to modern culture. . . . The individualism of anomie and breakdown of course has no social ethic attached to it; but individualism as a moral principle or ideal must offer some view of how the individual should live with others." (Cambridge: Harvard U P, 1992), 25, 44, 45.

54 Hertha Dawn Wong, *Sending My Heart Across the Years* (New York: Oxford U P, 1992), vi. Harold Noonan, in "Identity and the First Person," wrote: "I think that the destinction between using 'I' against the background of a criterion of identity, to refer to an object, and using it not in this way is what Wittgenstein in the *Blue Book* calls the distinction between the use of 'I' 'as subject.'" Cora Diamond and Jenny Teichman, *Intention and Intentionality* (Ithaca: Cornell U P, 1979), 62.

55 Hertha Dawn Wong, vi, 5, 6, 7, 16. Stephen Pevar wrote in the American Civil Liberties Handbook: "Courts have used a two-part test to determine who is an Indian. First, the person must have some Indian blood, that is, some identifiable Indian ancestry. Second, the Indian community must recognize this person as a Indian." *The Rights of Indians and Tribes* (Carbondale: Southern Illinois U P, 1992), 12.

56 Douglas Benson and John Hughes, "Method: Evidence and Inference-Evidence and Inference for Ethnomethodology," in *Ethnomethodology* ed. Graham Button (Cambridge: Cambridge U P, 1991), 119.

57 Anthony Kerby, *Narrative and the Self* (Bloomington: Indiana U P, 1991), 7.

58 Gilles Deleuze and Félix Guattari, *A Thousand Plateaus* (Minneapolis: U of Minnesota P, 1987), 76, 77. The authors wrote that language "is a map, not a tracing." My position is that maps are the philosophies of grammar, the map is a relative language with no referent; traces are shadows of coherent natural reason that are heard in language. Brian Massumi points out

in *A User's Guide to Capitalism and Schizophrenia* that the "self remains susceptible to identity crises brought on by confusions between 'inside' and 'outside.'" The language maps are outside, and the shadows are the silence, the transitive stories that wait inside natural reason and memories to be heard.

Mikhail Bakhtin, *Speech Genres and Other Late Essays* (Austin: U of Texas P, 1986), 85, 147. Bakhtin noted that words "can serve any speaker and be used for the most varied and directly contradictory evaluations on the part of the speakers." Wong is the narrator of the others in the languages of tribal identities; the simulations of narrative selves and the heteroglossia of others are the modern ritual contradictions in the literature of domi-nance. Bakhtin argues in "Author and Hero in Aesthetic Activity" that the "only thing left for me to do is to find a refuge in the *other* and to assemble—out of the *other*—the scattered pieces of my own givenness, in order to produce from them a parasitically consumed unity in the *other's* soul using the *other's* resources." *Art and Answerability* (Austin: U of Texas P, 1990), 126.

59   Francis Jacques, *Difference and Subjectivity* (New Haven: Yale U P, 1991), 26. "If 'I' is not a proper name shall we simply say then that it is a pro-noun? The grammatical category of pronouns is a ragbag, including even variables; and the suggestion given by the word's etymology that it can be replaced by a noun in a sentence while preserving the sense of the sentence, is false of 'I.' Shall we say that 'I' is a demonstrative?" wrote Anthony Kenny in "The First Person." Cora Diamond and Jenny Teichman, *Intention and Intentionality* (Ithaca: Cornell U P, 1979), 4, 5.

60   Cloud Man Horse, 1911, Minneapolis Institute of Arts, *I Wear the Morning Star: An Exhibition of American Indian Ghost Dance Objects* (Minneapo-lis: Minneapolis Institute of Arts, 1976), 18.

61   James Mooney, *The Ghost-Dance Religion* (Chicago: U of Chicago P, 1965), 19.

62   Mooney, 26.

Ruins of
Representation

A Rhetoric

of Obliquity

in African

& Caribbean

Women

Writers

_____

Michael G.

Cooke

W̶hat does Jacques Derrida mean, writing philosophy as if he were a cross between Immanuel Kant and James Joyce, tossing up an abstruse idealism along with puns, involuted structure, and a miscegenation of tongues? What is deconstruction saying when it says language is a self-undoing edifice? Does this leave us in a position very different from the dilemma of responding to a man who professes himself a liar?

But when deconstruction demands a perfect exactitude of reference in language, at the risk of radical rejection, it really conceals a political agenda. To make that demand of literature is something of a red herring, or rather a stalking-horse. In holding the most complex use of language to be *simply* unreliable, deconstruction is obliquely denying authority to more practical and more pressing uses of language. It is undermining political orthodoxy and dogmatism and in particular the credo of Nazism from which its two chief exponents had variously suffered.

That there is obliquity in deconstruction's basic attack on language leads us to recognize a paradoxical pathos about language itself. For all language is in some regards as self-insistent and as oblique as de-construction. Language uses its creator, the human mind, as its agent-victim to guarantee at once its obliquity (or diluting affiliation) and its self-insistence (or desire for direct fulfillment). Whatever may be said is tested by language's other creator, the plenary order of things and relationships and is tacitly put into doubt by its need for assent and confirmation from the interlocutor. The challenge of assent holds good even while, in another tilt, language can count on a willingness to effectuate its truth in the interlocutor. Out of that willingness, let us recall, prejudice is often born, and faith moves or at least makes mountains of religious observance. No less important, it is in the matrix of that willingness that government flourishes, As Thoreau trenchantly notes, government is "a tradition . . . endeavoring to transmit itself unimpaired to posterity, but each instant losing some of its integrity" and showing "how successfully men can be imposed upon, even impose on themselves, for their own advantage."[1]

Though pragmatic adjustments to the usual disparities of human experience may cause the imbalance of language to pass unheeded, it is not hard to see how the colonial situation would exacerbate these disparities and that imbalance to a point beyond ignoring.[2] One party has all the say, all the sway, the other becomes an obligatory echo, amounting to a silent partner in a most inequitable partnership. But just as when fire ants colonize electric wires only part of the system goes dead, while other remoter parts know it and can come in to make redress, so with sociopolitical colonization: there are never enough colonizers to complete or maintain the silent partners.

It can be disturbing but not surprising (given the willingness in the interlocutor to practice courtesy and manufacture truth) how long it needs for the remoter parts to rally to the cause in the colonial situation. Indeed, much has been left for the *post*-colonial setting and its retroactive fervor. We do not sufficiently honor Caliban for his precocity in keeping his resentment current, nor do we sufficiently scrutinize Caliban's contention that learning a language from Prospero means that he knows how to curse. Much subtler and much richer responses are anterior to cursing, with its essential monotony and desperation.

The magic wand of Prospero's language is also subject to the paradox of testing and obedience. The confrontation with Caliban may in this light take second place to *Miranda's* loving departure from Prosper(o) (ity): the play begins with her learning of her father's earlier shortcomings as a duke and concludes with his resume of his life prior to

Michael G.
Cooke

retiring "to my Milan, where/Every third thought shall be my grave."
In short, both circumstances and his own impulses serve to curtail
Prospero's ostensible authority.

And while it is clear that Miranda's instant love for Ferdinand, the
son of Prospero's enemy Alonso, supports a theme of reconciliation
in the play, it also implicitly entails a spontaneous deviation from
her father's interests. It is deviation not reconciliation that we see in
Romeo and Juliet. Miranda is not clamorous about it (indeed she is dis-
turbingly silent as Prospero insists that she "must now know farther"),[3]
but she does show an instinct for independence beneath the blithe
passivity of: "More to know/Did never meddle with my thoughts"
(1.2.21–22). For when informed that her family had fallen from the
power princely estate, she responds conventionally with a supicion of
"foul play," then at once asks: "Or blessed was't we did?" (1.2.60–61).

The woman's position, say even the Miranda[4] syndrome, has its own
complexity in the colonial and postcolonial environment. For the conceptions of women as double victims, that is, of the colonialists and
of their own men,[5] needs to be counterbalanced by a recognition that
women also were afforded a double handle on skepticism toward authority. The very subjection of their men to colonial rule could as easily
as not turn into a model for misgiving about any claims to superiority.
In addition a lot of female submission, though we take it as the mark
of victimization, really reflects a kind of inexorable contempt for men:
the men can do no better and one lets them be as they are in order to
be true to one's own knowing, and being, better than they. The effect
is a seesaw in the following arrangement, with men on top in apparent
strength but women on top in real strength.

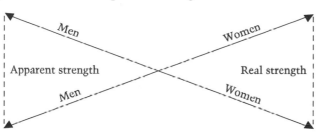

Masculine vulnerability breeds in the gap between apparent (social)
and real (spiritual) strength, but it is also in that gap that women culti-
vate apparent submission. This paper sets itself to shed some light on
the complex personal and cultural activity in that gap, with particular
reference to women's writing in West Africa and the Caribbean.

It is commonly held that, with the possible exception of the expatriate Buchi Emecheta, West African women do not exploit the vulnera-bility of the men in their writing,[6] but this seems to miss the way African and Caribbean women writers, in relation to men, rely on a structure of gradual, damaging revelation rather than a ploy of defiant confrontation. The African and Caribbean pattern may be traced along a trajectory from (a) curiosity, or the impulse to discovery and adap-tation,[7] to (b) absorption of (and indeed *with*) male-inspired values to (c) a modified reflection of (and *on*) those values to (d) a spontaneous questioning.

Such questioning is also male-inspired, but not male-embracing, and in the space where questioning occurs a new self-evaluation inevitably takes place. The rhetoric of eventual questioning occurs and revalua-tion is only delicately modulated from the rhetoric of curiosity and absorption. The *impact* of questioning is intense but is couched in language deceptively mild and oblique. ·

Out of a rhetoric of obliquity a challenge perhaps more radical than confrontation or cursing emerges, for the challenge is not Napoleonic but Godelian—not the effect of an ambitious antagonist but the de-velopment of an intrinsic weakness within the prevailing structure. The use of the rhetoric of obliquity as a probe of the system and of the self varies from writer to writer and from West Africa to the Carib-bean. The work of the Nigerian Flora Nwapa and the Ghanaian Ama Ata Aidoo, and that of the Jamaican Michelle Cliff and the Trinidadian Dionne Brand will provide a representative coverage of the case.

Flora Nwapa's *Efuru* (1966) begins with a swift personal decision and a flat, final assertion: "After a fortnight's courtship she agreed to marry him. . . . She told him not to bother about the dowry. They were going to proclaim themselves married and that was that."[8] But there is already something out of kilter, for these individuals have no names, but only category and gender designations: "the man," "the woman," "she" and "he." And it promptly proves that the world of the novel is one governed by tradition and hierarchy, with the status and roles of men and women graded according to strict stages and standards. Efuru, the title character, is "the woman" in question and she enjoys great privileges as the daughter of a "distinguished" family and is in fact trading on those privileges with her blitheness about tradition and hierarchy. Her whirlwind plan to marry Adizua, "the man" who is an unqualified suitor, only extends a practice of going her own way under the family's mantle (she has refused to marry at the customary time, for example, and neglected to take her "bath," or female circumcision).

Michael G.
Cooke

What is foundation, and what is the import of Efuru's blitheness? How deep does it run? Is she at some level making an oblique comment on hierarchy and tradition or is she a spoilt child?

Beginning with a problematically blithe decision and assertion *Efuru* ends with a startling, plangent questioning: "Efuru slept soundly that night. She dreamt of the woman of the lake, beauty, her long hair and her riches. . . . She [the woman of the lake] was happy, she was wealthy. She was beautiful. She gave women beauty and wealth but she had no child. She had never experienced joy of motherhood. Why then did the women worship her?" (221). As at the novel's outset the scene seems all security, with sound sleep and worldly blessings assured by the powerful water-goddess. But where at the outset the incongruity or conflict that arises is circumstantial, here it is forthright and analytical. It is as though Efuru's dream-life has been penetrated by the narrator, its content is: something in this whole scheme doesn't square. And either (a) there is no way to set things right, that is, the final question has no answer and the unfathomable rules the order of things, or (b) there is an answer that anyone can infer, but an answer without expression, perpetually withheld.

In either event the order of things is exposed to a demand for basic redefinition, while yet the degree of direct disturbance remains minimal. For the demand is couched in a doubly oblique rhetoric. The interrogative leaves not only itself but the action of the novel hanging indefinitely, and the fact that the question arises out of Efuru's dream state leaves *it* and all its freight open to dismissal.

To recognize the bleak forces radiating off and impinging on Efuru's conscious position at the close is not to be thrown into sheer irresolution about the bearing of the novel, or say rather its net effect. In a sense Efuru is proved "wrong" by the outcome of her self-willed marriage to Adizua—he turns out to be an uxorious good-for-nothing, and for that matter her second husband Eneberi is a runaway, liar, and cheat. Perhaps the traditional approach to marriage should have been honored? Efuru herself at one stage identifies with the traditional attitude toward childbearing, that is, that a childless woman is a failure and a disgrace.

But in fact she flourishes without husband or children (her only child dies in infancy). In sum, if Efuru is "wrong" to flout tradition in her marriage, that doesn't quite make tradition "right." *She* appears cumulatively right when, as she gets more beautiful and richer and more generous, the people begin to honor her, the supposed miscreant, as a

Rhetoric of
Obliquity

favorite of Uhamiri, the woman of the lake who significantly does not know "the joy of motherhood." Tradition emerges as less monolithic, less self-consistent than at first is admitted.[9]

A kind of slow, cumulative effect of oblique judgment becomes manifest here, to go along with the immediate obliquity of the novel's clinching interrogative. And we can recognize another mode of obliquity consonant with these, and that is obliquity by redefinition, for example, the term "distinguished" that is applied to Efuru's family and to other communities. The distinction here is badly tainted at its source, and when we learn this, late in the novel, Efuru's antic behavior seems more intelligible and the tradition she resists even more confused and vulnerable:[10]

> they were distinguished because they were privileged to have had contact with the slave dealers. Nwosu and the fisherman could not recollect what havoc the cannons and the guns and the hot drinks did for their people. All that happened, happened when they were children. Now, the shooting of the cannon did not only announce the death of a great man, but also announced that the great man's ancestors had dealings with the white men, who dealt in slaves.

The undermining of the "distinguished," even so, is couched in oblique rhetoric: "had contact with the slave dealers" and "had dealings with the white men, who dealt in slaves." Much remains implied, as many remain implicated, but none for sure, and nothing for sure except that the tradition the "distinguished" uphold has suffered an attack and a breakdown leading to an inheritance of somehow unreliable "men" and somehow intractable "women."[11] No wonder Ajanupu, of the knowing or unforgetting generation before Efuru's, is so fierce in pursuit of correct behavior; she is laboring to reconstitute the old tradition, and to undo its corruption.

What does the use of the rhetoric of obliquity in *Efuru* amount to? The novel plays complexly around the question of tradition, and as it ends with (1) a Western-trained doctor in effect superseding the dibia in authority and (2) *Efuru* taking her father's place as the main family member, it could seem to result in tradition's overthrow. But the most basic drive of *Efuru* is toward reflection and contemplation, and if the result of that contemplation can be "hate and resentment," such sentiments are frankly pronounced "foreign to . . . nature" (209).

The rhetoric of obliquity is aimed at tradition in particular the guise that is maintained by force, whether of habit or of arms. By the same token, a blunt opposition of defiance toward tradition, such as Efuru's

Michael G. Cooke

marriage to Adizua, meets with scant favor. The rhetoric of obliquity steadily grazes the fabric of a rigid traditionalism and a rigid antitraditionalism alike. In this way, the rhetoric of obliquity is not just the instrument for probing (and implicitly exposing and opposing) rigidity, but also the symbol, the necessity, of its own philosophy.

Ama Ata Aidoo's *Anowa* (1970) uses the Old Man and Old Woman (jointly termed "The-Mouth-that-Eats-Salt-and-Pepper") as a kind of chorus to give the action a frame of experience and cultural/historical depth. But the play really occupies itself with the marriage of a spoilt and self-willed young woman and follows the graph of love and trade in the life of the focal couple. Like Efuru, Anowa defies convention in remaining unmarried well beyond puberty and finally ups and elects to marry a "good-for-nothing" (Phase One, 15).[12] But unlike Efuru who emerges belatedly as a favorite of the woman (i.e., priestess) of the lake, Anowa will have none of becoming a "dancer priestess" and is strongly supported in this by her mother. Anowa's success at trade and fishing rests in diligence, not like Efuru's corroborated by the favor of the gods.

The question of slavery and of having a child also link *Anowa* and *Efuru*. But neither of these complex social questions has any great resonance beyond the negotiations of Anowa and her husband, Kofi Ako. The married pair are dramatically cut off from social and cultural contact, and as it purveys their travels and trials and triumphs and increasing tensions, *Anowa* seems to make the original home and society of the two principals an incidental backdrop more than a significant place. (Anowa says "One can belong to one's self without belonging to a place," and the production notes say "Costume" may be "anything African," with the option of "a set of Ghanaian costumes.") Slavery and childbearing fuel debates between Anowa and Kofi Ako as matters of choice or desire *for them*.

Slaves are a convenience for Kofi Ako as business expands. Anowa sees having slaves as an evil but explicitly declines to put her position in any historical or philosophical framework; "are there never things one can think out for oneself?" Her position, as Phase Three shows, is peculiar to herself and against her society's pragmatism on the subject (which causes her child's imagination nightmares [44–47]).

One further similarity between *Anowa* and *Efuru* calls for notice: the sudden revelation that comes to the title characters after long suffering and submission. Anowa's main revelation concerns Kofi Ako, and Efuru's concerns Eneberi, but here the similarity ends. For what Efuru understands about Eneberi's failings affects her conception of men and society, radiating through her outlook on the relationships and principles of her life and specifically underlying her sense of independence from her dead father as well as her inquiry into Uhamiri's paradoxical authority among the women. The marital situation focuses the social system for Efuru, not so with Anowa.

When Anowa divines Kofi Ako's impotence and faces him about it, there are spectators—including slaves—present. But Anowa is unaware of this. The scene is overpoweringly personal for her and for us. It explains for her, and for us (but not for her society) Kofi Ako's workaholism and his dependence on slaves as substitutes for his person. It explains his increasing unease with her unconventionality and independence, in that he needs her more and more to be unreflective and uncritical. And it explains his monogamous loyalty to Anowa and his anger at her repeated suggestion that he take other wives to secure himself children.

In sum, though *Anowa* contains numerous intimations of wider social critique, akin to *Efuru*, they are subordinate to the Anowa-Kofi Ako relationship, which is what the rhetoric of obliquity really addresses. One speech of Anowa's when Kofi Ako declares he will no longer be "working," is especially resonant: "Men whom Odomankoma create do not stop working; . . . yes, they do buy only when they are hit by illness or some misfortune. When their bodies have grown impotent with age" (Phase Two, 34). Though she has just observed that "these days you are always with your men," she is not inclined and we are not able to see the full implications of Kofi Ako's position. But the play's essential issues are intimated here: idleness, illness, misfortune, impotence. Idleness is chosen impotence, and impotence enforced idleness, with illness and misfortune standing as both causes and effects of idleness/impotence.

The question remains whether the slow, cumulative impact of judgment on Kofi Ako—the salient use of the rhetoric of obliquity in *Anowa*—obliquely extends to *men* at large. It may be noted that Kofi Ako embodies many features of the folkloric figure of the Complete Gentlemen, a "man" with a most prepossessing exterior fashioned from other people's parts (or labors, given Kofi Ako's use of slaves), but a "man" in himself hollow and deadly at the core. And certainly the other males of any significance in the play's unfolding, Anowa's father and the Old Man, seem pleasant and charming (especially in contrast with the irritable women). But *Anowa* amounts to something more complex than an exposure of the loathsomeness of winsome men, the impotence of their power.

Michael G.
Cooke

The final choral comments of the play stress the fact that Anowa was "true to herself," and objections are raised throughout, by Kofi Ako and her own mother, to Anowa's holding to her own views when custom and pragmatism counsel otherwise. On one level Kofi Ako's "impotence" has a counterpart in her "bare-footedness," with the key difference that she refuses to hide it and indeed maintains it when she could go dressed like a princess. "Bare-footedness" represents more than a personal eccentricity on Anowa's part. It conveys the fact that nothing in society either binds or projects her steps, her way. Kofi Ako, the empty man with the false front, is able to exploit Anowa's singularity to win her hand and promote his success; and his prominence and the juicy shock of his comeuppance may lead us to see the rhetoric of obliquity in *Anowa* as directed at him, or even at his kind. But it is more positively directed toward a struggle for individuality in the African woman, in an environment where such individuality— though compounded of favored traits like generosity, dedication, industry, lucidity, compassion, justice, and a leavening of dace—makes for mockery and exclusion and tragedy. To call Anowa "true to herself" only obliquely catches her character and her context. For she is also true to Kofi Ako, to the principle of "working," and, in her opposition to what might be called casual slavery, to the ideal of fairness and human dignity. The rhetoric of obliquity in *Anowa* challenges African society (one reason for making costume "anything African") not in an antimasculine, but in a forward-looking profeminine way.

The ultimate praise of Anowa does not, however, conceal the fact that the future for her way is bleak. The older women oppose her, and she has no children—ironically, only the slaves call her "mother." *Anowa* is more vividly set against the habits of its society than *Efuru*, but *Efuru* is more complexly laced with its society and culture than *Anowa*. Indeed, the power of social reflection makes *Efuru* wholly exceptional in its use of the rhetoric of obliquity.

In the Caribbean the subjunctive or introspective turn we have seen in *Anowa* comes out strongly even where there is an official social commitment. The reasons for this must include the fact that, in the Caribbean, social commitment is something of a new election rather than an old cultural matrix, and the personal act of election shows through (the reasons for introspection in Aidoo, conversely, include the fact that the social fabric is less closely fitted than heretofore, and the individual is thrown into higher relief).

At first blush Dionne Brand's *Winter Epigrams*[13] reads like a bewailing, indeed a belaboring of a capitalist, authoritarian system from a feminist Marxist standpoint. Place and state merge in a negative epiphany. Even lights represent a "sordid business" here in the Canadian north that contrasts so sharply with the Trinidad of Brand's birth and upbringing (though the popular warmth and grace of the tropical world have no substantial presence in the poems). When the Canadian "across the way" from Brand's place exhibits himself to her, and she remarks with astonishment: "how quickly we've established this intimacy" (*WE* 46), it's obvious that her expectations or experience of "intimacy" in the Caribbean contrast with such a perverse quickness. "In addition," as of early September in Canada "a smell of infirmity clasps the air" (*WE* 6). And finally the world of sound seems reduced to "only the sound of light poles/ . . . of the refrigerator/ . . . of the stereo/ . . . of the stove," so that "only, all the sounds seem to be connected by electric wires" (*WE* 38). The pathos of that final, detached "only" is charged by the advanced danger of "electric wires."

The negative bearing of Brand's everyday Canadian world—car lights, neighbors, the air, sounds—gets a political stamp when "street lights" are termed "fascist" (*WE* 39) and gets a heroic (or ludicrously self-inflated) public form when she is

> one of a hundred
> against the united states
> in a demo' for Nicaragua. (*WE* 42)

But that ostensibly political demonstration shifts into a rather subjective mode before our very eyes. The real emphasis falls upon the "one," the rest of the hundred receding into the background and the "united states" orthographically decapitated into a vague unsavory mass. The rhetoric of the scene is overtly political, abetted by the form of the epigram, but it is obliquely and resolutely lyrical in effect. Brand's epigrams are masks for lyrical spurtings, and it will prove that the lyrical underfreight of the pieces—what the rhetoric obliquely accomplishes—has little to do with their clamorous political surface.

Thus, one finds a lyrical person cropping out in the volume with a self-doubt very much at odds with the assertions of its politics. *Winter Epigrams* indeed begins as a declaration of radical doubt, of what is experientially and intrinsically unknown (as though to fulfill the deconstructionist's program while yet leaving it nothing to prove itself on). The very first poem introduces the elements of negation (white, dead, autumn-as-impending-winter) that Brand will develop into an attack on the capitalist North. But the poem obliquely recoils on itself, undermining its own effort to sing:

A white boy with a dead voice
sings about autumn.
Who knows what he means. (*WE* 1)

Her impatience, *her* antagonism get in the way of "what he means"
and seem to stem from doubts about her own meaning and purpose:

Ten months in the cold
waiting
I have forgotten, for what! (*WE* 3)

And again, more directly:

i have thought before of singing in a cafe,
i tried to come to Toronto/Yorkville—the Riverboat
where i thought it was hot and open. (*WE* 21)[14]

The "sick song" in *WE* 6 wants to lay blame at the door of the "cold
city," but its own abrupt image of a "warm . . . old hand" trying to bring
"calm" seems to suggest that the sickness is partially at least from personal, not meteorological longing. And two other poems in the series
tacitly confess the personal, lyrical bind that makes politics a facade,
a disguising option in the text. Brand gives a drunken "Black woman"
beggar her last "eleven cents" and "told her/ i knew she wasn't crazy
instead of embracing her" (*WE* 27, italics added). This detour from expressing affection is the counterpart of longing for the "old hand," as
helpless need becomes helpless incapacity for demonstration (except
political).

The second poem in question sees and still denies its lyrical bind:

At first I thought
it was because I had no money
and no job and no food
then realized that it was because of February again. (*WE* 52)

Here the rhetoric of obliquity is bold enough to come forward and
defy recognition. For February is not cause but metaphor of the absence of nurture. It is the starkest, most comprehensive signal of the
absence of the warming and calming "old hand." In this respect Brand's
being "afraid/of . . . [her own] tenderness" (*EEC* 42) and her "desperate" desire to love everybody (*EEC* 27) point to a need and a goal quite
other than the poems' announced concern. When Brand declares "I've
said too much already" (*EEC* 46), she hastens to cover this parapractic
confession of her willed ego-reticence and stalking-horse politics by

defiantly ("ah! what the hell") rattling off a list of more subjects for her to have say. What she says of herself describes precisely the position she creates for the reader: "things pass in the corners of my eyes / and I don't catch them" (*WE* 10).

It is possible, however, to catch Brand acknowledging that winter, the real and symbolic condition she curses, allows her to bring personal, lyrical things abroad under concealment:

> I can wear dirty clothes
> under my coat now,
> be who I am in my room,
> on the street. (*WE* 13)

It crosses her mind that "perhaps there'll be an accident though," and that "accident" conflates critical penetration of her oblique rhetoric with the synecdoche of her much-misséd "old hand"; for grandmothers in Brand's Guayguayare and throughout the Caribbean commonly tell young women in their families to be sure undergarments are always in best condition, in case an "accident" should befall them and the hospital have to change their clothes.

The idea of the "defense of Claudia" and the notion that these are all-embracing "love poems,"[15] in short the revolutionary feminism of the entire *Winter Epigrams* volume, should ultimately be regarded as the "coat" of Brand's work. And the "dirty clothes" (seen with the eyes of diffidence and sensitivity to shame) become equivalent to the inner figure "I am in my room" and should be sought in unguarded moments where snow in fact is lovely and magical (*WE* 41),[16] in "desperate" moments where a "radiator" must take the place of the absent "old hand" (*WE* 19),[17] and in the oblique reaching for the "moon" not only as a transcendence of winter but even of politics (*WE* 39, 40).

Winter Epigrams and *Epigrams to Ernesto Cardenal* are, in the normal way of engaged poems, both radiant and circuitous in their functioning. If it is proper, then, to say the volume is 'about' many things (not excluding politics), its hub and driving force seem closer to images of uprooted flowers and rotten fruit (*WE* 23 and *EEC* 41) than to anticapitalism and antiauthoritarianism. The warmth the poems long for is not a plane fare away in Guayguayare, Trinidad. The poems arrive at heatedness when they aspire to a warmth of human communication, caring, constancy. In other words, it is not surprising that Brand, though continually putting herself in *collective* situations, for example, as a demonstrator or as a beleaguered feminist (*EEC* 31), is continually isolating herself, insisting on the lyrical "I" vis-à-vis the rest. Her deracination in Canada only abets the suffering already there in her human loneliness.

Her poems then turn to establish contact and, possibly, "intimacy." We should not take the one-shot exhibitionist across the way as the whole story. As snow can be lovely, magical, so is winter (a) the source of poems and (b) a stimulus to the blind desire for love (*WE* 16), and (c) a "comrade" and *(horrible cogitatu)* potential "lover" (*WE* 54).

In the final analysis Brand like the Elizabethan Shakespeare (anathema in the Caribbean for his supposed maltreatment of the colonized person in *The Tempest*) puts her faith in immortality squarely in the lap of words. She contemplates *"winter suicide"* [18] and carefully stages herself performing one final action: "touching my dictionary." Surely that dictionary is the consummate maneuver of a writer wedded to the rhetoric of obliquity. The dictionary, or even half of it ("Vol. II the shorter/Oxford Marl-Z"),[19] allows the possibility of saying anything, everything, without the responsibility, the absolute exposure of speech.

In Michelle Cliff's *Abeng* [20] we once again see an overt concern with feminist and anti-imperialist politics, but here the locus of negation is not the North but the Caribbean itself with its heritage of slavery, sexism, and color/class inequities. Cliff, an expatriate like Brand, concentrates on bringing into play *in the Caribbean setting* a body of social-historical knowledge and an associated political indignation that she makes plain the people most affected are not in touch with (see esp. 140–42). She intersperses the story of Clare Savage's growing up with tendentious set pieces (see 14, 21, 27–28, 112, 113, passim), but she is speaking *about the situation* and not to the person of the women who crop up, variously ignorant and silent, in the later pages of the novel.

At bottom, it is not the condition of colonization or female subordination that *Abeng* is invested in, but the anterior, radical condition of being a woman. The formula might be rendered thus: a warped society produces a thwarted woman ("Kitty's . . . love . . . became a love . . . of necessity kept to herself" 128);[21] and the thwarted woman makes a failed mother everywhere in the text.

Abeng slowly accumulates and gears itself, behind its formal political convictions, to a vision of mother-loss and, answering to Clare Savage's female physiology rather than the commitments of the action, culminates in an image of mother-readiness [22] with Clare's menarche.

It is possible virtually to pinpoint the beginning of the turn to concern with mother-loss where Anne Frank and the Holocaust become tangled up with Clare Savage's own mother [23] and where Clare's "interest in the *why* of the Holocaust" proves to be "mostly influenced by the remoteness of Anne's mother" (79). The less epochal instances of mother-loss or mother-neglect in the text merge with this and are given a listing of their own

> Above all, a lady was aloof [see the "remoteness
> of Anne's mother"]. . . .
> So these women did not come forward because they
> were ladies. That was simple. . . .
> [Something] was missing. In [Clare's] own
> mother. In Anne Frank's mother. In all the [school]
> mistresses who only stood there, trying to turn
> their eyes from the sight of [the epileptic]
> Doreen smashing against the stones. (99)

The presence of the mongoose—dubbed "the true survivor" in Jamaica—takes on extraordinary resonance in *Abeng*, for the mongoose who survives its enemy, the bushmaster, by using "behavior [taught] by the mother mongoose" wipes out "all the snakes, and then . . . began to kill the chickens, and the birds, and the wild pigs" (113). The most positive mother figure we run across reeks death on the children of others.

Perhaps Abeng is ultimately less concerned with the *mode* of motherhood than with the shear, almost epiphanic reality of it. The novel ends with Clare Savage's menarche, and it is the point at which all the reticences of language and all the delicacies of sentiment Clare has acquired give way to what transcends learning, what is.

This is the moment that focuses Clare Savage's primary being, whereas all the political and historical concerns of the text seem to convey a second-order public stand. Here Clare gets a true image of herself, and she does it on her own in nature, does it with decisive indifference to any social, political, or philosophical position that might relate her to others: "her face was hot, and she dipped it in the water catching her own likeness even though it was barely light. . . . Something happened to her—was happening to her. And it didn't really matter that there was not another living soul to tell it to" (165–66).

Clare's menarche is obliquely foretold in a dream, and Abeng concludes, following the almost ecstatically blunt description of the menarche, with the declaration: "everyone we dream about we are." But this only raises anew problems of self and other, dream and reality. The other is becoming the self in the dream, while the self is becoming other in reality.

182

———

Michael G.
Cooke

We recall that the intensely social *Efuru* also ends with a dream, and a cryptic position on the order of things. And it becomes possible to see across the spectrum of uses to which the rhetoric of obliquity is put in recent African and Caribbean women's writing, a constant concern with identification in two guises: with the group and as the self. The rhetoric of obliquity provides a space (both practically and spiritually) for representation of the actual and for reflection upon it and becomes the *matrix* for the discovery of a self that, no matter how problematical its relationship with the group, at least identifies itself as itself. That re-flection implicitly leaves the rhetoric of obliquity, whatever problems it encounters with social, political, historical matters, as the expression of an irreducible and nondeconstructible Cartesian positive: I think, therefore I am.

Notes

1   *On the Duty of Civil Disobedience* (New Haven: Carl and Margaret Rollins, 1928), 2.
2   Robert Scholes in *Protocols of Reading* makes cogent objecton to the Derridean viewpoint in light of, or in the spirit of, such pragmatic adjustments (New Haven: Yale U P, 1989), 1–2, 30–87, passim. Sylvia Wynter provides a striking analysis of the way "countermeaning" develops out of the colonial situation, in "Beyond the Word of Man: Glisant and the New Discourse of the Antilles," *World Literature Today*, Autumn 1989, 639 passim.
3   *The Tempest*, 1.2.33. A pun on 'father' seems hard to avoid.
4   Not only in the Shakespearean but also in the jurisprudential reading. The Miranda ruling says in part: "you have a right to remain silent," but not an *obligation.* And anything said may be "used against" more than the particular speaker.
5   For a cogent summary of the case, see Miriam Tlali's *Crimen Injuria* and also in an analogous vein *Mules and Men* by Zora Neale Hurston.
6   As, say, African-American women do. It may be noted that in South Africa writers like Bessie Head and Miriam Tlali fall closer to the African-American than to the supposed West African position.
7   In a new place, experiments have shown, a hungry rat will leave food alone till it has done some basic exploration. Curiosity may be less superficial and more basic to survival than we give it credit for.
8   (London: Heinemann, 1966), 7.
9   Uhamiri, who emerges as an alternative to the standard view that only childbearing gives women real worth, also in her turn illustrates that every standard has an oblique alternative.
10 The public, dominant style of "worshippers of Uhamiri" is to go dressed all in white, rub white chalk over the body, and be continually wailing and shouting. But Efuru *chooses* not "to behave like that" and remembers other devotees who "behave normally" (147–48). Clearly the possessed worship-

pers are not enjoying the wealth and beauty supposed to be synonymous with Uhamiri.

11 The dibia, Enesha Agorua, seems to be on the verge of telling not only his family's but his society's story, during his interview with Efuru's father, Nwashike Ogene. But the latter uses his distinguished status to silence the man with the power to "see" and to speak: "Enesha Agorua," Nwashike Ogene urges, "don't talk any more" (152).

12 *Anowa* (London: Longman Drumbeat, 1970). The play consists of a prologue and three Phases.

13 *Winter Epigrams* and *Epigrams to Ernesto Cardenal: In Defense of Claudia* (Toronto: Wiliams-Wallace International 1983). The individual pieces will be designated by number and located by the abbreviation *WE* for *Winter Epigrams, EEC* for *Epigrams to Ernesto Cardenal.*

14 Not only barriers of person and place, but also demands of time are acknowledged as influences on her song: "griots take one hundred years/ to know what they say/ four hundred more to tell it" (*EEC* 34). Clearly Brand is conscious (but not part) of the griot tradition, which finally cannot encourage *her* in her lyrical impasse; it is not the griot but the tradition, owe half a millennium, that manages to "tell" what is known.

15 Actually, except for one non-committal instance in *WE,* the twelve embraces throughout *Winter Epigrams* are balked, fleeting, betraying, or hollow.

16 It is less the nature of snow than the lyricists mood, her total spiritual disposition, that brings on terms like "rapist" and "sabotage" in relation to snow (*WE* 5, 51).

17 That the old hand has a deep personal identity for Brand seems to be established in *EEC* 54: "Cardenal, the truth is that/even though you are not a country/*or my grandmother* . . . /or Guayguayare/I love you for the same things" (italics added).

18 The title of *WE* 45; this is one of the small handful of poems accorded the distinction of a title.

19 It is hard not to read that "Marl" as a source of fertilizer and bricks (growing and building) in relation to "Z," the end (or is it the symbol for zenith distance?).

20 *Abeng: A Novel* (Trumansburg, N.Y.: Crossing Press, 1984).

21 Or again: "the furious beam cast from the eye of the Black woman went as unnoticed as the shouts she made in the night" (153). Love and rage emerge, if at all, through the rhetoric of obliquity.

22 Occasionally the novel evinces a concern for homosexual possibilities, including a projection of female marriage by sex change (102–3; see also 101, 117) but those are little-girl speculations and are simply superseded by the primary preoccupation with the discovery of mother-readiness.

23 Initially on the strength of the coincidence that Kitty is Clare's mother's name as well as "the name that Anne Frank had given her diary" (80).

Différance

and the

Discourse of

"Community"

in Writings

by & about

the Ethnic

Other(s)

_____

Cordelia

Chávez

Candelaria

Community is an idealized term, understandably so, for as a common equivalent of "tribe" or "folk" or "we, the people," community recalls what is absent. The content or meaning of the "what is absent" harks back to ideas of family, home, and other desirable elements of childhood—imagined or not, but typically familiar and idealized—that are largely missing from the frantic present of adult experience. In the terms of attachment psychology, the "what" of community might even be seen to represent the original mother/infant dyad.[1]

In reconsidering the depiction of community in selected novels by U.S. writers marked by their ethnic-specific thematics, I have found useful Jacques Derrida's notion of *différance*[2] which proposes that the essential textuality of a given text resides both in its *difference* and *distance from* one sole determinable referent and in its *deferral of* meaning from one age or one reader to another. Rereadings of Henry Roth's *Call It Sleep*, Zora Neale Hurston's *Their Eyes Were Watching God*, and Rodolfo Anaya's *Bless Me, Ultima* disclose that the essential textuality comprising plot, character, and symbolic framework in these narratives is located in the tension(s) of *différance* produced by their portrayals of community. Their narrativity as texts of fiction (like the Derridean "écriture") develops in large measure from the dialectics between the problematics of community created in the story played off against its implied existence *somewhere* (e.g., home, the past, with someone, etc.) that, the texts ultimately suggest, exists only in the narrative. This dialectical tension subsumes more than a conflict between a depicted pastoral of lost possibility and an ironic real world of material experience, more than a contrast between a privileged many and a marginalized minority, more even than the opposition of civilized versus primitive worldviews. The tension emerges from *all* these polarities *amalgamated* and also from the psychological and cultural web of effects implicit in their dichotomization of identity.

For the protagonists of the three subject novels, the web of effects surrounding their place in their respective ethnic-identified community is tangled by conflicting meanings of blood, family, tribe, ego, and power, entanglements that are compounded by the fact and discourse of dominance which obtrudes upon them from the culture of political and socioeconomic power around them. These protagonists can thus never be completely "insiders" within either discourse. As a result, the sketches of community presented in these writings gain much of their energy and efficacy *as stories* from their articulation of yearning for the absent What.

But let me position myself at the original start of my rereading.

"Community" refers to a group of people associated together geographically and/or historically by common interests and traditions. The OED identifies two etymons: the early Latin *communis* meaning "fellowship, community of relations or feelings" and the medieval Latin *universitas* used concretely to name "a body of fellows or fellow-townsmen, . . . and this was its earlier use in English" (486). The early Latin meaning contains the intensionality of the idealized form expressing the idea of relations among closely knit persons. Emphasizing the positive values of close kinship and social solidarity, the intensional character of "community" is decidedly pastoral. The extensionality of the word comes from the second meaning, the one originally most common in English, and it has numerous applications: society, the state, people living in one locality with or without intercourse, a corporation, and so on.

The definition employed in this essay combines both intensional and extensional etymonic meanings to describe that place of known people which produced the protagonist who wants to leave it, but who

Cordelia
Chávez
Candelaria

yearns for it when absent, and is disappointed when s/he returns but, despite the disappointment, still desires it. In this conceptualization the ideal of community competes with the individual's clear-eyed perception of the space and human relations that produced her/him. As such it manifests the undecidability and contingency that lies at the center of *différance* and deconstruction. The meaning of experience with its multiple conflicts and ambiguities, like narratives, are quintessentially undeterminable in any unitary, final way. Analogously, when Derrida in his reading of Plato's decoding of *pharmakon* writes of "drug" in its meaning as both medicine and narcotic, remedy and poison, to preface his comments on referentiality, writing, and meaning, he is using it as a pre-text (i.e., pretext and prologue) for his personal anecdote about drug smuggling. By so doing he underscores the inability of a word, and by extension a language or texts of language, to say just *one* thing. They are always saying more, usually in opposition to themselves (like the intensionality/extensionality of the etymons of "community" and "drug") and thereby always demonstrating the principle of indeterminacy.

Before rereading community in *Call It Sleep, Their Eyes Were Watching God,* and *Bless Me, Ultima* through the lens of *différance,* however, I will consider salient earlier renderings of the subject. A preponderance of canonical pre-twentieth-century writings about American ethnic and racial minorities discloses markedly idealized portrayals of ethnoracial community. These narratives frequently contrast the idea of community harmony within the ethnic minority subset with the political and economic hegemony of a dominant (and dominating) society whose greater numbers and power weaken, and sometimes destroy, the valorized attributes of the minority culture. Writers as ideologically and stylistically diverse as Roger Williams, James Fenimore Cooper, Mark Twain, and Helen Hunt Jackson, each writing about different times and places, wrote in notably similar and romanticized ways about the idea of community among ethnic minorities.

One of the most exalted books of the American canon, Twain's *The Adventures of Huckleberry Finn* (1884) has been especially valued for its original treatment of racism, slavery, and apartheid in America as seen through the eyes of a boy and, with respect to form, for its use of vernacular codes of discourse. Twain was not particularly original, however, in his depiction of the noble Other and its attendant idealization of the Other's community. For example, the novel's only untarnished examples of the family affection associated with community occur in Jim's reminiscences about his wife and children, his plan to

Différance and
Discourse

reunite with them, and his dream of a liberated future with them.[3] "Jim talked out loud all the time . . . saying how the first thing he would do when he got to a free State he would go to saving up money and never spend a single cent, and when he got enough he would buy his wife, which was owned on a farm close to where Miss Watson lived; and they they would both work to buy the two children" (Twain 126). Notably, these examples of family community exist only as fantasies; all the other portrayals of slave life are fractured by the hate, racism, greed, and exploitation of actual Southern apartheid. Huck's relationship with Jim also shines with the feelings of friendly community, and, moreover, in the facts of the story Jim is Huck's only friend, for even his friendship with Tom Sawyer is fraught with anxiety and unpredictability. As others have noted, Huck and Jim's friendship cannot bear scrutiny for mimetic authenticity because, in antebellum America, it is plainly idealized.[4] It exists only as a fictional tracing, and, as an example of utopian community, it reflects the Derridean notion of *il n'y a pas déhors de texte*—that is, it is not referential to an actuality outside the text.

Twain's romantic model of Otherized community was inherited from previous tracings. The antinomian religious iconoclast Roger Williams (1603–83), for instance, was an early exponent of the noble savage interpretation of American Indians and their community. In "Of Salutation" (1643) he wrote that "there is a savor of civility and courtesy even amongst these wild Americans, both amongst themselves and towards strangers' (Williams, *Anthology of American Literature*, 74), a view that challenged the Anglo-European orthodoxy of the age that held that the indigenous Americans were barbaric and subhuman. Williams established an important polarity between white and dark that continued in later re/presentations of, as he saw it, the "Uncourteous Englishman" and the "Humane and courteous" dark-skinned "nature's sons" (74). This kinder Rousseauvian view of the New World "savages," while based on more enlightened notions of racially different people and some limited interaction with them, nonetheless derives a large measure of its appeal to contemporary readers from the very fact of its unorthodoxy. That is, it was as much ideologically based on the antinomian, anti-New England Calvinism idea of applying the Christian doctrine of brotherly love to the Indians as it was on any extended contact with or rigorous ethnography among them. While an improvement over the convert-and-conquest mentality toward the natives that predominated in the English colonies, it still

188
———
Cordelia
Chávez
Candelaria

suffers from its conceptual torque as an externally defined, paternalistic one-dimensionality.

Writing from a more consciously literary standpoint, James Fenimore Cooper creates similar noble Indians in his Walter Scott-influenced romances about North America. In *The Pioneers* (1823), the first of his Leatherstocking novels, he draws an Edenic community far outside the growing English settlement. Living in that suburban fantasy community are the last of the Mohicans Chingachgook, the White hunter Natty Bumppo, and the young aristocrat Edward Oliver Effingham. Despite the encroachment of "civilization" the three men live in the text's idyllic harmony because of Bumppo's intimate familiarity with Indian ways and because of Chingachgook's "savage" knowledge of nature, food, shelter, and native healing techniques (*The Pioneers* 74–85, 232–40). But the narrative is manifestly stylized and romantic and, hence, nonreferential, as Cooper himself once frankly admitted. Responding to a criticism that his books "give a more favorable picture of the red man than he deserves," Cooper wrote that his fictive Indians were based not on observations of people breathing the same air as he or of people he knew but, rather, they were "borrowed" from "an Account" written by a missionary to the Indians. He asserted that "a work of fiction has a fair right to the aid which can be obtained from a poetical view of the subject" and argued for "an author's privilege" in presenting "the *beau-ideal*" (Cooper, "Preface," 622–24).[5] He also declared that his "works aspire[d] to the elevation of romances" in the manner of Scott, thereby exemplifying a pre-Derridean (if blithe and unexamined) attitude toward (non-)referentiality.

A less literary motivation explains the related writings of William G. Ritch, a U.S. government official in the 1880s, who also constructed a myth of Indian nobility consistent with the Cooper paradigm. In a book written to publicize the territory of New Mexico to Easterners, he pitched the "wealth and wonder" of the land to prospective business interests and settlers. Commenting on Ritch's advertising pitch, historian Ramon A. Gutierrez writes that Ritch appropriated the Nahua legend of Aztlán to deliberately invent an apocryphal "legend of Montezuma" which contained "representations of an El Dorado that would appeal to capitalists and landless farmers" by engaging the "memories, hallucinations, and dreams" of the thousands of victims of "industrialized America who wanted to return to nature." So effective was the campaign, Gutierrez observes, that the concocted "Land of Enchantment" myth still draws tourists and immigrants into New Mexico by the thousands, and, ironically, "the myths became so powerful that now even the natives utter them as truth" (10).[6] This doubling back to a purely textual fantasy for a myth of ethnic identity parallels Cooper's admission that the source for his fictional Indians was a missionary text, not firsthand exposure with or of the "Other." According to Derrida this intellectual process functions less as mysticism than as the *true* nature of mimesis, or what he calls "mimicry imitating nothing," a position that emphasizes the gap between text and referent(s): that is, *différance*.

Many later writers[7] conflate the noble savage text of the Indian with the evolved text of Spanish/Mexican dignity to produce a new hybrid fiction of exemplary ethnic community. One such writer who wrote a perfect example of this idealization is Helen Hunt Jackson in *Ramona* (1888), a romance of an Hispanic/Mexican and an Indian community. Combining plot motifs from both *Pioneers* and *Huckleberry Finn* (that is, from the Morton saltbox of romance patterns that go back at least to Cervantes's *Don Quixote*), Jackson composes a story of outrage over the destruction of Mexican communities and "community" by U.S. expansionism. The novelist's protagonist, Ramona Ortega, an orphan mestiza mistreated by her adoptive mother, the haughty *doña* (and *dueña*) of a California hacienda, escapes with Alessandro, her full-blood Temecula husband. The convolutions and melodramas of their crisis-plagued odyssey permits Jackson to expound her enlightened message of social protest at the perfidies of American government policies and the White hordes attracted by the territory's gold. Instead of "lighting out to the territory" in the exact manner of Leatherstocking and Huck, the heroic Ramona, now widowed, marries her former foster brother and the newlyweds "light out to" Mexico together. Jackson's conclusion occurs in her epilogue to offer appropriate intertextuality with other romantic endings which, at the key moment of the narrative—that is to say at "The End," the author's last word to the reader—forefronts its fictiveness by reminding readers that the story *lies* (pun of *différance* intended) inside the book, not *dehors de texte*.

Underscoring the story's fictiveness at the end of these romances does not negate the fact that these novels originated in or were inspired by the sociopolitical material world. Twain and Jackson, especially, disclose a keen sense of the injustice of the U.S. government's institutionalization of apartheid that veers to moral indignation, as would be expected from writers with enlightened political sensibilities. But the political and psychological impetuses behind their writings do not, then, inevitably mean that their constructed texts equal a single literal material reality which we must read as unitary referents for their narratives. What they created was imagined alternatives to social injustice, alternatives which shift and change to accommodate the repertoires of knowledge each age and each reader brings to them. Furthermore, even though the deconstruction insistence on *il n'y a pas déhors de texte* may be, arguably, nonpolitical or apolitical and thus undermining of messages of social reform (e.g., *Ramona* and *Huckleberry Finn*), it is important to note that Derrida's theory is fundamentally iconoclastic and subversive. The uses to which it is put need not be necessarily unpolitical. One detractor, Michael Wood, of Derrida's theory admits that "the main appeal" of deconstruction is its "authoritative invitation to a dismantling of old gods and a deposing of old fathers" (30).[8] And Edward Said who has lodged cogent attacks on deconstruction's lack of interest in "dissolving the ethnocentrism of which on occasion it has spoken with noble clarity," still acknowledges Derrida's critical "perspicacity" and his effective "technique of trouble" (675).[9]

In its dismantling of logocentrism and the "metaphysics of presence," deconstruction provides *an other* vocabulary with which to critique the Canon, the valorized intellectual inheritance and paradigmatic identities of a given dominant/dominating culture. By positioning itself outside the credo of one real reality, one true philosophy, and an inelastic language of referentiality, deconstruction theory lends literary criticism an expressive calculus that is not dependent on a shared ideology or metaphysics as a precondition for its application. Conventional readings of the social reformism of, say, *Huckleberry Finn* and *Ramona*, built as they are on a thematics of liberal humanism, invite a shared ideology for their political efficacy. A Derridean rereading, on the other hand, finds what makes these writings stylistically effective and politically effectual is the combined force of their fictionality interlocked with their subversive *différance* in questioning and displacing received notions—even liberal ones—about apartheid, race, and culture.

Placing Twain, Williams, Cooper, Ritch, and Jackson side by side here is not intended either as an act of literary leveling nor as a process of intertextual copulation. I do intend to show that their treatments of the ethnoracial Other are, however, repetitions of the noble savage idea and therefore aesthetically incestuous. Generally these narratives have been read as depicting the inevitable hazards of what Twain called "snivelization," his epithet for a "Gilded Age" American progress characterized by uncritical acceptance of industrialization, technology, and

Différance and Discourse

White Christian political dominance. The writers' counter discourses thus tended to emphasize a vision of America-as-Eden only when it is distinguished from unquestioned Euro-American expansionism and mindless destruction of ethnically different cultures.

But what must be deconstructed in the aforementioned re/presentations of community is that they exist and *can only exist* within the narratives. That is what makes them, even Ritch's advertising catalog, fictions. The essence of their textuality is to show *an other* world, a more attractive and viable one, not to refer specifically either to an actual "erewhon" outside the text nor to a Platonic ideal of ethnoracial authenticity; they were not, after all, written as anthropology. Whether or not these writers thought they were building their fictional truths about a real or solely imagined space, what they accomplished were written texts highlighting the distance from, the margin between, their created fictive communities and anything outside them in the world of experience—although, in fact, something *déhors de texte* might have inspired the writing. Thus the critical perplex surrounding the effectiveness of the ending of *Huckleberry Finn*, for example, about which miles of ink has been written, is ultimately riveted in the novel's undecidability, its indeterminacy, its *différance*, particularly with respect to "community."

These are but several of many examples of literary idealizations of ethnic communities by dominant group and/or canonical writers presented as pre/text to my discussion of community in the Roth, Hurston, and Anaya novels. I read their novels as participating in the discourse of ethnopoetics, a perspective which describes the process of memorializing through literature and other art forms the varieties of ethnoracial experience and identity. Ethnopoetic writers and artists relate the conscious struggle to locate and preserve an ethnic-specific consciousness in the face of a dominant society's dominating language, conventions, and ubiquitous culture. Ethnopoets seek to locate their re/constructions (i.e., imagined configurations) of an aboriginal cultural past in the present tense of narrative discourse by foregrounding race, ethnicity, and notions of primordiality as explicit elements of literature and art. Concerned with reuniting the ruptured parts of culture perceived and imagined as a whole, ethnopoetics describes literature as diverse as Roth's *Call It Sleep* (1934),[10] Hurston's *Their Eyes Were Watching God* (1937),[11] and Anaya's *Bless Me, Ultima* (1972).[12] Distinguishable from one another by subject, plot, symbol, and form, these works nonetheless share the ethnopoetic preoccupation with ethno-

Cordelia
Chávez
Candelaria

racial identity, yearning for community, and imaginings of an originary primordial source.

Part of their effectiveness resides in their freshness and vigor in apprehending their respective ethnic subjects, particularly their inscriptions of "community." Rather than weaving narratives out of the noble savage threads of the canonical tradition described above, the three writers discussed below construct dense stories of individuals struggling for self-identity within ethnic families and communities defined as much by disharmony and *anti*-community as by unity. The stories thus expose the noble savage idea of undifferentiated communal harmony among ethnic minorities as a unitary myth of cultural constriction. Coincidentally[13] the three texts each open with crucial scenes of conflict that establish a tone and ambience of anticommunity that deepen the cultural and thematic elements of their respective stories.

Roth's *Call It Sleep* was rediscovered in 1960 when the novel was finally accorded its justified acclaim as an exemplar of proletarian fiction and modernist symbolism, the latter quality de-emphasized in the socialistic 1930s in favor of the implicit politics of its subject matter. The novel's tightly controlled narration, complex lyrical style, alternating linguistic codes, and psychology has elicited effusive praise since its rediscovery. Moving from straightforward omniscient description to limited third person to stream of consciousness narration, the narrative ranges over approximately six years in the lives of the Schearls, a Jewish immigrant family in a 1920s' New York ghetto. The novel's frame story—that is, the bulk of the novel told in four long chapters—is told from the point of view of the young son, David, who is engaged in oedipal struggle with his parents, recent immigrants struggling to adjust to each other as well as to their hostile American life. Because we see through David's eyes, his father's chronic job troubles and the parents' constant fighting are at first meaningful only as situational context to filter the boy's rite of passage as a first generation New York Jew, with all the cultural, historical, and psychological texture that fact implies. But later—with David—we piece together random pieces of information and oblique hints to learn that his father's anger, his mother's anxieties, and their constant conflict are directly linked to David's very identity: the issue of his paternity. Within the narrative's extended conceit of child-narrator typical of the bildungsroman form, the reader necessarily participates as perhaps the most important parent for, without the reader reading life into the boy's consciousness, David doesn't exist.

Call It Sleep opens with a brief frame prologue written in omniscient third person voice that, particularly germane to this essay, defines (anti-)community for the narrative. First, the prologue establishes sociohistorical context by introducing Genya and David Schearl arriving at Ellis Island from Austria in a scene of reunion with husband and father, Albert Schearl. As if with wide-angle lens, the omniscient narrator pans wide on the busy shipyard scene of arriving immigrants before tightening slowly to a hold on the Schearls. One of the most striking aspects of the prologue is the understated way Roth shifts point of view from the impersonal god's eye narrator to the specific viewpoints of three other shipyard observers of the reunion scene. The shift in perspective powerfully introduces the working-class voice(s) that dominate(s) the rest of the novel. As important, the shift forces the reader to alter modalities of reading from that of passive recipient of narrated scene to that of active participant voyeur.

> Except for [David's] hat, had the three newcomers been in a crowd, no one probably could have singled out the woman and child as newly arrived immigrants. They carried no sheets tied up in huge bundles, no bulky wicker baskets, no prized feather beds. . . . But despite this, despite their even less than commonplace appearance, *the two overalled men*, sprawled out and smoking cigarettes in the stern, eyed them curiously. And *the old peddler woman*, sitting with basket of oranges on knees, continually squinted her weak eyes in their direction. (10–11)

Cordelia
Chávez
Candelaria

My italics in the citation highlight the other shipyard observers who become limited narrators of the scene. Roth's shift to the subjective impressions of the three working-class people foreshadows the narrative's coming focus on David's perspective through which the entire remaining narrative unfolds. It is through the three observers that Roth sets up the family conflict, anticommunity, and ethnocentrism that dominates the plot. "The old peddler woman on the bench and the overalled men in the stern had seen enough husbands meeting their wives and children after long absence to know how such people ought to behave," the narrator writes to underscore the Schearls' uniqueness. "But these two stood silent, apart; the man staring with aloof, offended eyes grimly down at the water. . . . And his wife beside him regarding him uneasily, appealingly, . . . the child against her breast looking from one to the other with watchful, frightened eyes" (11). The three observers perceive characteristics of temperament in the family which adumbrate the emotional conflict and breakdown of family and Jewish community that crystallize to dominate David's consciousness.

The three see "something quite untypical" in the reunion that, deconstructed, discloses *différance*. What attracts their curiosity is the Schearl reunion's *difference from* other Ellis Island reunions they had witnessed, a difference that forces a *deferral of* meaning for the watchers—and the readers—who lack the information needed to explain the scene. At this point, the three witnesses can only conclude that "altogether it was a very curious meeting" (11), and then they disappear from David's story. Only later, rereading, do their defied expectations resonate in the rereader's mind as a "pre/text" of the novel's thematics; only then do we understand that the trio's misconceptions about the Schearl triangle exactly parallels the family's mutual lack of awareness of and sensitivity to each other's feelings and beliefs. Their insensitivity and gaps of insight, especially David's, explain their aloofness and lack of expressed affection which creates the tragic mood and tone of anticommunity that are the source of much of the novel's power. Like the three shipyard observers, the three family members are trapped inside their ignorance and preconceptions.

Call It Sleep thus posits the Derridean idea that individual belief is inevitably built on illusion and private memory, thereby leading to easy distortions of the practice of "love" and "community"—concepts based on the quite opposite values of sharing and reciprocity. This position recalls Derrida's point that the *true* nature of mimesis is "mimicry imitating nothing." For example, David cannot love his father because Albert acts as if he hates his son because he isn't sure if he *is* his son, an insecurity born of his own unacknowledged guilt about his role in his father's violent death. Unclear about her husband's private demons, Genya's distrust and misunderstanding of Albert stems from his chronic paranoia and fits of rage and from her fear that he might be insane after all. But because this is all presented from inside David's psyche, except for the opening frame, it is easy to accept the boy's distortions as definitive. Such a reading comprehends the novel as about the bad effects of neurotic parenting, about the sociopolitics of immigrant marginality, and/or about the artist as a boy. It is about those themes, of course, but what deepens and binds them in narrative coherence is Roth's dramatization of the chasms of *différance* inherent in language and discourse which mirror the chasms between people caused by interactions based on illusory, partial knowledge.

Children are perfect foils for expressing *différance* because of the natural gap between their innocence and their worldly experience and consciousness. David thinks and acts like a boy, as if the universe revolved around him. To him, the cellar holds exaggerated meaning because of his fear of the dark and his repulsion from the sexual games played there by the older boys. Similarly, in *cheder* his young mind magnifies the importance of the, to him, miraculous "page 68" of the Bible as the source of God. He also distorts his father's chronic frustration and anger into unrelieved hatred for him. But the reader knows that the boy is limited by his subjectivity and tunnel point of view, as were the three shipyard observers. The central effect of the novel is to produce a comparability of awakening consciousness between David's rite of passage and the reader's decoding of Roth's text, a process that ultimately, after the traumatic electrocution and its aftermath at the end, encourages recognition of the basic family bond hidden beneath (beyond?) David's understanding until the, very end when "A vague, remote pity stirred within his breast [for his father] like a wreathing, raveling smoke" (440). That *Call It Sleep* ends on a flicker of incipient family affection consequently *defers* the idea of community not to a literal referent *déhors de texte* but to a rereading of the narrative text itself. The novel thus captures the distance from, the margin between, the incipient feeling of community flickering in David's consciousness at the end and the hostile anticommunity that comprises his boyhood fears and insecurities until then.

Also foiling expectations of idealizations of ethnoracial community is Zora Neale Hurston's *Their Eyes Were Watching God* (1937) which, like *Call It Sleep*, has enjoyed a re(dis)covery since the 1970s. One reason the novel was earlier lost to an insignificant corner of twentieth-century American fiction was due to its dismissal by such important intellectuals as Richard Wright and Alain Locke who disparaged what they read as her overly "folklorized" treatment of African American experience. Alice Walker[14] and other feminists have since argued cogently that the negative criticism toward Hurston's writings derived as much from her feminism and *outré* personal lifestyle, which in the 1940s and 1950s were considered beyond the pale, as from anything she wrote. Accordingly, the recuperation of the novel and Hurston's entire body of writing constitutes an unignorable core of twentieth-century American fiction.

Presented as an extended flashback, *Their Eyes Were Watching God* embraces the rite of passage of Janie Mae Crawford (Killicks Starks Woods) from girlhood to adolescence, to womanhood, three marriages, widowhood, and finally to her self-reinvention through autobiography.

In portraying nearly four decades of Janie's life, Hurston also presents slices of black culture and experience in the Deep South taken from the writer's field study under the tutelage of anthropologist Franz Boas. Basing the novel on meticulous observations of her hometown, Eatonville, Florida, Hurston constructed the narrative as a black woman-identified (or, in Alice Walker's voice, "womanist") chronicle in which the dominating white order is diminished to an extraneous force not immediately visible in the lives of her characters. Because of this, Wright, Locke, and others have read the novel as unpolitical because of the absence of an explicitly black proletarian viewpoint. But it is actually boldly political in its feminism and also in its positioning of African Americans in the foreground of the text and not solely as marginalized victims of the dominant/dominating white order—a technique in many ways comparable to Henry Roth's inscription of immigrant Jewish ethnicity in *Call It Sleep*.

Also like Roth's novel, Hurston opens her narrative with a frame pre/text that introduces a complex (anti-)community of blacks that she textures and develops in the rest of the narrative. The frame comprises the first chapter and is told from three distinct narrative perspectives that feed into the frame story that occupies remaining chapters (two through twenty). The first perspective speaks the poetic voice of an omniscient narrator commenting with detached irony on "every man's wish" and the "mocked . . . life of men" (5). In three brief paragraphs of lyrical description moving like a wide-angle lens approach to a tight focus on Janie and her friend, Pheoby, the omniscient viewpoint shifts gradually into the second perspective, the limited point of view of the townfolk watching Janie return "home." Lined along the village street as evening darkens the scene, the townspeople watch her return to her old neighborhood with "judgment" in their eyes and the "envy they had stored up from other times" (10). This second viewpoint provides an outline of Janie's physical features and, through the shorthand of "the people's . . . burning statements" and their "killing tools" of "words walking without masters," a picture emerges of a prodigal daughter returning to the same unwelcome place that had made her leave in the first place. The third perspective evolves slowly from the townfolk's judgments into the welcoming comments of another townswoman, Janie's friend Pheoby Watson. The two women's animated conversation ultimately leads directly to the flashback that forms the bulk of the novel.

Like Roth's opening, Hurston's pre/text emphasizes alienation and societal disunity as a formative context for the protagonist's life. At first the townspeople's unfriendliness and Janie's aloofness hint at a haughtiness on her part that seems to justify their hostility. Pheoby's countering remarks, however, instantly provide a contrast of sentiment that legitimate Janie's conduct; "nobody don't know," she says, why Janie has returned or what happened to her while she was away, hence "judgment" is premature and invalid. Through Pheoby, at first just another minor character from Janie's past witnessing her return but who then becomes a major (if mostly silent) figure as Janie's confidante for the story—that is, the novel—she tells, the reader's own perspective shifts from that of passive observer to active participant.

In the flashback that forms Janie's self-story, Hurston does not present an idealized version of African American in-group communality, but, rather like Roth telling David Schearl's story, she presents a variegated portrayal of family love and neighborliness defined by conflict. Through vivid details of southern black-identified life and an evocative vernacular of several dialects of black speech, Janie's self-story emerges first as an abandoned child lovingly but strictly reared by her maternal grandmother then as a girl shaped into a woman by three marriages which end in one divorce, one widowhood, and finally her killing of Tea Cake Woods, her third "best" husband. The first person narrative, especially the plot twist of Tea Cake's violent death, requires the reader to weigh—simultaneously *with Pheoby*—the credibility of Janie's words and opinions, just like the judge and jury who acquit her for the self-defense killing of Tea Cake. By constructing a plot that completes its womanist theme through a necessary act of violence against a decent black man gone suddenly mad, Hurston insists on the integrity and authority of her feminist theme over and above sentimental notions of in-group "community." This was very bold in 1937, and it is still a fresh text largely because of this point of thematic author/ity.

As Mrs. Tea Cake Woods, Janie tells Pheoby, she discovered genuine love, despite Tea Cake's occasional bursts of temper and wife-battering. But the neurotic codependency of their intimacy did not permit her self-actualization, and her rite of passage to wholeness demands an ultimate act of independent *self*-preservation to complete Hurston's feminist theme.[15] Only with her very life threatened by Tea Cake's rabies-induced madness could she do what was needed to preserve her*self*, and only after the violent extreme of destroying her "onliest joy" could she return home again, finally whole. Her rite of passage thus moves logically from adolescence to autobiography, for

Cordelia
Chávez
Candelaria

it is the power and author/ity gained from sharing her life story with Pheoby that demonstrates her growth and evolved self-awareness.

Their Eyes Were Watching God stresses its textuality on every page, especially in the frame prologue with its three narrative styles and its focus on Janie and Pheoby, storyteller and listener positioned in mirror relationship to Hurston and the reader. Built around the tension and conflict Janie experiences within her community, the novel's plot is designed to advance the author's feminist theme and inside-out perspective on African American experience. As such, the narrative's meanings of "community" reside in its *différance*, in the problematics of "community" created in the story played off against a yearning *for* "community" *somewhere*, not in any implied or referential verisimilitude, but in the story itself which Janie relates. Accordingly, the bond between Pheoby and Janie also resides in its fictiveness, starting with the narrator/listener dyad that defines their relationship and which is emphasized by the artful, writerly womb symbols (bowl of food and pan of water) that emblematize both their femininity and their feminism. Hurston even deconstructs death in a writerly conceit at the end of the novel: "Tea Cake, with the sun for a shawl. Of course he wasn't dead. He could never be dead until she herself had finished feeling and thinking. The kiss of his memory made pictures . . . against the wall. . . . She pulled in her horizon like a great fish-net. Pulled it from around the waist of the world and draped it over her shoulder. So much of life in its meshes! She called in her soul to come and see" (286). Throughout, then, the symbols, the vernacular idioms alternating with the poetic language, the positioning of the women, the tidy symmetry of the plot, all constitutive elements forefront the novel's *différance*, the margin between the text and any referential context.

Similarly, Rudolfo Anaya's depiction of Mexican American (anti-) community in *Bless Me, Ultima* (1972) parallels Roth's and Hurston's fictionalization of the subject relative to their respective culture groups. He punctures facile idealizations of *familia* and *raza* solidarity to produce—in spite of his uncritical use of occasional gender stereotypes—a portrayal of Chicana/o[16] experience that, in Clifford Geertz's term, is "thick." The process begins in the first chapter, "Uno," which introduces the book's narrator, Antonio Marez, the boy who narrates an extended flashback (like Hurston's Janie and, implicitly, like Roth's David) about events that took place when he was seven and eight years old. The first chapter also establishes the theme of multiple conflict that Antonio must confront in his rite of passage into conscious-

Différance and Discourse

ness, the greater awareness and sophistication that are prerequisites for making his self-story flashback even possible.

The conflict ramifies from two broad subplots: the New Mexico village community's ambivalence toward Ultima, the old woman who comes to live with Antonio's family, and Antonio's struggle to mediate between the conflicting expectations of his parents. Although Ultima, a *curandera* or healer "knew the herbs and remedies of the ancients . . . [that] could heal the sick," her powers were often "misunderstood" by the locals and "suspected [to be] . . . witchcraft," that is, *brujería* (p. 4). Because of his loyalty to and respect for the old woman, Antonio is frequently caught in the crossfire, literal and figurative, of fear and hostility that she faces in the (anti-)community of Chicanos. The other major conflict of his boyhood concerns his parents' struggle to shape his life—his father's desire to mold him into a macho *vaquero* (horseman, cowboy) like the men of his adventurous, wild Márez clan versus his mother's desire that he become a priest in the more stable tradition of the Lunas, her clan of gentle, steady farmers. In the course of the narrative these conflicts spawn other antagonisms reflecting or producing gossip, anxiety, violence, and even murders that transform Antonio's boyhood years into traumatic crucibles from which (like the formative traumas of David Schearl and Janie Woods) he must forge an awakened consciousness. They also reveal a mean-spiritedness in the village that belies its surface pastorality and disclose hypocrisy within the Catholic church and among its followers that belies the apparent reverence of their faith.

But Anaya punctuates Antonio's narrative of conflict and anticommunity with rays of affirmation and the possibility of self-reinvention (cf. Janie's autobiography of self-realization) which can lead to discovery of personal authority. Importantly, these self-preserving options occur as emphatically autotelic reminders of the narrative's essential fictiveness, for they appear in the novel's highly stylized tropology of dream sequences and Indian/mestizo myths and legends. Dominated by the terrifying images and plot horrors characteristic of nightmares, the dream sequences "express Anaya's preoccupation with instinct and blood" as definitive markers of cultural/personal identity.[17] Anaya underscores their fictiveness by setting them off with prominent italics, by filling them with vivid often lurid oneiric imagery and tropes, by relating them in the language and style of complexly woven fairytales, and by linking them to the myths and legends Antonio learns from Ultima and, especially, from his friends Jasón and Cico. For example, the story of the golden carp—itself a stylized trope—helps the boy resolve his anxieties about God, faith, and religion, and along with his lessons about nature and healing from Ultima, contributes to his mediation of his parents' conflict over his future. The salient point for this essay, however, is that the novel's "social realism vanishes into the private realms of dream, fantasy, and primordial legend" (Candelaria 27), thereby defying referentiality and literalness to emphasize and exploit fictionality as a mechanism for personal reinvention.

As with the two previous titles, the reader discovers the essential narrativity of *Bless Me, Ultima*—that is, its plot, character, symbol, and narrative structure—in the tensions of *différance* resonating from Anaya's portrayal of conflicted community, or what I have been labeling "anticommunity." The narrativity of the novel as a fictive text arises largely from the dialectics of the story's anticommunity played off against the idealized Chicana/o mythos of *familia* and cultural solidarity that grew out of the ethnic nationalism of the 1960s' Chicano Renaissance. This dialectical tension amalgamates the *raza* pastoral of marginalized cultural wholeness with the irony of in-group anticommunity compounded by dominant white social privilege (read: the Church). The tension captures the psychological and epistemological web of effects which dichotomize Antonio's Márez v. Luna, Catholic v. pagan, boy-subject v. writer-observer identity. Like David in *Call It Sleep* and Janie in *Their Eyes Were Watching God*, Antonio's position in his ethnic-identified community is tangled by conflicted meanings of blood, family, tribe, ego, and power generating the multicultural discourse that shapes him.

Hence, none of the three protagonists are ever completely "insiders" within their respective communities, and as a result their narratives gain much of their energy and efficacy *as stories* from their articulation of yearning for the absent "insider" *What* of "community." The difference and distance from one single determinable referent and the continually contingent deferral of meaning for that *What*—in sum, their *différance* in articulating "community"—creates the excitement of fiction in these books and joins them to the intertextual conversation regarding ethnicity, race, and identity that stretches to Williams, Cooper, Ritch, Jackson, Twain, and others into the present century.

Notes

1 See Nancy Chodorow, *The Reproduction of Mothering*, and D. W. Winnicutt, "The Theory of the Parent-Infant Relationship," for summaries of psychoanalytic literature about the infant-mother dyad.

2 Jacques Derrida, "Différance" (1978), *Margins of Philosophy* (Chicago: U of Chicago P, 1982).

3 The affection and family relations portrayed among whites in the novel are all problematized by harsh undermining elements, especially hypocrisy.

4 See Daniel G. Hoffman, "The American Hero: His Masquerade" in Kartiganer and Griffith's *Theories of American Literature* (New York: Macmillan, 1972), 196–232; Henry Louis Gates, Jr., and William Boelhower, *Through a Glass Darkly: Ethnic Semiosis in American Literature* (Venezia, Italy: Helvetia, 1984), and Richard Ruland and Malcolm Bradbury, *From Puritanism to Postmodernism: A History of American Literature* (New York: Viking, 1991), 198–201.

5 James Fenimore Cooper, "Preface to the Leather-Stocking Tales," Anthology of American Literature, ed. George McMichael et al. (New York: Macmillan, 1980).

6 Ramón Gutiérrez, "Aztlan, Montezuma, and New Mexico: The Political Uses of American Indian Mythology," *Aztlan: Essays on the Chicano Homeland*, ed. Rudolfo Anaya and Francisco Lomelí (Albuquerque: Academia, 1989), 172–232.

7 For example, Hart Crane, Bret Harte, Jack Kerouac, Denise Levertov, Hanial Long, Frank Norris, Katherine Anne Porter, Wallace Stevens, and others.

8 Michael Wood, "Deconstructing Derrida," *New York Review of Books* 24.3 (March 3, 1977), 27–30.

9 Edward Said, "The Problem with Textuality: Two Exemplary Positions," *Critical Inquiry* 4.4 (Summer 1978), 673–714.

10 Henry Roth, *Call It Sleep* (1934; New York: Avon, 1964).

11 Zora Neale Hurston, *Their Eyes Were Watching God* (1937; Urbana: U of Illinois P, 1978).

12 Rudolfo Anaya, *Bless Me, Ultima* (Berkeley: Tonatiuh, 1972).

13 I think "coincidentally" but perhaps not, since one of the original attractions for me of discussing these three novels together was their similar construction of threshold scenes of conflicted anticommunity.

14 Alice Walker, *In Search of Our Mothers' Gardens: Womanist Prose* (New York: Harcourt, 1983).

15 Patricia Burke cogently argues this point in her "Jungian Journey of Self-Affirmation in *Their Eyes Were Watching God*," *Multiethnic Literature of the United States: Critical Introductions and Classroom Resources*, ed. Cordelia Candelaria (Boulder: U Colorado, 1989), 95–115.

16 "Chicana/o" is a gender inclusive conflation of "Chicana" and "Chicano" to refer to politically conscientized Mexican Americans.

17 Cordelia Candelaria, "Rudolfo A. Anaya," *Dictionary of Literary Biography*, vol. 82 (Detroit: Bruccoli Clark, 1989), 27.

Dialogism

and

Schizophrenia

_____

Tzvetan Todorov

*Translated
by Michael B.
Smith*

Τhe rather pedantic term, *dialogism*, designates the duplicity of voices that can be heard through every utterance, the plurality of discourses characteristic of all speaking subjects. Its presence in my title is also a way of paying respects to the man who introduced the word and has done so much to shed light on the phenomenon it designates: the Russian thinker Mikhail Bakhtin. The questions I would like to raise here concern, not the structure of dialogism, but the system of values one never fails to attach to it— the assessment made of it.

In the not very remote past, everything taken to resemble what we now call dialogism was considered a defect. Need I recall Gobineau's invectives against mixed races or those of Barrès against the uprooted? Rather as a curiosity I will quote the following more recent phrase by Malraux, which is, moreover, based on another authority: "Colonel Lawrence used to say, on the basis of his experience, that every man truly belonging to two cultures . . . lost his soul." If I do not spend any more time on such affirmations, it is not because they are no longer made, nor because the positions from which they set out are not power-ful, but because I share no common ground with them. I cannot engage them in dialogue. If I were to concern myself with them, I would end up exposing them, pointing them out with an accusing finger, cloth-ing myself in indignation or satire. But there is another reason for this refusal, more pertinent here. These attitudes, despite their presence or even their frequency, today appear to me to belong historically to the past. They are in keeping with the great patriotic movement of the bourgeois states—a movement certainly not over, but whose end is in sight, if only on the ideological plane. Who, in our day and age, would not prefer to side with dialogue, cultural pluralism, and toler-ance for other voices? On this score, governmental declarations and the demands of the artistic avant-garde are in agreement.

The reason I bring up this latter group is because there is a kind of euphoric proliferation in the groups that are self-proclaimed avant-gardes, in France at least; and there has been a plethora of works, these last years, that speak of the beauty of *mestizaje*, eulogize cosmopoli-tanism or voice the polylogue's passion. There is a propensity to define "écriture" as a crossing of borders, a migration, an exile. And I read, in the works of one of the epigones of this trend, an invitation to writers to "strike out into the unbounded polyphony in which all languages are foreign, and distinct languages do not exist" (Scarpetta 183).[1] It is pre-cisely that new *doxa* of widespread polyphony, that universal mixing of languages, that unconditional endorsement of mixing that I would like to take as my starting point: not in order to favor its opposite and praise Gobineau or Barrès, but rather to question the significance and accuracy of these affirmations, while abstaining, admittedly, from a discussion of literature.

The first case I would like to bring up in this context is a passive form of dissidence, typical of the majority of the inhabitants of totali-tarian countries. This was my situation, but now more than eighteen years have passed. Hence the tone I adopt in speaking about it is rather impersonal, since it is no longer possible for me to resume that pos-ture today. My memory has generalized my own case, mixing it with the cases of people close to me and with images drawn from reading as well. The situation is one of having two alternative discourses: one public, the other private. Public discourse is that same one used by television, radio, and the press. It is the one heard at political meetings and the one to use in all official situations. Private discourse is used at home, among friends, or for every area ideology does not enter, such as sports or fishing. The two discourses, which are characterized by a call for totality similar to that by the two languages of a bilingual, differ in vocabulary, partially in syntax, but especially in the way they are used. Private discourse is governed by the requirement that may be called the truth of correspondence: statements must describe the world or designate the position of the speaking subject in the most precise manner possible. Public discourse, by contrast, is governed by the quest for the truth of conformity: in order to be assessed, an utterance is not compared with an empirical experience but with other discourses, given in advance and known to all, with an opinion that is right about everything.

In order to describe this situation more accurately, I would like to compare it to several similar ones. Let us call the first of these, borrowing a term from George Orwell, "doublethink." Orwell, in his novel *1984*, has us imagine that the Party has introduced a technique for mind manipulation called doublethink. For tactical reasons inherent in its form of dictatorship, the Party often announces contradictory affirmations, while at the same time declaring them to be totally consistent. How can these two linguistic acts be reconciled? That is precisely where the doublethink technique comes into play. The following is one of Orwell's descriptions: "To know and not to know, to be conscious of complete truthfulness while telling carefully constructed lies, to hold simultaneously two opinions which canceled out, knowing them to be contradictory and believing both of them, to use logic against logic, to repudiate morality while laying claim to it" (32). That is remarkably reminiscent of this other description, by Bertold Brecht, who is, however, the champion rather than the adversary of a totalitarian system. "He who fights for communism / must know how to fight and how not to fight / how to tell truth and how not to tell the truth / how to serve and not serve / how to keep his promises and not to keep them / how to face danger and flee it / how to make himself recognized and how remain invisible." In a word, this "technique" allows you to dispense with the law of noncontradiction, to pretend there is coherence where incoherence reigns. Faced with these two irreconcilable givens—contradictory utterances on the one hand and the requirement of noncontradiction on the other—the Party chooses to override the latter, not by accepting contradiction, but by conditioning reason not to notice it when the Party Line is concerned.

Another comparison that comes readily to mind is the comparison with dissidence—but active, not passive dissidence in this case. Confronted with two irreconcilable givens—the incoherence of the world and the coherence of thought—the Party chooses to act against the latter. The dissidents, on the other hand, have chosen the opposite. They maintain the integrity of thought and cry out against the contradictions of the world in which they live. These considerations bring us quite close to an eventual situation described by Bakhtin himself (or by his collaborator and friend V. N. Voloshinov). In a study entitled "The Structure of the Utterance," published in 1930 (Bakhtin and Voloshinov both claimed to be orthodox Marxists at the time), they study "the dialogical character of internal discourse." After having recognized this characteristic, they hypothesize a kind of pathological variant of it, in which the internal voices, instead of corresponding to precise and stable ideological options, are prompted only by contingent relations with the circumstances of the moment (by the truth of correspondence?). "In especially unfavorable social conditions, such a cleavage between the person and the ideological environment that provides its nourishment can ultimately lead to the complete disintegration of consciousness, to disorder or insanity" (Todorov 70).[2]

"Unbounded polyphony," therefore, according to the account just given, leads to schizophrenia, taken in its commonly understood sense of split personality, mental incoherence, and attendant distress. Doublethink is also a kind of madness, since it implies a decision to accept incoherence or even contradictions. It is like a vaccine the Party wants to use to inoculate everyone.

In order that incoherence of thought might harmonize with the incoherence of the world, we would thus be immunized. But madness is defined quite differently in the two camps. Whereas Orwell and the dissidents define madness (which they see at work in Party politics) by means of an internal and qualitative criterion (namely, the acceptance of contradiction), the party identifies the dissidents' insanity (since it locks them up in psychiatric hospitals) by means of an external and purely quantitative criterion: they don't think the way everyone should, so they must be crazy. To be against the system is to be against the norm, to be abnormal.

The doublethink imposed by the Party requires that there only be one type of discourse throughout the subject's life, a discourse which accepts contradiction as its modus operandi. Active dissidents, for their part, also practice one type of discourse under all circumstances. They speak out against the contradictions and incoherence of the outer world, but respect the law of noncontradiction. Passive dissidence, by contrast has two sorts of discourse, usually in contradiction with each other, but each in perfect coherence with the context in which it is used. The first form of discourse knows only the truth of conformity;

the second, only the truth of correspondence. Only this discourse of passive dissidence practices both alternatively.

What I have just described is an idealized situation. In real life, things are far more complex, even though the overall structure may remain recognizable. I have posited, as clear and distinct entities, the Party on one side and the (active or passive) dissident on the other. These oppositions are easily maintained on a discursive plane, but they become far more problematic the moment real people are involved. The Party member, too, of course, has a public and a private mode of discourse, as do the functionaries of the Party (whose members Orwell refers to as "the Inner Party"). What varies is the threshold of separation between the two types of discourse. The border between public and private also fluctuates: there is a huge difference between the speech uttered in the galleries of congress and that exchanged between colleagues at their place of work, both public situations nonetheless. At one moment, public discourse may be established to interpret films, books, or historical facts, while at another, it may extend to the area of personal relations: there is one and only one way to conform to the norm in love or friendship! The truth of correspondence, which is deemed essential to private discourse, is often nothing but the truth of an other conformism, anterior and exterior to the current one. Totalitarianism, as it can be observed today, is never really total. While we witness its general, overall presence, we notice at the same time its countless inconsistencies, its "imperfections," so to speak.

During a meeting between two people it is exceptional for a homogeneous discourse to spring up on both sides or, conversely, for two entirely different discourses to confront one another. There is really always one discursive hierarchy articulating another similar, but not identical, discursive hierarchy. The remarkable thing is that the shift from one discourse to another, the choice of verbal register, is perfectly mastered by everyone and anyone, without it having been learned at school or having even been named. This leads us to suppose that beyond the enunciative precincts of each particular discourse, public or private, there is yet another, higher regulative agency, which determines the right mixture of public and private for any given utterance.

This functional distribution, which is characteristic of passive dissidence, and a sane response to a schizophrenic situation, can fail. What threatens it is clearly the blurring of carefully drawn lines between discursive levels, the breakdown of the discursive hierarchy. If the regulating agency fails to identify the public and the private correctly, all is lost. The subject falls into a form of insanity that is not cultural but personal, which may be less interesting from a historical point of view but far more painful to live through. No longer able to stand the tension caused by the constant need to switch over from one hookup to another, he ends up letting go, at which point public discourse invades private consciousness, producing an immediate collapse, a permanent contamination. In a world based on the ideal of unity, maintaining duality is risky: abandoning it, especially since this is the result of caving in under pressure rather than premeditated acceptance, denies the subject access to even minimal coherence. This is perhaps where the subject of totalitarian countries can be distinguished from his equivalent in other countries. It is not that the latter is unaware of the division brought about within his discourse by the split between truth of correspondence and truth of conformity, but in his case the penalty for breaking the rules, for impulsive obliteration of the boundaries, is less harsh.

Now I move on to the second case of dialogical practice: my present experience. My making myself into an example may call for a few words of explanation. Born in Bulgaria, I have lived in France since 1963. In May 1981, exactly eighteen years after I left, I went back to my native country for the first time, for a ten-day Bulgarian Studies conference. For the sake of completeness, I will add that during this time I stayed with my parents in the same house I used to live in.

The experience I am describing is that of an exile, returning to his country after a lengthy absence. (Let me also point out that I was a "circumstantial" exile, neither a political nor an economic exile.) Through a series of chance occurrences, my experience was brought to a kind of climax which induced me to analyze it. Some people go down into the depths of caves to observe how organisms react in extraordinary circumstances; this helps them better understand normal functioning. Similarly, during those ten days in May, I was the subject of an unusual experiment: not a descent of eighteen hundred meters underground, but a return to a place I had left eighteen years earlier. The extraordinary circumstances in this case are: the length of the absence, the completeness of the break for those eighteen years,[3] and my reentry, during those ten days, into precisely the same material conditions I had been in eighteen years earlier. That is why now, without taking any particular interest in my own biography, I feel more or less obliged to tabulate my impressions.

An exile, back in his native country, is not at all like a visiting foreigner nor even like the foreigner he himself once was at the beginning of his exile. When I arrived in France in 1963, I knew virtually noth-

Tzvetan
Todorov

ing about that country. I was an outsider, within French society, with which I only became familiar over time. There was never a sudden transformation in my relationship with that society, but a gradual transition from the position of *outsider* to that of *insider* (the *out* and the *in* always being, of course, relative terms); and then one day I realized I was no longer an outsider, not at least in the same sense as before. Over the years, my second language had replaced my first language without a violent jolt. Now the experience of the returning exile is quite the opposite. He discovers suddenly, overnight, that he has an insider's view of two different cultures, two different societies. I need only return to Sofia for everything to become immediately familiar to me; I can bypass the preliminary adaptation process. I am just as fluent in Bulgarian as I am in French, and I feel a part of both cultures.

These, one might think, are the ideal conditions for internal dialogue to flourish, for reaping the benefits of bilingualism, since in my case the subject had overcome all the hurdles of misunderstanding and enjoyed the advantages of a clearly expanded verbal universe. As Bakhtin wished (in other passages than the one quoted above) and as today's advocates for unbounded polyphony claim, neither discourse, neither language truly contains the other by subjugation. I should have been living in the euphoria of disharmony. We like to say, a bit hyperbolically: "I feel French with the French. American among Americans, Moroccan when I'm with Moroccans." And we take a certain pride in being able, in this way, to show different facets of the same personality, our ability to understand others and to identify with them. Yet in my case the hyperbole came true: I could be French with the French and Bulgarian with the Bulgarians. Each of my two personalities could manifest itself in one of my two languages.

Though I may hesitate on the correct interpretation of certain aspects of my experience during this homecoming, one thing is beyond doubt: the experience was one of malaise and psychological oppression. It is that malaise, that difficulty of being, that I would like, rather than explain, to describe here. I hasten to add, to avoid a likely misunderstanding, that the source of the uneasiness I am speaking of does not seem to me to be political, in the strict sense of the word, that is, connected with the different political structures of France and Bulgaria. I do not mean to discuss a problem of censorship here. I had a premonition of this malaise even before leaving for Sofia, as I was preparing my remarks for the conference to which I had been invited. Since the theme of the convention was "Bulgaria," I was confronted with the question of the value of nationalism. My position (obviously

Dialogism and
Schizophrenia

I am simplifying) was that the autochthon was always blind to his own identity; the history of a people was never anything but the sum of external influence it had undergone; in any case it was better to live the present rather than try to resuscitate the past. In short, it was not a good idea to shut oneself up within traditional national values. I wrote that unhesitatingly. The problems arose when I began translating my talk, originally written in my acquired language, French, into Bulgarian, my native tongue. It wasn't so much a question of vocabulary or syntax, but in changing languages I noticed that I had changed my imagined audience. And at that moment I realized that the Bulgarian intellectuals to whom my discourse was addressed could not understand the meaning I intended. The condemnation of attachment to national values changes significance according to whether you live in a small country (your own) placed within the sphere of influence of a larger one or whether you live abroad, in a different country, where you are (or think you are) sheltered from any threat by a more powerful neighbor. Paris is certainly a place that favors the euphoric renunciation of nationalist values: Sofia much less so.

To a lesser degree, this problem is a familiar one to all speakers and writers: one's discourse must be modified as a function of the intended audience or readership. But in this case, the modification my projected listeners seemed to be suggesting to me was more than that. It required that I change an affirmation into its direct opposite. I understood the position of the Bulgarian intellectuals, and had I been in their situation, mine probably would have been the same. But I was not in their situation. I lived in Paris, not Sofia, and thought quite differently. Only how could I tell this to them? Should I have acted as though I had only my present, French personality, expressing my opinion without taking into account what I knew of their eventual reaction? But that would have amounted to denying my inner access to Bulgarian culture. Should I have spoken as if I had never left Sofia? That would have been like pretending the last eighteen years of my life had never taken place. Should I have tried to combine the two positions, thus seeking a neutral path? Combining "A" and "not A" has its costs. The only other option was silence.

The same malaise would come over me in another form during conversations I had with friends in Sofia. One of them might be complaining about living conditions. When that happens in Paris, I can offer all sorts of suggestions to my interlocutor. My suggestions may be more or less convincing, but in any case they arise from a background of shared experience. Therefore he, or she, is willing to listen. In Sofia it was different. If I tried to "put myself in the shoes" of my interlocutor, and therefore in those of my Bulgarian personality as well, I found myself making particularly "Bulgarian" suggestions. But I felt that I was being listened to with skepticism. It was as if I could hear his skeptical silence (or sometimes his skeptical voice) speaking to me, saying: "If things are really that simple, why don't you stay here yourself, and try out your own remedy?" I couldn't very well stand there and say to the person in that situation: "Oh, well, so much for your problems. I'll be on a plane for Paris on Monday." That was in fact the case, and I suddenly felt like saying so, whether because I couldn't find a solution to his problem or to get away from that skeptical smile. But no, I could not say that, not only because it is impolite, but also because in doing so I would have put myself exclusively in the position of my French personality, the one only passing through Sofia. Could I perhaps blend the two perspectives? Though I am French and Bulgarian at the same time, I can only be in Paris or Sofia at any given moment. Ubiquity is not yet within my reach. The tenor of my remarks is too dependent upon their place of utterance for my whereabouts to be irrelevant. My twin affiliation produces but one effect: in my own eyes it renders inauthentic each of my two modes of discourse, since each can correspond to but half my being. I am indeed double. And so it is that once again I am locked in an oppressive silence.

In the course of other conversations I notice that, in answering questions about life in France, I can only speak comfortably about aspects that are similar to life in Bulgaria or about negative aspects. (These two categories overlap to a great extent: bureaucracy, elitist mentality, nepotism.) Yet I seem to choke on any of the traits I could boast of, any of the positive elements. This is because in the former case I am speaking from a position equally accessible to my French and my Bulgarian personality, whereas in the latter it is the Frenchman alone who speaks in me. But being Bulgarian also, I put myself in the place of my interlocutors and suffer the limitations thus imposed. Again, the double parole proves impossible, and I find myself split into two halves, one as unreal as the other.

Old friends I met, undoubtedly desiring to please me, but perhaps also sincerely, would tell me, "You haven't changed one bit! You're exactly the same as you were!" But hearing that did not please me. It was a way of denying the existence of those last eighteen years, pretending they never took place, and that I had not acquired a second personality. My mother gave me a pair of my shoes that she has kept in a drawer, so I could work in the garden. I put them on. No doubt about it, they were mine, worn just the way all of mine are. They fit perfectly. I was recognized, accepted. We'd take up conversations broken off eighteen years earlier. Everything conspired to make me believe those years simply did not exist, that they were a dream, a fantasy, from which I was now being wakened. I felt as if any minute I'd be offered a job, I'd settle in, perhaps get married. . . . On the contrary, what I would like is for people not to recognize me, for them to be amazed at the changes that have taken place. I felt positively relieved talking on the phone to the French cultural adviser: I could speak French: I was not dreaming! The gentleman even knows my name; he knew I was coming. So my French existence was not a fantasy! And although the subject of the conversation was rather mundane (how to get more French books sent to Bulgarian libraries without increasing the budget), I felt the warmth of the implied complicity of our conversation. My existence had been confirmed. If I lose my place of utterance, I can no longer speak. I speak not, therefore I am not.

Space (my "elsewhere") was threatened with banishment. As for time, it had never seemed so long to me before. Those ten days lasted almost eighteen years. With every passing evening, I felt as if I had aged by several years. For every conversation, every meeting made me imagine the years I might have experienced in Bulgaria, or rather made me actually remember what I had experienced those years I had not known, instead of the ones I did know in Paris. For I did not learn history the way a foreigner would, or a distant family relative, to whom everything must be told because he comes from outside. No, I learned it from within, by all the things that go without saying, by allusions, by imagination. That ability I had to reimmerse myself immediately, totally, in the Bulgaria I had left behind, cast as unreal before my own eyes my experience of the recent past and my French identity. It was impossible to create a whole being out of those two halves: it was one or the other.

The dominant impression, then, was of incompatibility. My two languages, my two kinds of discourse were, from a certain point of view, too close. Either was capable of mediating the totality of my experience, and neither was clearly subordinate to the other. Here, one presided, there, the other took over. But neither ruled unconditionally. They were too much alike, and therefore could do nothing but take the other's place: they could not be combined. Thus the insistence of the impression that one of those lives must be a dream. When I am in Sofia, it is life in France that seems like a dream, and I experience the same impossibility of going back one feels upon awakening from a dream. And I often catch myself thinking, when I meet a new person in Sofia, "another ghost" or "I am a ghost," which comes to the same thing. That reminds me of a story by Henry James, "The Jolly Corner," in which the main character, returning to his homeland thirty-three years later, sees real ghosts. . . . Back in Paris, it is precisely when I first wake up that I am the most disturbed. I don't know which world I have to enter. My mother writes me now: "Today I wonder whether you were really here, or if it wasn't all a dream." Yes, a dream or madness, perhaps because I really only pretend to live here or there? A dream or madness: Are these not simply ways of reacting to the schizophrenic situation itself? As in the case of passive dissidence, mental incoherence is perfectly coherent with the incoherence of the world.

Each of my two languages was an entirety, and that is precisely what made them uncombinable, incapable of forming a new totality. Before that visit my knowledge of Bulgarian had not in the least made life in France impossible for me. The use of my mother tongue was strictly confined within functional limits. A few words at the end of a conversation with the several Bulgarians I know in Paris; correspondence with my parents; reading of an occasional book; the multiplication table and curse words: those are about the only circumstances in which I cling to Bulgarian in France. I can also very easily imagine the reverse situation: living in Bulgaria, I become a translator from French or speak to foreign visitors or become a specialist in French history. But of course that is not what I actually did during my ten-day visit. During that time, I did not give up any of my French personality, and I acquired, or reintegrated, a Bulgarian personality that was every bit as total. It was too much for a sole being like me! One of the two lives would have to oust the other entirely. To avoid that feeling in Sofia, I sought refuge whenever possible in physical labor, beyond the reach of social contact. I cut grass in the garden, trimmed trees, moved earth, somewhat as we do when, ill at ease in unaccustomed circumstances, we are quick to volunteer to peel the potatoes or accept an invitation to a game of table tennis, happy at least to recover an integrity of the body.

The equality of voices makes me feel the breath of insanity. Their asymmetry, their hierarchy, on the other hand, is reassuring. And I distinctly feel that just as my bilingualism, or my dialogism, helps constitute my present personality, so does a certain hierarchy (but not just any one). A publishing company in Sofia asked me to write the preface to an anthology of French literary criticism. I hesitate to accept, I beat around the bush, although in France I am quite accustomed to the role of preface-writer. The problem is, the hierarchy with which I am familiar would be turned upside down. I know how to integrate the Bulgarian voice (or another) into the French setting, not the reverse. My present identity is located in Paris, not Sofia.

I have reached the end of my remarks, though not a conclusion. In the first case I considered passive dissidence, the two discourses could not function harmoniously unless each was held in place within a strict hierarchy. In the second case I examined, involving a return to one's native country, the two discourses, which were also two languages, drove me toward madness as long as I was unable to assign distinct functions to each of them. Thus it should be clear why, while refusing to endorse the notion that one who belongs to two cultures loses his soul, I doubt that having two voices, two languages, is a privilege guaranteeing access to modernity. I wonder whether a bilingualism based on the neutrality and perfect reversibility of the two languages is not a false hope, or at least an exception. Perhaps the liberating effect of such bilingualism implies not only a psychic commonalty of the speaking subject in both instances, but also an articulation, a clear angle of separation between them, a strict division of tasks—a hierarchy, in short. I believe I saw silence and insanity looming on the horizon of boundless polyphony, and I found them oppressive, which is doubtless why I prefer the bounds of dialogue.

214

Tzvetan
Todorov

Notes

1. *Eloge du cosmopolitisme* (Paris: Garsset, 1981).
2. *Mikail Bakhtin: The Dialogical Prinicple* (Minneapolis: U of Minnesota P, 1984).
3. There is no Bulgarian community in Paris, or else I never found out about it, having little interest in doing so; news travels poorly between Sofia and Paris, due to the "iron curtain." There is, in fact, less connection between Paris and Sofia than between Paris and Rabat, for example.

Bilingualism

& Dialogism:

Another

Reading of

Lorna Dee

Cervantes's

Poetry

Ada Savin

T he "consistent fineness" of Lorna Dee Cervantes's poetry has aroused a wide response among literary critics.[1] Thus Marta Sánchez considers the opposition between the militant Chicana and the lyrical poet to be the major paradigm underlying the poems' inner tension, a view which fails to account for the diverse intersecting voices in Cervantes's poetry. And Cordelia Candelaria's otherwise insightful analysis of the *Emplumada* poems similarly falls short of providing a cohesive analysis of the manifold threads that are interwoven into the author's poetic persona.

This essay will attempt to provide a different angle of approach to bilingual or interlingual (Chicano) poetry drawing on Mikhail Bakhtin's dialogic interpretation of language and literature. An examination of Cervantes's work within this theoretical framework will hopefully throw a more encompassing light on her poetry. By the same token it could open up the whole field of bi- or interlingual (Chicano) literature, to a wider ranging Bakhtin-oriented approach.

As is generally known Bakthin considered dialogism in literature to be essentially the domain of prose, and more specifically of the novel. Thus in "Discourse in the Novel" he juxtaposes poetry to prose, arguing that the former "chooses not to look beyond the boundaries of its own language" (*Dialogic Imagination* 399); hence "the possibility of another vocabulary, another semantics . . . of other linguistic points of view is . . . foreign to poetic style" (285).[2] Bakhtin thus concludes that poetic style "is fully adequate to a single language and a single linguistic consciousness" (286). I would argue that the very material, content, and form of bilingual poetry in general, and of Chicano poetry in particular, run counter to Bakhtin's statements.

In "From the Prehistory of Novelistic Discourse" the Russian theorist argued that polyglossia and the parodic literary forms were instrumental in destroying "impermeable monoglossia" and in establishing a distance between language and reality. "In place of a single, unitary sealed-off Ptolemaic world of language, there appeared the open Galilean world of many languages, mutually animating each other" (65).

No doubt, this process found its most fertile soil in the modern novel. However, it also allowed for a considerable expansion of the poetic language. In his *Songs and Sonnets*, John Donne encompassed a surprising variety of discourses (trade, law, astronomy), albeit submitting them all to a unitary self. And it is no accident that it was T. S. Eliot who revived our interest in Donne's poetry. Eliot himself is representative of our century's social, political, and cultural upheavals of which the bi- or multilingual writer is an eloquent literary symbol. As George Steiner has pointed out, the bilingual tradition in a larger sense goes back to the use of Latin and French (besides one's native language) by the European elite until the late eighteenth century.[3] Literary productions frequently made use of these languages or were pregnant with learned references to one of the "high" languages (in a way T. S. Eliot's bookish bilingualism continues this tradition).

The advent of nationalism in the nineteenth century brought a shift in the attitude toward language, which came to be seen as the embodiment of a nation's *Geist*, history, and specific worldview. The writer, as special master of the language, thus embodied the genius of his native idiom. A so-called symbiotic relationship linked the two. "For the writer to become bi- or multilingual in the modern way, genuine shifts of sensibility and personal status had to occur" (Steiner 4). Whether voluntary or forced "commuters" in the world, some of the most prominent twentieth century writers are "poets unhoused and wanderers across languages" (Steiner 11).

Beckett or Nabokov, Pound or Celan have distanced themselves from their own language and at times adopted another idiom, thereby disassociating poetic authority from the use of a single tongue. To return to Bakhtin, one can no longer talk in the case of Celan or Nabokov about a "single linguistic consciousness." Their work achieves a certain quality of transparency: no matter which language they write in, the "other" language shines through producing, as it were, an effect of refraction. That "incomplete commitment of oneself, of one's full meaning, to a given language," which Bakhtin claimed for the novelist only, is clearly manifest in the poetic style of Celan. With him bilingualism is no longer a bookish, referential means of including other languages and cultures into the literary work; it has become the very expression of a divided self's mode of existence.

But what about poets living under the sociopolitical and cultural circumstances of an active polyglossia? Their multilingualism is necessarily of the existential kind; their poetry acts out the living contact between the cultures in contact and their respective languages. As Tino Villanueva has pointed out, bilingual Chicano texts are to be viewed in the universal tradition of the multilingual literature of medieval Spain, Norman England, or the recently discovered New World. "What is reflected in these poets' work is their individual and historical continuity in two cultures" (*Imagine* xxxvi).[4] Bilingual Chicano literature then is a literary expression of the upheaval in the collective status of a whole community. It enacts on the poetic level the past and ongoing conflict between an internally colonized population and the dominant society. Power relationships are at work and language, given its pragmatic and symbolic power, becomes an essential battle horse. The alternate use of Spanish and English in Chicano literature is indicative of a process of identity search through a dialogization of the two cultures. On the other hand, the specific use of each language consistently undermines the official authoritative discourse, whether mainstream American or Mexican. Indeed, according to Bakhtin, speech diversity achieves its full creative consciousness under conditions of an active polyglossia: "Two myths perish simultaneously: the myth of a language that presumes to be the only language, and the myth of a language that presumes to be completely unified" (68).

Indeed from a Bakhtinian point of view, bilingualism in literature could be considered as a particular, extreme case of dialogism. Thus Bakhtinian analysis of the Chicano novel would focus on the double-voiced bilingual discourse, pointing out its peculiar functions. It is bilingual Chicano poetry which appears more intriguing in the Bakhtinian perspective, as it raises certain questions left unanswered by the Russian theorist: What happens to the unitary poetic self in the bilingual poem? Can we still talk about a "unitary, monologically sealed-off" language? About a single linguistic consciousness?

In the following pages I will discuss these issues by addressing some of Cervantes's poems. Insofar as Tzvetan Todorov's reflections on bilingualism and identity in his essay "Dialogism and Schizophrenia"[5] bear on his personal experience of a return to the homeland, they can serve to illuminate similar concerns in Cervantes's poetry. While Todorov, after an unsettling experience in his country of origin, seems to have found the key to a balanced bilingual self in a clear articulation between his two linguistic and cultural identities, Cervantes has a more difficult task to face in that she is confronted day after day with an ambivalent reality which throws her identity into permanent question. The historico-political context is burdensome, the cultural conflict is painfully alive. In her case then, it is impossible to keep the two identities clearly apart; hence, like other Chicano poets, she attempts to mix elements of both cultures in a move toward a hybrid, border identity.

Emplumada, Lorna Dee Cervantes's first collection of poems, remains, nine years after its publication, an eloquent literary expression of the Chicanos' paradigmatic quest for self-definition.[6] In Cervantes's poetry this existential search is manifest in a pendulumlike movement in which time and space, languages and cultures are continually refracted. Thus in "Oaxaca, 1974" the painful, buried memory of the past surfaces, significantly, in two languages. "Es la culpa de los antepasados. Blame it on the old ones." Though Cervantes writes mainly in English, two distinct voices are heard throughout her "identity" poems. In "Refugee Ship" and its Spanish counterpart, "Barco De Refugiados," the existential quandary is made explicit: the feeling is one of overwhelming estrangement from one's essential identity markers: name, physical appearance, and language.

> Mama raised me without language.
> I'm orphaned from my Spanish name
> The words are foreign, stumbling
> on my tongue. I see in the mirror
> my reflection: bronzed skin, black
> hair.

Cervantes, the poet, is bound to tame the English language, to "steal/obedient words obligatory words" ("Visions of Mexico") from an a priori foreign language, in which she is paradoxically more eloquent. The very fact of incorporating this issue within her poems demonstrates her relative distance from each of the two languages. Thus, her use of English and Spanish contradicts Bakhtin's definition of the poetic idiom, which "must be a directly intentional language, unitary and singular" (287). The world of Cervantes's poetry is not "illumined by one unitary and indisputable discourse" (286). It is rather inter-illuminated by two linguistic consciousnesses at work. Her poetic discourse is fragmented, divided, lying somewhere in the interspace between two cultures. The text itself becomes a form of cultural interaction while the poet's consciousness is the battleground (to use a militarized term, à la Bakhtin) of conflicting cultural forces which are constantly dialogized.

Several oppositions, appearing implicitly or explicitly in Cervantes's poems illustrate the scope of her dialogizing effort:

Spanish—English
South—North
Past—Present
Ancient—Modern
Sensitive—Sensible
Fertile—Sterile
Oral—Literate
Mythology—Science

The imaginary back-and-forth movement between two traditions becomes a dialogue—whether internal and temporal (between past and present, her ancestors and her present self) or external and spatial (between North and South, the United States and Mexico). The other oppositions mentioned above locate themselves within this paradigm.

In "Visions of Mexico While at a Writing Symposium in Port Townsend, Washington," the oral-literate dyad most strikingly defines the Chicano poet's ambivalent position. Coming "from a long line of eloquent illiterates / whose history reveals what words don't say," Cervantes needs her "tower of words" to fulfill her task as a scribe, a mediator between North and South. Likewise, in "Poema para los Californios Muertos," she is the depository of her ancestors' past history on the "raped tierra" and an estranged witness to the present reality.

These older towns die
into stretches of freeway.
The high scaffolding cuts a clean

cesarean
across belly valleys and fertile dust.
What a bastard child,
this city
lost in the soft
llorando de las madres.

The "identity" poems convey a feeling of restlessness and tension
that accompanies the poet's imaginary back-and-forth movement between two traditions. We are manifestly no longer concerned with a
hermetic, pure, and unitary voice. Double-voicedness it would seem is
inherent to the Chicano poet's condition. To a certain extent Cervantes
seems to comply with Todorov's demand for a functional hierarchy
between a bilingual's two languages: Spanish surfaces in intimate, traditional contexts while English functions as the intellectual, rational
language of eloquence. But again, Cervantes's case is more dramatic
since she is not able to function entirely (whether linguistically or
psychologically) in either one of the two cultures.

In Mexico she is called names, "But México gags, / ¡Esputa! on this
bland pochaseed" ("Oaxaca, 1974"), while she herself does not really
belong there—"My sense of this land can only ripple through my
veins" ("Visions of Mexico"). "The words are foreign, stumbling / on
my tongue" ("Refugee Ship"). In the United States she feels a victim
of racism—"I'm marked by the color of my skin"—("Poem for the
Young White Man"). She does not belong this far North where she
sees nothing but strangers around her. Cervantes is painfully aware of
and sensitive to her ancestral roots which lie deep in the Californian
ground. Her Mexican ancestors are buried underneath the new freeway
that intersects the barrio. Once she almost yielded to the temptation of
fleeing this memory-ridden land, but the call of the ancient Californios
proved stronger:

Maybe it's here
en los campos extraños de esta ciudad
where I'll find it, that part of me
mown under
like a corpse
or a loose seed.
("Freeway 280")

Cervantes makes frequent use of internal, temporal dialogue between her ancestors or an earlier self and her present self. But the scope

of the dialogue is larger, both spatially and temporally. "Coming from a long line of eloquent illiterates," she has acquired a literate culture and is in the process of reinventing an identity that transcends the Rio Grande border. The *Americas* are her and her people's rediscovered continent.

"Visions of Mexico While at a Writing Symposium in Port Townsend, Washington" is a dialogic poem par excellence. Cervantes moves back and forth, in time and space, between the two countries, as if looking for the best vantage point from which to speak out. She realizes that, in spite of her natural, spontaneous attachment to Mexico, her locus of discourse is North of the Rio Grande, her own land by birthright. In the last lines of the poem, Cervantes seems to invoke an imaginary addressee, presumably an Anglo, who would be capable of understanding the meaning of her migration:

> as pain sends seabirds south from the cold
> I come north
> to gather my feathers
> for quills

Thus, it is through her writing in English, interspersed with some reappropriated Spanish—evidence of her painful attachment to two cultures—that she can attempt to convey her people's genuine experience.

In "Poem for the Young White Man Who Asked Me How I, an Intelligent, Well-Read Person Could Believe in the War Between Races" the dialogue is external. The poet impatiently addresses a young Anglo whose answers are implicit; we can easily imagine them. Cervantes's tone is persuasive. She becomes a *poète engagé* almost against her will. Marked by the color of her skin, she "cannot reason these scars away" and write about "the blessings of human understanding" from an ivory tower. Anger, bewilderment, and contained rage express themselves in a series of affirmations and negations:

> Every day I am deluged with reminders
> that this is not
> my land
> and this is my land.
> I do not believe in the war between races
> but in this country
> there is war.

Bilingualism and
Dialogism

In only one instance throughout the *Emplumada* poems does Cervantes surrender to despair, to apathy, and that is the only time when she chooses to write the same poem twice, in Spanish *and* in English, as if only the juxtaposition of the two versions could possibly convey her existential plight. In "Barco De Refugiados"—"Refugee Ship" she feels more estranged than ever from her Mexican heritage, from her present environment, and from her own self. Unable to feel the ground beneath her feet, to communicate with the people around her, she feels like a captive aboard the refugee ship: "The ship that will never dock/ El barco que nunca atraca."

Cervantes's double-voiced discourse is manifest in her intimate poetry as well. Also manifest is an underlying tension springing from the confrontation between the existential and the ethnic dimensions of the poet's identity (the woman and the Chicana). Thus two women seem to be speaking in poems such as "The Body As Braille" or "Astro-no-mía."[7] One is the heiress of a people endowed with an intuitive, esoteric knowledge of the surrounding world. The other has been exposed to modern education, to a scientific approach to nature. Cervantes's poetic intuition and craft lie in the unresolved, ambiguous way in which she transcends the apparent dichotomy. In "Astro-no-mía" there is a puzzling in-built pun in the hyphenated spelling of the title announcing an imaginative escape to the stars followed by the inevitable comeback to earthly life. Here is the daring end of the poem:

But all I could remember was that man,
Orion, helplessly shooting his shaft
into my lit house from the bow.
Y Yo? Hay bow. Y ya voy.

In the very last line Cervantes blends her two linguistic consciousnesses into one utterance (through a process of hybridization) creating, as it were, the effect of a crypto-language. Indeed, as George Steiner aptly put it: "The polyglot mind undercuts the lines of division between languages by reaching inward, to the symbiotic core" (*Extraterritorial* 119).[8] I would like to think that if, in violation of all chronology, Mikhail Bakhtin had read Cervantes's poems, he could not have overlooked the distinctly feminine voice discernible in her poetic discourse. He would probably have added it as an important source to the other voices making up the contrapuntal chorus of great literature.

Examining Lorna Dee Cervantes's poetry along with other bilingual poets' writings, one is struck by what seems to be the emergence of a new poetics. From a Bakhtinian perspective this could be indicative of a period of shift in the literary poetic language in that these works undermine the official authoritarian and conservative discourse. According to Bakhtin's dialogic view of language, bilingual poetry thus functions as a decentralizing, centrifugal force that runs counter to the unifying, normalizing tendencies in language. As a poetics it tends to disintegrate the unity, the monoglot nature of traditional poetic forms. I would say that the exceptionality of the best of interlingual Chicano poetry lies in the "contradiction-ridden tension-filled" poetic utterance dialogizing two cultures.

Notes

1 See Marta Sánchez, *Contemporary Chicana Poetry: A Critical Approach to an Emerging Literature* (Berkeley: U of California P, 1985), and Cordelia Candelaria, *Chicano Poetry: A Critical Introduction* (Westport: Greenwood Press, 1986).
2 Mikhail Bakhtin, *Dialogic Imagination*, ed. Michael Holquist (Austin: U of Texas P, 1981).
3 George Steiner, *After Babel* (Oxford: Oxford U P, 1975).
4 Tino Villanueva, Introduction, *Imagine* 1.1 (1984).
5 See present anthology, Todorov.
6 *Empurrnula* (Pittsburgh: U of Pittsburgh P, 1981).
7 "Astro-no-mía," *Americas Review* 15 (1975).
8 George Steiner, *Extraterritorial* (New York: Faber, 1972).

Bilingualism and
Dialogism

Dialogical

Strategies,

Monological

Goals: Chicano

Literature

_____

Bruce-Novoa

Although contemporary Chicano literature is considered one of many manifestations of the civil rights struggle and the general cultural reorientation of the 1960s, the tactics employed in the literature to carry out those social projects remain mostly ignored by criticism. My intention here is to explore the contradictory tension between certain political and cultural goals of the ethnic awakening known as the Chicano movement[1] and the rhetorical strategies to accomplish them used in some representative texts of Chicano literature.

To convert the people of Mexican descent residing in the United States into a cohesive nationalistic group was a necessary first step for any concerted action by Chicano activists. It was not a simple matter, but one that required the development of strategies in which centrifugal and centripetal forces could be created and then directed. Inner harmony and union had to be produced, while simultaneously provoking an attitude of difference based on that inner union which could be turned into opposition to the exterior other, the majority of U.S. society. The goal of the inner-oriented strategies was to produce monological unity; that of the exterior-oriented was to fragment the supposedly monolithic/monologic Anglo American culture by forcing it to dialogue with the residents of Mexican ethnicity, a dialogue which in itself would constitute a de facto recognition of the Chicano as an interlocutor. While the latter tactics were dialogic in as much as they fomented a rhetorical interchange between two distinguishable subjects, the former postulated the ideal of forming an integrated group capable of maintaining itself separate from that Other. Eventually, however, as the novelty wore thin, the interior/exterior dichotomy of We versus They proved difficult and, in the end, impossible to sustain.

In the mid 1960s, when the Black Civil Rights struggle and other avatars of the counterculture movement created an environment of social reform that appeared inevitable, Mexican Americans began to participate in the process. However, this population had never taken action in a united manner outside of narrowly limited regional zones, which explains the urgent need to create a nationally unifying strategy. The politics of confrontation, characteristic of the 1960s, required massive support from a community that perceived itself as united and was willing to act as such. While the blacks seemed to have achieved that goal, as much through their history of slavery and repression as through their racial tie, Mexican American had not achieved anything similar.

The first goal, therefore, was unity. This was reflected in the term *Chicano* chosen by political activists to replace other popular self-denominators, like *Mexican, Mexicano,* or *Mexican American.* Yet the existence of these alternatives was merely the surface manifestation of profound differences in self-conception in segments of the community each pretended to encompass. To be *Mexican* outside of Mexico converts one into an exile or expatriate, distanced from the source of authentic national culture. The proximity to Mexico also makes it probable that anyone who continues to call him or herself *Mexican* will encounter a resident of that country who can unmask the U.S. pretender with a well aimed accusation of impostor. Mexicans have invented pejorative terms like *Pocho* for people of Mexican descent in the United States. It is a cultural trap that true Mexicans can spring on U.S. would-be Mexicans to distance and alienate them at any moment. The term *Mexican American,* although it rightfully names both nationalities in play, also emphasizes disjunction and duality. Moreover, it evokes the traditional U.S. process of assimilation. In the 1960s, to call oneself *Mexican American* came under attack by political activists who synonymized the term with the affirmation of the gradual loss of the differentiating cultural and ethnic characteristics, the exact

Bruce-Novoa

ones that the disciples of the new ethnic consciousness intended to emphasize as unifying principles.

The term *Chicano* encapsuled dual strategies: while it united an imagined community interiorly, simultaneously it differentiated the group, not only from the Anglo Americans, but also from the national culture of Mexico. At first, its ambiguity, both in English and in Spanish was an advantage. The term proved unique, easily distinguishable from that of any other group, thus creating Chicanos as a recognizable Other. Yet the lack of specificity for the members themselves made it necessary to provide some system of identification, permitting that the term be utilized in rites of initiation—or indoctrination. The name and the ideals that it represented required concretization in objects of cultural production, and literature responded.

To achieve ideal unity, authors, reflecting an attitude popular among political activists of the nationalist bent, adopted a tribal rhetoric. They delimited the national space within a clear borderline that excluded the enemy, who resided in alien territory full of menace.[2] In this context, the process of assimilation—the transformation of the immigrant into a participant in Usonian society through the appropriation of the customs and values of the host group—was perceived as a sinister plot to eradicate Chicano culture, offering, as supposedly had been done earlier with European immigrants, full participation in society solely to those who submitted to this character-adjusting process.

Traditionally, U.S. society has managed to assimilate immigrants gradually over several generations.[3] In spite of the intense and disturbing pressure brought to bare on those who pass through the assimilation process, historically immigrants have resigned themselves to the transformation almost stoically, complaining about the temporary pain while simultaneously accepting it in name of the better future in which they or their children will receive the rewards promised to those who incorporate themselves into the dominant group. During the process, they inhabit a space of transition, a purgatory of adaptation whose sign could well be a term ambiguous with respect both to the position and the process: *inter*. During this transition phase, the immigrant tries to maintain—sometimes fanatically—elements associated with source nation, such as festival days, social customs, language, and material objects, especially foods which often require home preparation of imported basic goods. This umbilical-cord behavior keeps the immigrant connected to what is held in the memory as the now distant "authentic culture." These elements are exactly what distinguish the immigrants as ethnics, serving as signs of difference

Dialogical
Strategies,
Monological
Goals

within the surrounding dominant social order. The fact that they are remembered, practiced, or consumed with such intense need and pleasure as different from the surrounding society make them no longer national traits but U.S. traits, their particular value and significance determined by this country and not the country of the group's origin. Eventually these elements will either be homogenized within the vast and multivariegated weave of diversity accepted as the national character of the United States, restricted to domestic use within the security of the home, or relegated to the relative isolation of the streets of the ethnic neighborhood where those elements acquire the character, not merely of nostalgic memories, but of active signifying code of social interaction. In addition, this code assumes the added significance of being the source of survival within a perceived situation of threat from the outside.

Across a wide spectrum, Chicano activists, from cultural nationalists to Marxists or Maoists, tried to radicalize the perception of the assimilation process, reducing the space and duration of the gradual transition to a thin line crossed instantaneously. That is, there was an attempt to eliminate those features of the assimilation process which allow a person to be in transition from one culture to another, holding on to the old while already participating to some extent in the new—one could say that the goal was to eliminate the characteristic U.S. space of ethnicity.

This type of radical politics required a clear confrontation of We versus They along the lines of tribal cosmicization into distinctly opposed groups each with its own space.[4] Lotman and Uspenksii, although discussing a different national context, describe something similar: "The basic cultural values (ideological, political, and religious) of medieval Russia were distributed in a bipolar field and divided by a sharp boundary without an axiologically neutral zone" (31).[5] Lotman, himself trapped in ideologically binary structures, underscores the lack of transition space in this radical opposition, emphasizing that these groups customarily conceptualize a boundary, not as a line shared equally by the inhabitants on either side, but rather as a zone closed to both; instead of an open zone of transit, the border marks "the break in the continuity of space, with the property of inaccessibility" (Lotman 111).[6] According to this scheme, the act of crossing the cultural frontier became a fearful violation of the group's security, a betrayal of its integrity as well as that of the individual. To guard against this threat, the tribe traditionally created tabus, stigmatizing the exodus as a crime of abandonment and treason against the group of origin.

To prevent the other group, the receiving one that inhabits "cultural chaos," from continually attracting immigrants with promises of eventual integration and participatory rights, the same rhetoric also has to create in the receiving group the desire to keep the immigrant at a distance. This is often done by exasperating hatred, fear, and misunderstanding between the groups. In the rhetoric of militant confrontation, the goal was to produce an environment of menace within which assimilation was represented as both a suicidal self-betrayal for either group and a dangerous invasion of either's home space by an alien and menacing other.

This tribal orientation lends itself to hierarchical structures. Those who occupy the cultural center serve as models of authenticity and have the power to impose loyalty tests on all participants within the space, long established or newly arrived. By eliminating the transition zone, they can censure the slightest divergence from the rules and impose strict obedience. Members continually have to check their behavior against the central paradigm; similarity is conceived of as proximity to the *axis mundi* and distance from the enemy. Those who inhabit the periphery of the circle, nearest the enemy, as well as those who straddle the border and openly incarnate the assimilation process—biologically or culturally—are always suspected of treason.

While the binary opposition can be considered de facto dialogic, the goal of this structuring practice is monological: to catalyze unity based on the strict adherence to communal customs and the modes of behavior defined as distinct from those of the Other. Some Chicanos even have insisted that our culture is unique, an ideal only possible in the equally ideal space of the word as a fiction of impossible desire and a utopian ideology of separatism. Within this cosmic vision, the other pole of existence is not an alternate system in a dialogue of equals, but rather a locus of negativity and of the outlawed values of a solitary system which locates them in an exterior zone, extraterritorial, making them tabu for the authentically faithful members of the community. This tabued zone is chaos, described by Eliade as simultaneously within and out of the system, recognized, yes, but as something beyond the inner group's grasp. Inhabitants of the interior space are not permitted access to the outside zone, which they know only as a figure characterized by negativity (Lotman and Uspenskii 34). To achieve this, some works attack the assimilation process as a fraud. They redefine assimilation within a system of strict bipolarity in which the Anglo American keeps the Chicano fixed at the pole of negativity. The strategy then practices an inversion of the supposed reality to appropriate positivity for Chicanos while shifting negativity to the Other.

Examples of this rhetoric in Chicano literature of the 1960s and 1970s abound, but here I will limit myself to three. Two, Rodolfo Gonzales's *Yo soy Joiquín/I Am Joaquín* (1967) and Sergio Elizondo's *Perros y antiperros* (1972), are openly creative works. They were both popular and academic readings in the 1970s, figuring as fundamental texts in early Chicano literature courses.[7] The third, Américo Paredes's *With His Pistol in His Hand, A Border Ballad and its Hero* (1958), an academic monograph, was less popular in those early years.[8] However, over time it and its author have become key influences on Chicano criticism, becoming the objects of almost a cult following which makes them exempt from objective critical study.[9]

Sergio Elizondo announced clearly the confrontation between two antagonistic and mutually exclusive groups in the title *Perros y antiperros* [Dogs and Antidogs] of his collection of poetry. Metaphorically it represented the opposition of a They/inhuman against a We/human. If that were not sufficient, there could be no mistaking his intent after reading the collection, with its culminating satirical degradation of Anglo-American society in the poem "Camino de perfección/ The Way to Perfection." The attack is brutal. According to Elizondo, the essence of Usonian culture can be summarized in the key image of artificiality: Anglo-American life is centered around plastic. Elizondo draws a cultural boundary and asks Chicanos to decide on which side they want to live. While the tactic is dialogical in as much as it is directed against the dominant code and utilizes a comparative structure that juxtaposes the Chicano to the Anglo-American, Elizondo's goal is to eliminate the negative influences—the presence itself—of the Anglo-American Other.

As Elizondo sees it, Chicanos's obsession with Anglo-Americans is the fundamental vice that undermines the culture, because it privileges the Other as the positive model for imitation while internalizing the negativity inherent in the binary opposition of the system. This forces Chicanos into always reacting to the actions of the Other, thus reducing Chicano culture to dependency on the Anglo-American social agenda. Elizondo seeks to reorient Chicanos' perception toward a monological concentration on the self in which the Anglo-American Other would be the negative, tabued pole. To achieve this end Elizondo reduces the Anglo-American to a nonhuman brute. Meanwhile, the Chicano We is affirmed by invoking historical memory to trace the

Bruce-Novoa

Mexican-U.S. confrontation and to make manifest the tradition of resistance based on human values which have characterized our culture.

Elizondo's collection of poems attempts to guide Chicanos toward their own center where they can recuperate those positive values upon which can be based a cultural renaissance. From this center Chicanos can position Anglo-American culture well outside their own circle, far off in the zone of tabued negativity. Armed with this new consciousness, it becomes possible to degrade the Other as inhuman, undesirable, even pathetic, and in the last analysis scarcely worth entering into a dialogue with because it has nothing to offer in exchange. All things Anglo-American are reencoded under the sign of negativity, the They being reduced to a pack of savage beasts at worst and pitiful animals at best. If Elizondo's strategy succeeds, it should be impossible to envy or esteem Anglo-Americans (96–115).[10] At the same time, the attack radicalizes the relations in the eyes of the Anglo-Americans. In the terms Elizondo imposes on the intercultural situation, Anglo-Americans can see Chicanos only as unassimilable and, thus, dangerous and undesirable.

Gonzales's *Yo soy Joaquín/I Am Joaquín*, the first major work of literature from the Chicano civil rights struggle, functions in a similar manner. It begins by depicting Chicanos as dominated by the Anglo-American society, pawns of an economic system that uses them only for its own profit. The situation is monological from the start, with Chicanos occupying the position of negativity: lost, manipulated, dragged about, starved, and poor. Faced with a seemingly impossible situation, in which all power flows from the center and allows no response from the periphery, the poem's persona must first create the possibility of a two-way flow of ideas. To do so he must create an active subject position for the Chicano marginal other, thus making possible the situation for a dialogue. This is achieved by offering choices to the reader between remaining in the position of silent and powerless oppression suffered by those who delude themselves into believing they can literally work themselves closer to the pole of power or of rejecting that position and finding an alternative. Slowly, the alternative takes shape, although ambiguously at the poem's early stage. The structure of choice between two ways of reacting to a situation realizes the purpose of establishing a dialogical possibility. By the end of the introductory section, within this bipolar structure, an inversion of values is initiated through the use of an image intended to shift negativity to the dominant society. This is achieved through the metaphor of the great inhuman monster of progress by whom Chicanos are oppressed. And in the bipolarity of opposites, if They are negative, then We are positive.

With the monological center transformed into one of two possible poles of choice, one of which is assigned negative value, the selection seems determined. Yet, the implicit question is what action is appropriate other than mere dialogue with power, which could slip into the previous imbalance. Exposure to power seduces by providing a minimum of rewards and holding out promises of eventual incorporation. The poem's persona responds by setting the example: he rejects the illusory promises, retires from the dialogue with dominant society, and retreats into "the circle of life, my people" (3). Within that circle there are no non-Chicanos—in the Spanish version the people are called "my race." Furthermore, everything is oriented toward the center of the self, group identity. This self-centered focus results from the appearance of a new axis mundi, the wisdom of the wise elders. In their collective memory, maintained through oral tradition, the persona will learn the story of the group, its genealogy, and the dynamic process of its evolution. Since struggle is inherent in this history, a strategy of survival is discovered. In this instance, that strategy is one of miscegenation, or mestizaje, first of invading Spaniards and native Indians, and later of rich and poor. The mixing process was, however, not of sexual blending but one of bloody warfare over the rights to land, yet the mixture was achieved and a nation formed.

The values discovered from tradition are survival skills projected into the future, that is, into the present of the poem's persona where they can be used as tactics for the new struggle in the United States. While the poem continually moves back in time to trace the thread of history, it also moves forward to the present to renew contact with the situation in the United States. This back and forth movement is itself a process of discourse, a weave between the poles of Mexican past and U.S. present, a dialogue of possible worlds. But the poem does not aim at the simple goal of equal rights in the legal or social sense, but of property rights in the national sense. The dialogical structure only serves to build the case for a withdrawal into a monological national state separate from the United States, although equally separate from Mexico as well.

I Am Joaquín's version of the appearance of the Chicano people as a nation—posited as the regeneration of the authentic Mexican nation betrayed by the winner of the Mexican Revolution of 1910-20—should not mistakenly be read as yet one more ethnic dialogue with the Anglo

American Other within the great tradition of U.S. assimilation, but as the opposite, a rejection of any proposal to dialogue. The poem justifies this position by its discovery of the Anglo American's prior rejection of the Mexican invitation to enter into a process of cultural exchange; Anglo Americans are depicted as taking what is offered but giving nothing in exchange. So dialogue with the Anglo American is said to be futile. This lesson taught by the elders should shake Chicanos out of the illusion of assimilation. Supposedly history teaches that another alternative must be followed, that of separatism, of a complete withdrawal into an independent, ethnically cleansed national state. Meanwhile, the first step is the affirmation of a separate racial group: "My blood is pure" (20) the poem affirms near the end, invoking a strict tabu against further miscegenation. Assimilation is thus rejected, replaced with a call to bloody war against the Anglo American oppressor. To insure that no Chicano will move toward the enemy slowly, the demarcation line between groups is drawn as a thin border separating two monological spaces between which dialogue has been suspended and forbidden (Bruce-Novoa, *Response to Chaos*, 48–68).

The two texts sought to eliminate the Anglo American Other from Chicano space by redefining both groups as they interrelated. This, of course, required confrontation, contrast, a jockeying for position, in other words, a dialogic interchange. For example, both evoke the traditional, popular concept of U.S. national development as an expansion of Anglo American culture from the Atlantic coast westward into an unpopulated wilderness. This concept is so ingrained in the Anglo American psyche as an essential narrative context for all other historical events that it can be seen to constitute one of the *ideologemes* of U.S. culture.[11] Yet, within it lies another microelement without which this *ideologeme* would be impossible to maintain—hence, an element essential to the Usonian character—that of the savage *hinterland*, unpopulated in the sense that it contained no "people," but only wandering nomadic aborigine with no permanent settlements, and thus still closer to animals than humans. This wilderness supposedly awaited the forces of civilization to claim it for human habitation. This one-way historical development against which no human response supposedly was voiced follows the same monological structure discussed above. And it is exactly this microelement that suffers redefinition when Chicano history is introduced as the story of a space within present U.S. territory delimited cartographically, administered as part of a vast legal system stretching around the world and with permanent settlements—in short, it documents the historic presence of a competing civilization. While westward development of the United states is impossible to negate—no one would seriously attempt to erase the mass migration of peoples that filled in the U.S. map in a generally westerly drift—the *ideologeme* dependent on a vacated frontier cannot, however, continue as before. What has been depicted as the natural and therefore innocent expansion of a civilized group through an uninhabited wilderness is transformed into an invasion by one state of its neighbor, who often responded with resistance against the incursion—although not always, but even the history of those segments who welcomed incorporation into the United States disproves the wilderness *ideologeme*. The monological expansion, human versus nature, becomes a dialogical struggle of human versus human, of culture versus culture. This subverts the entire structure built on the founding *ideologeme*. If we take into account the tremendous significance traditionally invested in this *ideologeme* and the systems of cultural production structured on it—the canon of U.S. literary studies for instance—we can appreciate the impact of the subversion.

To expect this maneuver to totally debunk the U.S. national image would be too idealistic and dangerously naive. However, for Chicano literature and the nationalist project of certain Chicano activists, what matters is the fact that a new possibility has been introduced into the game of national identity. This provokes a revaluation of the historical concept of the nation because a new player must be accounted for, the Chicano. This presence relativizes the historical process by infusing instability. Lotman and Upenskii summarize well this effect: "Polemics with opposing ideologies inevitably becomes an important element in the self-definition of any cultural phenomena. In the process of such polemics one's position is formulated along with a revealing transformation of the position of the opponents" (40).

In the third example, *With His Pistol in His Hands: A Border Ballad and Its Hero*, Américo Paredes utilizes similar strategies to study the tradition of the romance, or corrido, in south Texas. He opens a dialogue, not only with the popular image of the Texas Rangers, but with the official elitist writing that lent the aura of academic authority to what was, according to Paredes, essentially a romantic fiction. Specifically, Paredes targeted for attack Professor Walter Prescott Webb, whose *The Texas Rangers* was considered the authoritative text on the subject (José Saldívar 51–53; Limón 29).[12] Yet, as we might expect, once again this dialogical strategy sought to establish a monological structure within which the author occupied the positive center and

Prescott Webb is relegated to outside the field of academic discussion of the subject, having been branded as unscholarly.

Paredes wrote his text during the 1950s when he was a junior professor at the University of Texas, the major institution of his native state. He set out to debunk the most renown historian in Texas at the time, Prescott Webb. Systematically he subverted Webb's reputation by questioning his objectivity, the reliability of his sources, and, thus, the validity of his conclusions. The purpose was not just to counter the supposed facts about the Texas Rangers with others, but to attack the man himself. Paredes selected sections of *The Texas Rangers* that served his purpose of displaying the author's prejudice against Mexicans. Then, he mercilessly ironized the author through his commentaries. "Professor Webb does not mean to be disparaging. One wonders what his opinion might have been when he was in a less scholarly mood and not looking at the Mexican from the objective point of view of the historian" (17). The result is to show Prescott Webb as a scholar unworthy of our trust because of his inability to distance himself from his personal prejudice when writing. Paredes offers, in contrast, alternative versions of the relations between the Rangers and the Mexican people who inhabited the Rio Grande Valley of Texas, those whom Paredes calls *border people*. With a feigned humility, Paredes presents his own information with self-critical irony. "I do not claim for these little tidbits the documented authenticity that Ranger historians claim for their stories. What we have here is frankly partisan and exaggerated without a doubt, but it does throw some light on Mexican attitudes toward the Rangers which many Texans may scarcely suspect. And it may be that these attitudes are not without some basis in fact" (25). This affirmation if followed up by another: "The Rangers have been known to exaggerate not only the number of Mexicans they engaged but those they actually killed and whose bodies could be produced, presumably." Readers experience a dialogic juxtaposition of images: the direct and humble veracity of the common people, for whom the author serves as encarnated voice, pitted against the written, arrogant exaggerations of heroism on the part of the elitist academic. Furthermore, in a fashion similar to José Limón's reading of Paredes's work, we can read this confrontation as a struggle between a courageous novice professor against the old, established historian. The former's goal was to eliminate Prescott Webb, which would leave the field in his own hands. Paredes had no intention of sharing the field as a space of dialogue, which could have been the case if he had focused strictly

235
———
Dialogical
Strategies,
Monological
Goals

on contradicting facts. He wanted his foe to be excluded from further consideration. Paredes's line of Manichean difference is fraught with nationalistic reverberations: the *Border People* have to side with him or be considered traitors to their own community, for which Paredes considers himself the authentic spokesman.

Renato Rosaldo insightfully selected citations from Paredes's text to demonstrate, one, the medieval patriarchal order of strict heirarchical authority invoked by the author for his hero figure—and, following Limón's logic, for himself—and two, to show his intolerance for other types of expression within the community.[13] As in *Yo soy Joaquín*, readers are forced to choose sides between supporting the ethnic group or betraying it. Rosaldo correctly asserts that this type of monological authority is deconstructed by Chicano authors who came later. This implied change in context could lead one to assume that in the moment of Paredes's writing the system he constructed was representative of a real cultural order. However, Rosaldo provides one quotation in which Paredes attacks contemporary Chicano singing—what he calls Pachuco singing—thus demonstrating that even at the time of Paredes's writing the cultural community was dialogical not monological. And lest one think that Paredes's vision of the past is any less problematic, Rosaldo places a endnote in which he refers readers to David Montejano's work on the history of Texas for a "less idealized view of primordial south Texas Mexican society" (Rosaldo 241). In that text one finds little if any support for the existence of the Paredes utopian patriarchy or Ramón Saldívar's organic society.[14]

In each of these examples, dialogical tactics attempt to distinguish between the Other and We, establishing a situation in which the two dialogue. Thus, the Chicano appears as a subject in control of its self-expression. Eventually, however, they swing the focus around to themselves, eliminating dialogue in favor of a monological interior unity. Nevertheless, in each case the text generates within itself contradictory inner resistance which subverts the monological ideal.

Contradiction occurs first in the language in which the texts appear. Two of the texts, Paredes's and Gonzales's, were written in English, and two were published in bilingual editions, Gonzales's and Elizondo's. Grouped together as foundation texts of Chicano literature, they produce dialogical intertextual echoes within the space of that literature that force readers to cross a frontier of difference otherwise held to be rigid and strict, that of preferred—that is, native—language. The two that appeared in bilingual formats, with the two versions juxtaposed verse by verse, produce a dialogue between the languages. With the

Bruce-Novoa

two languages side by side, a visual interaction, a synecdoche for cultural interaction, arises within the space of the reading. The text can be read monolingually, readers choosing one or the other version, or bilingually by reading one and then the other. But the reality of the text is interlingual in as much as the two versions interrelate to create a truly dialogical structure that accurately reflects the context from which the text arose and to which it redirects itself.[15] Continually they remind us that the readers to whom the text directs itself are, if not in fact at least ideally, products and producers of a mixture of Spanish and English which ultimately is the essence of the group's cultural definition.

That Paredes decided to write and publish his text not only in English, but couched in academic diction, testifies to his desire to position himself in the elitist space of dominant society, to which he directs his book. The book opens for itself a space in U.S. academic circles, accepting, tacitly if not explicitly, that this space and no other —neither the Mexican nor that of popular culture—can be its only context. And while Gonzales's and Elizondo's poems can be read as separatists manifestos that ask Chicanos to distance themselves from dominant society and reject middle-class values, Paredes's book positions itself outside the group and culture it pretends to define as its community. His text appears within the dominant Anglo American academic structure it supposedly attacks. The mere fact of its existence within that space subverts the binary structure of strict opposition. The goal of monological unity dissipates under the light of dialogical reality.

While the three texts proclaim that one distinctive characteristic of Chicano culture is its oral essence in contrast to the written character of Anglo American culture, they participate in the practice of writing and fully intend to take advantage of their written quality. Hence, they document the disappearance of the cultural sign they conceptually privilege, participating in the process of transforming the oral into its antithesis. For example, while they highlight oral ritual as a key to Chicano culture, they themselves encode it only as a memory of what is no longer dominant, an absence in their own texts. When they encode the content of the oral tradition in written texts, these writers privilege the content over the method of transmission. That is to say, when they emphasize information as data and facts, they diminish the importance of the communal ritual which supposedly was the source of their information. Tacitly, upon lamenting the disappearance of the traditional ritual that centered the community through the spoken word, they promote its extinction by facilitating the content of the cultural message of that tradition to readers without requiring of them their participation in the ritual practice of which the information once was an intricate part. And if we take seriously the essential unity of form and content, then the result is a cultural product split apart and vitiated when judged from traditional perspective of its origin—or, from another perspective less reactionary, its is now a hybrid culture, necessarily dialogical.

On the level of content, in *Yo soy Joaquín* one also finds indication that within the supposedly secure ethnic circle not all is well. The threats to Chicano culture come not only from the outside, but arise from the tendency of members of the group to engage in activities which lead them to break the circle and exit. It should not come as a surprise that a product of the 1960s would express conflicts in terms of a generation gap. The poem's persona assumes the identity of an adult perturbed by the lack of communication with the young members of his family: "I see my children disappear/ behind the shroud of mediocrity/ never to look back and remember me" (19). These tensions are only the surface signs of more profound conflicts dividing the adults themselves into opposition groups. The persona expresses this in the form of his conflictive, divided self: "I look at myself/ and see part of me/ who rejects my father and my mother/ and dissolves into the melting pot/ to disappear in shame" (13). To eliminate these internal conflicts would require an intergenerational dialogue: "I must fight/ And win this struggle/ for my sons, and they/ must know from me/ Who I am" (19). However, an even more fundamental dialogue must be realized first before the generation can attempt theirs. The persona, himself the victim of a cultural malady of the lack of self-knowledge, must transcend his alienation from his own tradition and history. In the very center of *Yo soy Joaquín* we find the need for dialogical tactics within the persona's being. The reorientation toward the past to search for a "mechanism that works against natural time" (Lotman and Upenskii 65), although apparently monological, is in effect dialogical in its juxtaposition of the contemporary modes of assimilation and the ancient modes of resistance against assimilation. And although what is sought is the creation of a monological unity capable of embracing time and history, the intradialogical dynamics are obvious.

The same dynamic is found in Elizondo's *Perros y antiperros*. The poet defines his role as the guide capable of reorienting the young who he sees as in the process of drifting away from the core of values that would give them a historical and cultural identity. Paredes seems less direct, although the fact that he must enunciate again a system of values that draw a demarcation line of loyalties implies that he perceives the need to confront his own community with a clear decision that leaves no space where one might accommodate gradually to the Other. Certainly José Limón's and Renato Rosaldo's readings impute to him a desire to act as heroic role model for the community he wanted to represent. And his attack on young, urban Chicanos reveals a sense of perceived intracultural threat akin to Elizondo's and Gonzales's: "these pachucos nowadays, mumbling damn-foolishness into a microphone; it is not done that way. . . . And when you sing, sing songs like *El Corrido de Gregorio Cortez*. There's a song that makes the hackles rise. You can almost see him there—Gregorio Cortez, with his pistol in his hand" (34). The metonymic association of the author with the model singer, who in turn metamorposes into the heroic protagonist is clear. Like in Octavio Paz's *The Labyrinth of Solitude*, the specter of the Pachuco is raised to signify cultural degradation, and then the reader is offered the alternative: to follow the author back to a mythic hero whose comportment is to be emulated in the present. The *Yo soy Gregorio Cortez* and the *Yo soy Joaquín* function similarly to encarnate the literary hero-protagonist in the author-singer of the tale, centering the community of readers around the figure as model.

The intra-ethnic tension existed from the start of contemporary Chicano literature criticism, although both Chicanos and others preferred—and still prefer—not to focus on it. The tendency is to support the ideal of unity and stress the value of resistance. But, as the literature and its criticism matures, the plurality of voices makes it more difficult to ignore both the dialogical character of Chicana the cultural production and the monological desires with their illusory claims. The implicit rejection of monological cultural unity in such texts as *Pocho* by José Antonio Villarreal or *City of Night* by John Rechy once were explained as an aberration produced by their author's cultural alienation characteristic of the period before Chicano activism in the 1960s, but this explanation falters in the face of Oscar Zeta Acosta's fiction from the early 1970s. Since it was impossible to eliminate an author like Acosta, who possessed Chicano credentials as a political activist in the community and whose books addressed directly the cultural and political struggles of the 1960s, the response was simply to ignore him, leaving him out of critical discussion of Chicano literature. Critics focused their attention on texts which supported the ideal of ethnic unity or which lent themselves to facile denunciation. Yet, even in *Bless Me, Ultima*, . . . *y no se lo tragó la tierra* and *Estampas*

Dialogical
Strategies,
Monological
Goals

del valle the respective Chicano communities depicted are in conflict with themselves.

To the women, however, goes the credit for having enunciated the situation most clearly. Bernice Zamora and Lorna Dee Cervantes, the most significant poets from the first two decades of contemporary Chicano literature,[16] began their respective collection with images of patriarchal rituals from which Chicanos exclude Chicanas. Women are treated like the negative Other, voiceless and less than fully human in that they are not empowered with subjectivity. In short, both women begin with the statement of the Chicano man's desire for a monological system and then proceed to force it into a dialogue with women. The intracultural conflict is clearly revealed. In a similar fashion, the first contemporary novel by a Chicana, Berta Ornelas's *Come Down From the Mound*, opens with a confrontation between the male and female protagonists.[17] Their conflict becomes the central narrative line, playing itself out in sexual and political terms. Significantly, the narrative often focuses on playful, though aggressive, dialogue between the sexes. These texts can be read as efforts by Chicanas to dialogue with a Chicano male chauvinist literary tradition, although each female writer arrives at a different conclusion about the possibility of achieving the goal of communication between the sexes. What is significant here is that the monological goals of that literary tradition are subverted when Chicanas reveal the fissures in the interior circle. Any positive response to the questions the women raise require dialogical strategies if the culture is to survive.

Chicanos authors, both female and male, contradict the monological ideal of a unitary Chicano ethnicity by infusing it with a relativizing heteroglossia. Paredes's text exemplifies well the effects of heteroglossia. While the author juxtaposes alternate versions of the past to attack Prescott Webb, readers who are not predisposed to surrender blindly to Paredes's rhetoric must ask themselves if the text does not suffer from the same vices that the author has attacked in his rival. There is something humorously ironic in Paredes's accusation that Prescott Webb's writing is "frankly partisan and exaggerated," considering his open partisanship for the Mexican American cause and the exaggerated way in which he goes beyond scholarly argumentation to personal invective. His tone of ironic subversion disseminates throughout the text, undermining his objectivity and infusing his statements with doubt, relativizing it.[18] That the corrido, in which Paredes places so much stock, systematically reduces historical data to the formulas of

Bruce-Novoa

popular songs and narrative cliches moves history itself to the field of documentary fiction at best.[19]

The impact of discourse, of dialogue, of heteroglossia on the monological goals is devastating on the nationalist political program. Everything in these texts is relativized. The discursive quality of heteroglossia produces dialogism.

> Dialogism is the characteristic epistemological mode of a world dominated by heteroglossia. Everything means, is understood, as part of a greater whole—there is a constant interaction between meaning, all of which have the potential of conditioning others. Which will affect the other, how it will do so and in what degree is what is actually settled at the moment of utterance. This dialogic imperative, mandated by the pre-existence of the language world relative to any of its current inhabitants, insures that there can be no actual monologue. One may, like a primitive tribe that knows only its own limits, be deluded into thinking there is one language, or one may, as grammarians, certain political figures and normative framers of 'literary languages' do, seek in a sophisticated way to achieve a unitary language. In both cases the unitariness is relative to the overpowering force of heteroglossia, and thus dialogism. . . . A word, discourse, language or culture undergoes 'dialogization' when it becomes relativized, de-privileged, aware of competing definitions for the same things. Undialogized language is authoritative or absolute. (426)[20]

However, this devastation of the limited ideals of monologic nationalism permit the rise of the liberating and realistic need to embrace the widely diverse totality of the Chicano communities. Dialogical strategies, used to relativize the texts of the Other, undermine the absolutist ideal of unitary truth. Once the dialogic realm is established, retreating back to a zone of monological authority is almost impossible.

Heteroglossia is the undeniable state of contemporary culture. Dialogized language makes the return to the monological a nostalgic illusion. What began as an effort to subvert the Other through dialogic tactics as a necessary step toward nationalism has resulted in the proliferation of texts representing the pluralistic tendencies of the Chicano communities. Instead of a fixed and strict border, Chicano cultural production has opened an expansive space of inter- and intracultural communication in which dialogue is the rule and heteroglossia the norm. But the feared assimilation also undergoes a redefinition into

Dialogical
Strategies,
Monological
Goals

the process of transculturation . . . yet another name for cultural dialogism.

Notes

1 Chicano intellectuals now question the term *movement*, rejecting the ideological singularity and monological culture it implies. No such unity existed, rather many local manifestations which never achieved enough coherence among themselves to justify the terminology. And it could not have arisen because a single monological Chicano culture has never existed which could serve as a base for the new one. The term, then, turns out to have been an example of the rhetoric of desire of unity, a utopian strategy, idealistic and ultimately unrealizable, a classic reification of the logocentric dream of hegemony.

2 "One of the outstanding characteristics of traditional societies is the opposition that they assume between their inhabited territory and the unknown and the indeterminate space that surrounds it. The former is the world (more precisely, our world), the cosmos; everything outside it is no longer a cosmos but a sort of 'other world,' a foreign, chaotic space, peopled by ghosts, demons, 'foreigners' (who assimilated to demons and the souls of the dead." Mircea Eliade, (*The Sacred and the Profane* [New York: Harcourt, 1959]), 29.

3 It would be difficult to deny that assimilation—acculturation or transculturation or whatever name might be given to the process—has functioned for the large numbers of immigrants, but one should also accept the fact that no one formula for the process applies universally nor that assimilation ever means total disappearance of traces or origins. "Hansen law," enunciated by Marcus Lee Hansen in 1938, postulated that the first three generations of a family of immigrants followed a fixed pattern of assimilation. He summarized it in the often cited "what the son wants to forget, the grandson wants to remember" in "The Third Generation in America," *Commentary 14* (November 1952), 495. Although this is still referred to as a "law," criticism has shown it to be only Hansen's opinion, Werner Sollors, *Beyond Ethnicity, Consent and Descent in American Culture* (New York: Oxford U P, 1986), 208–36.

4 Mircea Eliade uses cosmicization to signify the organization of social space around sacred principles called *axis mundi*, in *The Sacred and the Profane*, 32. The centralizing power of the *axis mundi* is monological in that all power flows from it unilaterally, defining everything within the social space in relation to itself, as well as tracing an outside boundary which serves to limit the range of movement permitted to the inhabitants. Beyond the borders lies a space defined as chaos and inhabited by demons. To exit across the border into chaos is equivalent to entering the realm of death. The relationship of cosmos to chaos is binary, but the attribution of significance is monological.

5 Iurii Lotman and Boris Uspenskii, "Binary Models in the Dynamics of Russian Culture (to the End of the Eighteenth Century)," *The Semiotics of*

242
———
Bruce-Novoa

Russian Cultural History, ed. Alexander D. Nakhimovsky and Alice Stone Nakhimovsky (Ithaca: Cornell U P, 1985), 30–66.

6   Jurij Lotman, "On Metalanguage of a Typological Description of Culture," *Semiotics* 14.2 (1975), 97–123.

7   Rodolfo Gonzales, *I Am Joaquín, An Epic Poem* (Denver: El Gallo Newspaper, 1967), and Sergio Elizondo, *Perros y antiperros* (Berkeley: Quinto Sol, 1972).

8   Américo Paredes, *With a Pistol in His Hands: A Border Ballad and Its Hero* (Austin: U of Texas P, 1958).

9   Paredes is most often cited as an authority whose opinions stand as definitive statements. As such he has received attention from colleagues and admirers. Roger D. Abrahams and Richard Bauman place Paredes in the key position of transmitter of what they call "doing folklore Texas-style" to a younger generation. They also credit him with originating the emphasis on "performance-oriented folkloristics." They close their essay by stating: "We all consider ourselves the heirs of the long and honorable lineage of Texas folklorists, but Américo Paredes is the one who made us what we are," Roger D. Abrahams and Richard Bauman, "Doing Folklore Texas-Style," in *"And Other Neighborly Names," Social Process and Cultural Images in Texas Folklore*, ed. Richard Bauman and Roger D. Abrahams (Austin: U of Texas P, 1981), 3–7. In "The Return of the Mexican Ballad: Américo Paredes and His Autobiographical Text as Persuasive Political Performance," José Limón raises Paredes to the status of cultural hero, the performer of model action. Ramón Saldívar takes Paredes's work on the resistance figure of Gregorio Cortez as a source for the paradigm of Chicano narrative itself, a body of writing produced in many different areas of the United States and by a highly heterogeneous population with little if any common experiences to tie them to Paredes and his south Texas context. Teresa McKenna similarly exalts Paredes depiction of the dynamics of his specific area and one particular cultural product of it into a universal concept in that he offers "an encompassing view of an area which geographically, as well as politically and culturally, stands as figure and metaphor for the transition between nations and the complex of connections which continue to exist for all Mexicans whether border residents or not" (in José David Saldívar, 54). José David Saldívar practices a similar strategy of universalization, although he does not go as far as to extend the applicability of the model to all nations as McKenna does: "Paredes's *With His Pistol in His Hand* thus is the first sophisticated Chicano narrative to begin to overturn established authority in Texas and the Southwest" (José David Saldívar 55–56).

To balance these admiring perspectives one might refer to Renato Rosaldo's precautionary comments that preface his treatment of Paredes's text: "From the perspective of feminist thought in the late 1980's, Paredes's work now appears dated in its idealization of a primordial patriarchy, and ahead of its time in so clearly seeing the interplay of culture and power. To project a heterogeneous, changing heritage into the future, 'we' Chicanos must continually reread past narratives in order to recover courageous early works without reifying them as sacred relics more fit for veneration than dialogue and debate" (Rosaldo 151). After briefly depicting Paredes's vision of what Ramón Saldívar calls the organic community of south Texas, Rosaldo adds: "If taken literally, Paredes's view of the frontier social order seems both pre-feminist and as implausible as a classic ethnography written and read in accord with classic norms. . . . Read as poetic vision, however, the account of primordial south Texas Mexican society establishes the terms of verbally constructing the warrior hero as a figure of resistance. It enables Paredes to develop a conception of manhood rhetorically endowed with the mythic capacity to combat Anglo-Texan anti-Mexican prejudice" (Rosaldo 151). It is in the line of Rosaldo's admonition against reifying Paredes that my analysis of the effects of Paredes's rhetorical strategy is carried out. This does not lessen the significance of Paredes's work, just as the analyses of Gonzales and Elizondo in no way diminishes their and their work's contributions and importance to Chicano cultural production.

10   Bruce-Novoa, *Chicano Poetry: A Response to Chaos* (Austin: U of Texas P, 1982).

11   Fredric Jameson defines ideologeme as "The smallest intelligible unit of the essentially antagonistic collective discóurse of social classes" (76); and "The ideologeme is an amphibious formation, whose essential structural characteristic may be described as its possibility to manifest itself either as a pseudoidea—a conceptual or belief system, an abstract value, an opinion or prejudice—or as a protonarrative, a kind of ultimate class fantasy about the 'collective characters' which are the classes in opposition" (87).

12   José David Saldívar, *The Dialectics of Our America: Genealogy, Cultural Critique and Literary History* (Durham: Duke U P, 1991); José Limón, "The Return of the Mexican Ballad: Américo Paredes and His Anthropological Text as Persuasive Political Performance," Stanford Center for Chicano Research, Working Paper 16, 1986.

13   Ronato Rosaldo, *Culture and Truth: The Remaking of Social Analysis* (Boston: Beacon, 1989).

14   John Holmes McDowell's often cited study, "The *Corrido* of Greater Mexico as Discourse, Music, and Event," begins with a warning to readers that the essay utilizes "two serviceable fictions: first, in assuming that there is such a thing as 'the' *corrido*; and, second, in positing the existence of 'ballad communities'" (44). These are both concepts derived from Paredes's work. Significantly McDowell's caveat alerts readers to the danger of reducing the mutifaceted genre of *corridos* to one basic form— although he goes on to indulge in this very reduction along Paredes's lines. The explanation of his second point is worth our attention in that it directly addresses the creation of a historical fiction organized according to the monological structure I have been explaining here.

It may well be that ballad communities have existed and continue to exist, although it seems peculiar to characterize a necessarily diverse group of people on the basis of one genre in their expressive repertoire. Américo Paredes provides a useful concept when he speaks of a ballad tradition as a "crystallization" of traditional ballads at one particular time and place into a whole ballad corpus, which by its very weight impresses itself on the consciousness of the people. "Such a ballad tradition, we surmise, existed along the lower Rio Grande border into the early decades of the present century. But the conceptual leap from ballad tradition to ballad community is difficult to justify from concrete ethnographic data." (45)

Once again we are reminded that Paredes's vision is more poetic than historic, as Rosaldo points out. And that poetic vision sought to organize what McDowell correctly characterizes as a diverse group of people around only one form of action-reaction based on the experience of one small region. McDowell questions the existence of such a reality outside the fictional text. I question its existence within the rhetorical structure of the text itself.

15 In my first essay on Chicano literature I rejected the popular terminology of "bilingualism" in favor of "interlingualism." In another essay on Tino Villanueva I explained that the first two sections of his book *Hay otra voz poems* seem to be bilingual "in that the poems are in either one language or the other, while the last section contains only one poem ('Escape') which is written only in Spanish. The mixing of two languages I call interlingualism, because the two languages are put into a state of tension which produces a third, an 'inter' possibility of languages. 'Bilingualism' implies moving from one language code to another; 'interlingualism' implies the constant tension of the two at once. In truth, although the first two sections of *Hay otra voz poems* are technically bilingual in structure, the total experience of the reading is interlingual, but only in the last section does the surface of the text itself become obviously interlingual" in "The Other Voice of Silence: Tino Villanueva," *Modern Chicano Writers*, ed. Joseph Sommers (New York: Prentice Hall, 1979), 133.

16 Bernice Zamora, *Restless Serpents* (Menlo Park: Diseños Literarios, 1976), and Lorna Dee Cervantes, *Emplumada* (Pittsburgh: U of Pittsburgh P, 1982).

17 Berta Ornelas, *Come Down From the Mound* (Phoenix: Miter, 1975).

18 José David Saldívar correctly notes that in his text Paredes's ideological drama "relies for much of its persuasive success on the author's irreverent sense of humor and irony" (54).

19 Paredes takes a position on the origin of the corrido in which he insists that it was invented on the Texan-Mexican border during the second half of the nineteenth century. His rejection of the logical roots in the Spanish romance and the older Mexican corridos also undermines his position on other matters. Also, see note seven above for a discussion of John Holmes McDowell's comments on the "serviceable fictions" associated with Paredes's construction of community around a corrido tradition.

20 Mikhail Bakhtin, *The Dialogic Imagination*, ed. Michael Holquist (Austin: U of Texas P, 1981).

Bilingualism

as Satire

in Nineteenth-

Century

Chicano

Poetry

T he bilingualism of the following four Chicano poems from the U.S. Southwest during the 1800s reflects the historical concern by Chicanos of our complex linguistic context.[1] These four bilingual poems come from approximately 540 poems I collected printed in approximately twenty-five Spanish-language newspapers published in California, Colorado, New Mexico, and Texas between 1848–1906.[2] We see in these bilingual constructions varied, imaginative, and effective experimentation representing a rich linguistic legacy, worthy precursors to the complex contemporary bilingual poetry of such Chicano writers as Alurista, Tino Villanueva, and José Montoya.

Luis A. Torres

The four bilingual Chicano poems under consideration are printed here in chronological order, with my English translations:[3]

I. "El Cura aprendiendo inglés, or, the Yankee Dul," by El Cura de Tamajona, published July 29, 1864, in the newspaper *El Nuevo Mundo*, San Francisco, California. This poem is trilingual, Spanish, French, and English.

El Cura aprendiendo inglés
The Yankee Dul

Poned cortinas,
Pronto, Monsieur,
Mi gola blanca,
Mi traje azul,
Viva el imperio,
Me ahogo, ¡ay Jesús!
—Yo no te entende,
Dijo el atún.
(Que era un Yankazo
Como abedul.
Con cada pata
Como un almud.). . .
Vieca. . . ¿no danzas?
Zi Yankee dul.

Ensayen danzas
De aire andaluz,
Salas gritaba
Con inquietud,
—Mas ronco acento,
Le dijo chust,
(Era el yancote)
No haya rum, rum,
Ensayen todos
Zi Yankee dul.

Señor Austriaco,
¿Qué bailas tú?
¿Serán enanos?
¿Será Mambrú?
¿Bailas Mazurca? . . .
¿Bailas? ¿No hay mus?
Baila un Palomo
Con Padedú,
Te hará la Algara
Currucutú,
—O un bailecito
Bailarú yoú . . .

Luis A.
Torres

Que es de mi tierra . . .
Zi Yankee dul.

¡Oh que bonito!
Cuánta inquietud
Y hermosa orquesta
Que es el *non plus.*
Mas la dirije
Lincoln y puf
En vez del *Sacra*
—Y en vez de augus
Tos nobles . . . acentos,
¿Qué es? ¡¡¡Pataplum!!!
Toca Paniagua
Zi Yankee dul!!!!

¡Con qué atacabas
A O'Donojú
Traidor Almonte!
¿Que también tú
Le haces al Austria
La *portabá?* . . .
Barres lacayo,
Tinta de pús
Tronos sainetes
Resté sans cu
Abajo . . . y dancen
Zi Yankee dul.
     El Cura de Tamajona

The Priest Learning English
The Yankee Doodle

"Hang up the drapes,
Hurry, Monsieur,
My white epaulet,
My blue suit,
Long Live the Empire!
Oh Jesus! I am choking!"
"I can't understand you,"
The idiot said.
(He was a huge Yankee

Big as an Oak,
Each foot
Half an acre in size.)
"Old lady . . . Will you dance?
The Yankee Doodle? "

"Rehearse dances
Of an Andalusian flair,"
Monsieur Salas
Nervously hollered.
But a hoarse accent
Told him, "Hush,"
(It was the huge Yankee)
"No time for la-di-da.
Everyone, rehearse
The Yankee Doodle."

Austrian lord,
What do you dance?
Dances for dwarves?
Do you dance the Mambru?
Do you dance the Mazurca? . . .
Will you dance at all?
Will we dally in the salon?
Dance a Palomo
With a Pas De Deux!
The Algara will make you
Currucutú,
Or will you dance
This little dance. . . .
One from my country. . . .
The Yankee Doodle?

Oh how lovely!
What a clamor your
Lovely orchestra plays,
Most disconcerting.
For it is directed by
Lincoln, thank God!
Instead of the
Sacred Coronation
And instead of the sacro-

Luis A.
Torres

Sanct . . . sounds,
What is it? Footstomping!!!
Good buddies, will you play
The Yankee Doodle!!!

With what did you attack
O'Donojú, you
Traitorous Almonte!
Will you too
Make a mouthpiece
of Austria? . . .
Lackey, color
These farcical thrones
Yellow like pus.
You'll end up
With nothing where you
Sit on your throne
Below . . . and all will dance
The Yankee Doodle.
      El Cura de Tamajona

II. "Desde que llegué," Anonymous, published September 23, 1886, in the newspaper *El Anunciador de Trinidad*, Trinidad, Colorado.

Desde que llegué

Desde que llegué á este puesto
Empecé a aprender inglés,
Y estoy tan adelantado,
Que ya puedo decir *yes.*
Sé contar perfectamente
Desde el *numer one* al *ten,*
Saludar con el *good morning,*
Quede vd. con Diós *my friend.*
Decirle á una niña hermosa
Muy *nice* me parece usté,
Y se le gusta mi modo,
Mi mano le cederé;
Pero de todo el idioma
(Y hablo con ingenuidad)
La palabra más sonora
Es el *money,* ¿no es verdad?
      "A."

Since I Arrived

From the moment I arrived here
I started to learn English,
And I have learned so quickly
That I can already say *yes.*
I know how to count perfectly
From *number one* through *ten,*
Greet someone with *good morning,*
May God go with you *my friend.*
I can tell a pretty girl,
"You seem very *nice* to me,"
And if she likes my manners,
I will ask her to be mine;
But of all the words in English
(And I say it most sincerely)
The one that rings with harmony
Is surely the word *money,*
Don't you agree?
      "A."

III. "Lo que dirá," by T. A. Tornillo, published October 15, 1892, in the newspaper *El Hispano Americano,* Las Vegas, New Mexico.

Lo que dirá

Y que el pueblo vea
That T. B. Catron don't get there.

El 8 de Noviembre lo dirá
Si al pueblo, Catron, mancillará.

El pueblo on that day will blare
Que el panzón never got there.

Because a ladrón banquero
Is not the choice of el borreguero.

For his bursting lungs
Can't silence truth telling tongues.

In silence mute el 8 buscará
Peace in a hiding place do su despecho ahogará.

Poor Tom, tu sino es la dura suerte,
And on the 8th., recibirás tu muerte.
    T. A. Tornillo

What He Will Say

And the people will see everywhere
That T. B. Catron don't get there.

On the 8th of November we will see
If Catron can disgrace our community.

The people on that day will blare
That the fatso never got there.

Because a thieving banker
Is not the choice of the sheepherder.

For his bursting lungs
Can't silence truth telling tongues.

In silence mute he will search on the 8th
Peace in a hiding place to choke on his wrath.

Poor Tom, hard luck is your destiny,
And on the 8th, you will surely die.
    T. A. Tornillo

IV. "Mi Gusto," by "A," published October 19, 1899, in the newspaper
La Voz del Valle, Antonito, Colorado.

Mi gusto

No me hables ¡por Diós! así . . .
¿Por qué me hablas al revés?
Di con tu boquita "sí,"
Pero no me digas "yes."

Si no quieres verme mudo,
Saludas ¿cómo estás tú?
Yo no entiendo tu saludo
"Good morning, how do you do?"

¡No por Diós! linda paisana,
No desprecies nuestra lengua,
Sería en ti mal gusto y mengua
Querer ser americana.

Que yo, a las mexicanitas,
Las aprecio muy deberas;
Trigueñas o morenitas
Me gustan mas que las hueras.
   "A."

What I Like

Do not speak to me, dear God, in English!
Has your language been reversed?
Tell me with your lips so dainty "sí,"
But please never tell me "Yes."

If you don't want me to be mute,
Greet me with "¿cómo estás tú?"
I don't understand your greeting,
"Good morning, how do you do?"

No, dear God! my dear compatriot,
Never disparage our Spanish tongue;
You would commit a sad disgrace
To wish to become Anglicized.

For I have always truly treasured
The sweet young Mexican maidens;
Their hair so dark and skin so brown,
I love them more than Anglo girls.
   "A."

Luis A.
Torres

These four bilingual poems are unique among nineteenth-century Chicano poetry, for such construction was extremely rare. Of the approximately 540 poems I collected from this period, only these four were truly bilingual; one additional poem, "La influencia de los greenbacks," published in *El Clarin Mexicano*, from Santa Fe, New Mexico, August 10, 1873, employs two English words but is almost entirely monolingual Spanish.[4] It is a mark of how far afield contemporary Chicanos have strayed from their linguistic Spanish roots when we realize that from 1846–1906 less than one percent of the poetry printed in these representative twenty-five newspapers was even bilingual, and none was entirely in English.

One of the major considerations determining the poets' use of bilingualism in these poems was to serve as a warning against the increasing loss of the Chicano culture. The time span within which these poems were written is a factor in determining their degree of bilingualism. The poems cover thirty-five years, from the trilingual "El Cura aprendiendo inglés," in 1864, with little English wording; to "Desde que llegué," in 1886, with brief English phrases; to the penultimate poem "Lo que dirá," in 1892, in which the bilingualism is almost perfectly balanced; to "Mi gusto," in 1899, which grudgingly employs English phrases. So with the passing of time, the quantity of English in these poems generally increases which heightens in the poems the concern of acculturation. The last poem, "Mi gusto," is a prime example of this concern; the loss of Spanish and its substitution with English is the chief feared manifestation of this acculturation with the bilingualism used satirically against those who would lose their Spanish in favor of learning English.

The four poems represent the three Southwestern states of California, New Mexico, and Colorado over a period of thirty-five years, yet they have many common characteristics of theme and poetic form. Perhaps the single most significant aspect of these poems, other than their bilingual form, is their humor, providing added testimony to the humor exhibited in so much early nineteenth-century Chicano poetry.[5] These poems are satirical, and as is endemic to satire, all four are laced with social commentary and are socially engaged. Their satirical elements are evident. For example, as Northrop Frye said in "The Nature of Satire," the elements essential to satire are wit and an object of attack, followed by a balance of tone between hatred and gaiety (16).[6] These four poems are marked by a tone poised between anger against their presumed antagonists and the humor the poets are able to engender by one of the basic strategies of satire, the reduction, or cutting down to size, of the object of attack.[7] Irony is an additional method of reduction, and the bilingualism itself of these poems is ironic in that the poets used the languages spoken by their presumed antagonists, English in all four poems including French in "El Cura aprendiendo inglés." These poets were satirizing enemies of enormous power and influence—T. B. Catron in "Lo que dirá" and Maximilian in "El Cura aprendiendo inglés"—and the encroaching political, economic, and social power represented by the English language itself in "Mi gusto" and "Desde que llegué." Thus, in their diminution of their objects of attack, the poets were able to provide for the Chicano community an abstracted reduction of their enemies to conceptually isolate the threat to the community.

Such methods of satire through bilingual construction can be seen, for example, in "Lo que dirá," or "What He Will Say," written against

Thomas B. Catron, one of the leaders in New Mexico of the Santa Fe Ring of the 1880s. Catron is at once a specific target of the satire, yet emblematic of the Anglo-American politicians controlling the Santa Fe Ring against which the Chicanos were fighting. Speaking of Catron and of the large influx of Anglo-Americans into New Mexico during the period, Rudolfo Acuña in *Occupied America* describes the occupation of New Mexico and stresses that political cliques were created to facilitate the theft of the land and suggests that most were subservient to the Santa Fe Ring which

> controlled the governor and most of the office holders in the territory. . . . Thomas B. Catron, the ring's official leader, and mastermind of its New Mexico operation, arrived in New Mexico in the late 1860's, eventually becoming United States attorney general for the territory. 'Thoughout his life in New Mexico, Catron wielded more power than any other single individual in the territory. Through land grant litigation and by purchases he acquired more than one million acres of land' (57).[8]

The Republican Catron's 1892 campaign for delegate-in-Congress was the specific object of satire in "Lo que dirá." The poet's wishes were fulfilled, for Catron's campaign was defeated. According to Rosenbaum, in *Mexicano Resistance in the Southwest*, in the 1892 elections, "Catron's shadow covered everything else. Pilloried for his enormous wealth based on land stolen from *los pobres*, his intimidation of *mexicano* jurors, and his use of harassment and assassination, Catron symbolized in San Miguel County the worst evils of Anglo encroachment; he lost by the widest margin of any candidate" (133).[9]

The poem works effectively as satire largely because of the bilingualism. The use of English in this poem verges on satirical parody in that the language of the Anglo-American Catron is mimicked and held up to ridicule. An additional element of satire is evident in this poem, as in the three others, in the use of antiliterary words, the harsh, nearly scurrilous language in the attempt to diminish the object being satirized,[10] such as in "Lo que dirá" the words "panzón" ("fatso"), "ladrón" ("thieving"), "Poor Tom," and "recibirás tu muerte" (literally "you will receive your death"). Hodgart, in *Satire*, suggests a rough style of language is a staple in the history of satirical language "to match the violence of [the writers'] feelings and the grotesqueness of their subjects. The critical doctrine that satire should be harsh and rough, because it attacks vicious men" (141)[11] has been an accepted linguistic form of

Luis A.
Torres

satirical language, here compounded and made more intricate by the bilingualism of these poems.

The bilingualism in "Lo que dirá," representative of the additional three poems, sets an "Us v. Them" ideology, with Spanish words characterizing the Chicano "Us" and English words characterizing the Anglo-American "Them." Such a dichotomy is necessary for extrapoetic purposes, chiefly to solidify the Chicano society in their struggle against the adverse effects brought about by the "Them" in the poems. For example, the poet T. A. Tornillo—almost certainly a pen name, perhaps translatable as "I Will Screw You"—uses Spanish when he refers to the concerns of the Chicanos as when he says, "Y que el pueblo vea" [And the people will see], and switches in the next line to English when he refers to the Anglo-American antagonist Tom Catron in, "That T. B. Catron don't get there" (the apparent grammatical lapse intensifies the parody through antiliterary language). The tone created by the linguistic shift is that Catron does not deserve to be addressed in Spanish, for his English-speaking world is opposed to the Spanish-speaking community, an opposition here reversed through language.

This "Us v. Them" theme, attacking individuals in "Lo que dirá" and "El Cura aprendiendo inglés," has a broader target in "Desde que llegué" and "Mi gusto"; the English language itself is satirized and parodied through the bilingualism. The main object of attack in these two poems is the danger of acculturation, for they feared that an increased acceptance of the English language by the Chicano people would trigger an acceptance of the attendant Anglo-American culture. This fear provides the humor created in "Desde que llegué" and the plaintive warning in "Mi gusto."

A large measure of the successful tone in "Desde que llegué" is the delicate irony of the author's self-deprecating humor. He ostensibly takes pride in his ability to utter the most basic of English words such as "yes," to count from one through ten, and to offer salutations and compliments. He draws a persona of a simpleton, a portrait which remains consistent until the last three lines. If the reader has unwittingly accepted the persona's character, the reader is primed for the effective reversal in the last three lines, especially in the last line which has the effect of a periodic sentence. Following the reader's belief that the persona is indeed a simpleton, the last line reverses our expectations of him completely, for we are surprised that he is perceptive enough to deduce the heart of the English-speaking society—"*money*"! This satirical rebuttal against the materialism and greed the poet believes

Bilingualism
as Satire

are the chief motivations of the Anglo-American society ridicules the culture represented by the English language of the previous part of the poem.

Similarly to "Desde que llegué," "Mi gusto" looks on the prospect of the Chicanos' adoption of the English language as a threatening trend toward acculturation, a prospect to be feared. However, the tone with which the two poems treat the threat is antithetical, self-deprecatingly humorous in "Desde que llegué" but darkly sardonic in "Mi gusto."

The poet of "Mi gusto" might well intend his invective against English to be directed against those Chicanos who would follow the "simpleton" persona in "Desde que llegué." In the first stanza, the poet of "Mi gusto" pointedly instructs the young woman he is addressing, "Tell me with your lips so dainty, 'Si,' / But please never tell me 'Yes,'" thus ridiculing a similar simplistic linguistic performance the persona of "Desde que llegué" ostensibly was proud of accomplishing, the ability to say "Yes." In the second stanza, he warns the young woman he will be struck speechless if she addresses him in English with "Good morning, how do you do," a similarity, again, to what the persona of "Desde que llegué" was proud of accomplishing, the ability to say "Good morning." The poet of "Mi gusto" continues in the third stanza with a pointed admonishment that the young woman not "disparage" the Spanish language, followed by a direct warning that she should not become Anglicized, such acculturation residing in her benign acceptance of the English language, for presumably she is not aware of the threat posed by English: with the use of the English language comes the acceptance of the attendant Anglo-American culture. He ends with a reaffirmation of the Mexican culture, looking inward to the people as a bulwark of safety against the linguistic threat which would imply cultural and social disintegration.

Among these four poems, the language varieties go beyond rudimentary bilingualism into linguistic diversity, most evident in "El Cura aprendiendo inglés," or, "the Yankee Dul." In this respect, these early bilingual experiments are remarkably similar to the various forms evident in contemporary Chicano poetics. Linguistic scholars and critics of contemporary Chicano literature have cited the wide variety of language use among Chicanos, far beyond plain bilingualism to multilingualism. For example, Cordelia Candelaria in remarks about the poet Alurista's language use suggests its most obvious feature is its bilingualism and says that upon closer inspection what is apparent is its

Luis A.
Torres

*multi*lingualism, its polyphonic codes of sound and sense, its complex use of at least six different language systems: 1. Standard edited American English. 2. English slang. . . . 3. Standard Spanish. 4. Dialectal Spanish (regional vernaculars including *caló*). 5. English/Spanish or Spanish/English bilingualism. 6. An amalgam of pre-American indigenous languages, mostly noun forms in Nahua and Mayan. . . . [T]he phonological, morphological, syntactic, and semantic possibilities of Chicano poetry are astonishingly flexible and extensive. (*Chicano Poetry: A Critical Introduction* 73)[12]

Similarly, Rosaura Sanchez, in *Chicano Discourse*, expands further upon the theme of multilingualism in suggesting that within one of these dialects—caló—four distinct varieties are evident based on geographical locale and finds that, "in the artistic and literary fields, Chicanos have raised it to another level and made it a literary code as well" (129–34).[13]

I do not suggest here that the language use of these early writers is as complex as that of contemporary Chicano poets. However, these early poems reveal the inherent linguistic complexity of our people in the 1800s which would amplify and become elaborated during the intervening period between the 1864 "El Cura aprendiendo inglés" and contemporary Chicano poetry; such complexity would lead to the extensive language varieties today. In the single poem "El Cura aprendiendo inglés," for example, we see a symbolic answer to the question, Where did our contemporary multilingualism originate? In its trilingualism of Spanish, French, and some English, and its blending of Mexican, Spanish, United States, French, and Austrian social features, it serves as a microcosm of the linguistic and cultural milieus affecting our historical and contemporary communities. The multiple levels of meaning created by the linguistic blends are ingenious, a tour de force of language use for the period.

The author of this poem is "El Cura de Tamajona," or, "The Priest from Tamajona," a pseudonym. He published six poems, satires of Maximilian and his wife Carlota, in the San Francisco newspaper *El Nuevo Mundo*, all in July 1864. El Cura was either a native San Franciscan with close ties to Mexico or an exile in San Francisco fleeing the French/Austrian invasion of Mexico.

The purpose of the poem is to satirize the supposed elegance of the French and Austrian cultures. The dance that is being staged by the presumed royalty is viciously ridiculed. Such coveted refinement is mocked even by the subtitle of the poem, "The Yankee Dul," or, "The Yankee Doodle," a tune posited as inherently inelegant—or even as *anti*-elegant. In the last two stanzas, the veneer of refinement completely disintegrates, the writing becoming nearly unintelligible, reflecting the desired collapse of the usurper's throne.

The first hint of satire is in the fifth and sixth lines, when the speaker—presumably Maximilian—says in line five, " 'Long Live the Empire!' " and immediately in line six says, "Oh Jesus! I am choking!" as if one will choke just by wishing "the Empire" well. This tone continues in a slur against Carlota when, at the end of the stanza, Maximilian in preparing himself to dance asks, "Old lady . . . Will you dance?" The "Old lady," one assumes, is his wife Carlota who held pretensions to beauty.

In the second stanza the preparation for the dance continues with the coterie rehearsing dances "Of an Andalusian flair," a mark of Maximilian's attempt at an international culture, one evoking the Spanish colonization of Mexico. But the dance participants will ultimately dance "The Yankee Dul" in an apparent attempt at further broadening their veneer of culture.

In the third stanza, the first eight lines continue the preparation for the presentation of the dances, such as the Mambru, the Mazurca, or a Palomo with the ballet "Padedú" (Pas de Deux). In the last four lines of the stanza, the attention shifts to the narrator of the poem, as he asks,

> "Or will you dance
> A little dance. . . .
> The dance from my land. . . .
> *The Yankee Doodle!*"

The effect of the narrator's juxtaposing the European dances with the American tune "The Yankee Doodle" is the further reduction of the French and Austrian cultures' elegance.

Of major interest in the third stanza is the bilingualism in the twelfth line, "Bailará yoú." The "yoú" is, of course, the English word "you," with the accent mark on the letter "-ú" of the Spanish equivalent "tú," the informal word of address. The formal address, "usted" in place of "tú" or "you," would be more fitting for a true monarch, as Maximilian wished to be. However, the narrator in his bilingual construction of combining the informal "tú" with "you" to create the coined word "yoú" is telling Maximilian that his pretensions to the throne are just that—pretensions.

In the fourth stanza, the poet satirizes the music and the orchestra, calling it noisy but beautiful and *"non plus"* in French, suggesting its equal no longer exists. A further example of his complex language use is in the words, "Y en vez de augus / Tos nobles . . . ." The words "augus" and "Tos," if combined, would be "augustos," in English "august" or "noble." But he splits the word, and the "Tos" could be read as "Es*tos* nobles . . . acentos," but since he says in the previous line, "En vez de," he is saying, literally, "instead of these noble accents [or sounds]," the sounds are noise, since he then asks, "¿Que es? ¡¡¡Pataplum!!!" ("what / Is [the sound]? Footstomping!!!") He therefore gives us two readings by his splitting of "Augustos," intended to diminish the "August" pretensions of the usurper.

In the fifth stanza, he loses all pretense of a satire meant to reduce Maximilian and instead directly attacks him. He says, "Con que atacabas / A O'Donojú." Since the poet has used trilingualism previously, the name "O'Donojú" (instead of the Irish equivalent "O'Donohue") can be read as a play on the Spanish enunciation of the English "I don't know who," a phrase which casts Maximilian as even more traitorous, implying he has attacked everyone indiscriminately. The satire continues until the ninth line when the attack against Maximilian is complete in the words "tronos sainetes," or "farcical thrones," followed by the French phrase *"Reste sans cu / Abajo,"* literally, "You will be left without a tail / Below . . . ." With this reduced image, and belittled by the parodying use of the French phrase symbolizing his French patrons, Maximilian is left a ridiculed figure, transfigured from the elegant portrait at the beginning of the poem. Thus ends this vicious, complex, and linguistically ingenious satire against the usurper.

The four satirical poems studied here served to emphasize for their communities the theme of separation from the objects of attack, marks of warning against linguistic and social acculturation. In linguistic experimentation and powerful social statement, these poems stand as eminently innovative to serve as worthy precursors to the multilingual experimentation of contemporary Chicano poetry. Thematically these early poems may stand as models for our contemporary works, for their poets turned inward toward the Chicano people to form a solidarity in response to their rapidly evolving social plight. Aesthetically, they also provided us with the model of how and where we may find our artistic resolutions: We must develop our aesthetic standard from the multifaceted linguistic reality of our own people.

Notes

1 I will use the contemporary term "Chicano" in reference to the people of Mexican descent living in the United States during the nineteenth century even though the term did not come into widespread use until the latter half of the twentieth century. I do so to emphasize the aesthetic and cultural continuity from the nineteenth century through today.

2 Of approximately 540 poems, at least half were originally written in the present-day boundary of the United States Southwest; the remainder were either written in other Spanish-speaking countries or were anonymously written, and their location of origin is impossible to determine.

3 I have aimed largely for literal translations, but I have also tried to create English poems which would stand on their own. Also, I have transcribed these poems faithfully as they were printed in the newspapers with the exception of adding minor corrections such as diacritical marks where such marks were not included in the newspaper printing.

4 "La influencia de los greenbacks" is essentially monolingual Spanish, but it is bilingual in spirit. The only two words in this poem of fifteen four-line stanzas that are English are "Greenbacks" and the loan word "cheques" for "checks." However, these two words are frequently repeated, and they dominate the poem. The influence of English upon acculturation toward what the words "greenbacks" and "cheques" imply informs the poem.

5 The humor of nineteenth-century Chicano poetry can be seen in the poetry from California. Of a total of approximately 125 California poems from 1855–1882 I collected which I could document as indigenous, I chose 71 such poems as the basis of a study. Of these, I listed 7 in the "Humorous" category, and several others which were politically satirical could likewise have been so categorized.

6 Northrop Frye, "The Nature of Satire," *Satire: Theory and Practice*, ed. Charles A. Allen and George D. Stephens, (Belmont: Wadsworth, 1962).

7 See Hodgart, *Satire*, pages 147 and 157, for the strategy of reduction in satire and aphorisms.

8 Rudolfo Acuña, *Occupied America* (New York: Harper and Row, 1981).

9 Robert J. Rosenbaum, *Mexicano Resistance in the Southwest* (Austin: U of Texas P, 1981).

10 See Frye for references to this technique of satire, *Anatomy of Satire*, 18.

11 Matthew Hodgart, *Satire* (New York: McGraw-Hill, 1969).

12 Cordelia Candelaria, *Chicano Poetry: A Critical Introduction* (Westport: Greenwood P, 1986).

13 Rosaura Sanchez, *Chicano Discourse: Socio-historic Perspectives* (Rowley: Newbury House, 1983).

Luis A.
Torres

Makes no difference whether you speak Spanish through the streets of Quito, Havana, Mexico City, Madrid, or Managua—you're caught. Or, for that matter, East L.A. or the *Barrio* in Manhattan. We eat and dream in Spanish.

Language is usually seen as a portent of evolution, something that sets us above and apart from the rest of creation. Today, after more than fifty years juggling words, I see it more as a trap, as a leash defining the limits of my understanding and reducing my ability to relate and live with other language-bound creatures. Born in Spanish—in Havana, Cuba—I considered myself bilingual since my mother was English speaking. It was a private, domestic illusion. Spanish determined the confines of my values and attitudes. I am doomed to the language and its grooves.

During my years as a student at Columbia and the New School, I missed the fault; I failed again to see it when I translated my novel *Memorias del subdesarrollo* into *Inconsolable Memories*. It is not the meaning of words or the structure of sentences. It is the way we load

Nacer

en

Español

Edmundo

Desnoes

and fire words. Only now, after uprooting myself from Cuba for a decade, and finding myself unable to take root in Manhattan, I am growing a bifocal vision.

Language survives through time and space, travels through history and geography, accompanying us as closely as our own shadow, sometimes behind and othertimes ahead of us, yet always bending our perspective. Language goes beyond the awesome differences between *macho* and male; it goes beyond etymological breakdowns. What keeps it alive is how we use and abuse it.

Its Latin matrix makes Spanish highly rhetorical, in itself as well as compared to English; it lingers longer on words because language is cognitively more decisive within the culture—it even takes longer to enunciate polysyllables than monosyllables. We spend more time in language, feel its weight upon us, and believe in throwing it around, as if words were weapons, stones, or limbs able to embrace.

Spanish became a nation in the fifteenth century when it overwhelmed—with Santiago and *cojones*—the more highly developed Moors and decided with the same sweeping faith and arrogance to expel the Jews. The Moors were technologically more advanced; the Jews were intellectually at the head of Europe. Spanish locked itself into courage and faith and assumed they were the main Christian virtues—and the language perpetuated the passion. The same linguistic worldview crossed the Atlantic and established itself in our *Nuevo Mundo*. The view still operates in Latin America; Fidel Castro and his bearded rebels *reconquistaron* the island under the same banner and drove away a superior culture, in economic and technological terms, with self-righteous courage. Only *in* Spanish could they have driven away English-speaking interests; only the Spanish language would take upon itself a challenge the rest of the world considered absurd and impossible, given Cuba's size—the expulsion of the United States in the name of its archenemy, socialism.

Spanish has never been able to properly embrace representative democracy because republicanism is a civil organization of society; only when we embrace a church, today communism, are we able to dent world opinion.

Language carries ideology longer than social institutions; in spite of its linear and sequential nature, it includes a circular motion, a wrapping itself around its own discourse. It functions at times as a particle and at others as a wave. Spanish-born individuals are anarchic particles that operate as waves of faith and courage when moved to action. Language *is not* indestructible, it is only more resilient, resistant to change than laws, institutions, or modes of production. Spanish is stubborn and English is pragmatic. No two European languages could be more radically bifurcated.

Spanish doesn't take failure easily. Failure doesn't teach us a lesson; failure humiliates us, and if we can't have it our way we surrender to corruption and opportunism. Language sustains a binary system of values, *sí* and *no*, and therefore the other side of faith and courage is disbelief and opportunism; when we don't believe we are easily corrupted and survive by lies and astute behavior. The binary system is down to earth—crude realism or the sublime—stubborn arrogance.

The split and the clash between Spanish and English, as established views of the world, began in 1588 with the defeat of the *Armada Invencible*. English is a practice; Spanish is a project. Francis Bacon, less than thirty years later, in 1620, confirmed the practice that defeated the Spanish project. Since *Dios* is a concept, a guide to action, nevertheless a concept, it must rely heavily on language—and language is what Bacon dethroned, replacing it with practice, science, acting upon the environment, not upon the *alma*. (I use *Dios* and *alma*, not as style, not to remind you of the undercurrent of Spanish in my thinking, but because *Dios* and *alma* are absolutes, loaded with passion and sexuality, public entities—while God and soul are private, relative, personal entities.) The Mediterranean world, the Greeks, were trapped in words, and Bacon insisted on a *Novum Organum*; Plato and Aristotle "assuredly have that which is characteristic of boys; they are prompt to prattle but cannot generate; for their wisdom abounds in words but is barren of works." That was a lethal blow to Spanish, to our "words" and "prattle." What Bacon said of the Greeks could be said today of the Spanish-speaking people; for all our cultural claims, we have not produced "a single experiment which tends to relieve and benefit the condition of man." When presented with this proposition in the thirties, Miguel de Unamuno, the Spanish philosopher, exclaimed proudly: "*Que inventen ellos*," "let them (the rest of Europe) invent." As we approach the millennium, Spanish is being left behind in production, merchandising, exchange of information, and individual freedoms. We are peripheral to a planetary thrust that is embracing even China and the Soviet Union.

For a moment, during the Kennedy years, political alternatives seemed to be appearing in the South, in Latin America. "To Kennedy," writes Richard N. Goodwin, "as to the swollen, bellicose Castro, Latin America was destined to be a principal battleground between systems of government." This is no longer the case. (The Pacific Rim, as a focus of investment and world attention, is what Latin America was twenty years ago.)

Communism, the last form of absolutism, is, or was, the last hope of Latin America. Spanish, with its gusto for guts and its need for ideological commitment, is ideally suited to enter the Marxist-Leninist church. In Cuba, during the sixties, we studied the main Marxist thinkers. Marx, in Spanish, sounded to us as the Bible rendered by Cipriano de Valera, the Spanish priest who translated the scriptures in the sixteenth century; Lenin was read and understood as if he were a reincarnation of San Ignacio de Loyola; and Rosa Luxemburg, as Sor Juana Inés de la Cruz.

It is not only the nuance of words that we betray when we translate a text. It is not a matter of words and meaning; the betrayal lies in the way we exchange words, value, and believe them. Madame de Stael, for whom conversation was a *raison d'être*, found, to her astonishment, that Germans used words and language merely as an instrument, as a means of communication. In France, she explains, "words are not merely, as they are in other countries, a means to communicate ideas, feelings, and needs, but an instrument one likes to play and which revives the spirit, just as does music in some nations, and strong liquors in others."

The French believe language is a rational absolute; the Spanish use it as an absolute to impose truth in the plaza. For Madame de Stael it was almost what it is today for Spanish-speaking people; Germaine believed her books, given her genius, would make Napoleon forgive her for conspiring and allow her to return to Paris and establish a shadow government in her salon. Conversation, language, was, for Madame de Stael "a certain way in which people act upon one another, a quick give-and-take of pleasure, a way of speaking as soon as one thinks, of rejoicing in oneself in the immediate present, of being applauded without making an effort." This ability "to act upon one another," "of being applauded without making an effort" has been neglected by most linguistic studies, yet it enjoys good health amongst Spanish-speaking nations and their communities abroad. Bilingualism is no answer; the second language is merely absorbed into the ways and means of the old.

This function of language makes the countries of Latin America resilient and even hostile to key elements in global development and ignorant of postmodern behavior. We can produce and do produce political and literary figures of world stature. The political leaders operate upon society through words, values, and ideas. Revolution seems the opposite of idle prattle, yet it takes place when prattle can become reality; when words are trusted, revolutions take place. The new structures created by social upheavals—since the independence wars of the nineteenth century—have failed to change our basic reliance on language as truth, of courage as the supreme test of virtue. This spirit is inimical to science, for it fails to see the coexistence of contradictory endeavors and visions as a creative factor in civil society.

Language, Spanish, conditions us to see what happens around us from a given perspective. Our values become absolutes and no corroboration is necessary, therefore no change is possible. Auerbach, in his study of the "representation of reality in Western literature" describes lucidly the basic difference between Spanish and English "reality." A careful reading of his chapters on Hamlet and Don Quixote exposes the basic attitudes assumed by each historical language. In "The Weary Prince," Auerbach argues that Shakespeare "includes earthly reality" in *Hamlet* but always "his purpose goes far beyond the representation of reality; . . . he embraces reality but he transcends it." Cervantes is more crudely popular and down to earth, but his character, Don Quixote, refuses to accept the test of reality and imposes his *idée fixe* upon the challenge of the objective world. When Sancho Panza shows three peasant women on donkeys to the "Caballero de la triste figura" as Dulcinea and two of her ladies—Don Quixote immediately has the answer, the lady of his dreams is enchanted by an evil knight. He is able to impose a sublime vision upon a pedestrian reality.

A vision, an *idée fixe* is a thing of the mind, therefore shaped by language. "In this sense Spanish realism is more decidedly popular, more filled with the life of the people, than English realism of the same period." This leads Auerbach to dismiss the contribution of Spanish to the modern world: "Yet in the history of the literary conquest of modern reality, the literature of Spain's great century is not particularly important—much less so than Shakespeare, or even Dante, Rabelais, or Montaigne." And with a devastating blow places Spain in the impotent real of magical realism: "It turns the world into a magic stage (Spanish literature of the *siglo de oro*). And on that magic stage—this again is very significant for its relation to modern realism—a fixed order reigns, despite all the elements of adventure and miracle. In the world, it is true, everything is a dream, but nothing is a riddle demanding to be solved. There are passions and conflicts but there are no problems."

This is the major wound of Spanish as a language/worldview. Realistic and fantastic in the same breath; after five hundred years this binary trap survives in both politics and in the literature of Alejo Carpentier,

Gabriel García Márquez, and even Jorge Luis Borges. These writers have succeeded in and through language, through ideas, through Spanish.

The purest literary example of this fugue is the Cuban poet Jose Lezama Lima. The atrophied realism of Gongora's *Soledades* is carried to a total break with reality. Reality, for Lezama, is an excuse to start writing a poem; nothing more. As words speed up in a dense accumulation of metaphors—"as a train traveling on a ribbon of silk over a precipice"—the poem is able to do away with reality. Poetry ends being self-generated, absolute. "La oscura lucha con el pez concluye, su boca finge de la noche orilla." Language sucks in reality and ends by freezing it.

Pablo Neruda is no exception. In his autobiography, the Chilean poet defines language as ideology, words as a living organism: "No se puede vivir toda una vida con un idioma, moviéndose longitudenalmente, explorándolo, hurgándole el pelo y la barriga, sin que esta intimidad forme parte del organismo." ("You can't spend your entire life with a language, moving lengthwise, exploring it, scratching its hair and its belly, without this intimacy becoming part of your organism.") Words come to life and this "intimacy" with language becomes our ideological nature. Words are the only ones able to fulfill our thirst for the absolute: "Soy omnívoro de sentimientos, de seres, de libros, de acontecimientos y batallas. Me comería toda la tierra. Me bebería todo el mar." ("I'm omnivorous for feelings, for beings, for books, for events and battles. I could eat the entire earth. I could drink up the entire ocean.") This absolute can never be achieved amongst dense material things, only amongst breathing words.

Edmundo
Desnoes

Economics, science, and politics are pivotal to our century—yet only politics, as an earthly religion, is central to Spanish synapses. Although economics actively shapes our lives, very few Spanish-speaking individuals—in both Europe and America—understand the abstract power of money. In a list of the one hundred most economically powerful men in the world—not a single individual was born in Spanish. There are wealthy men and women in our language, but their wealth is passive, hidden in Swiss banks (ex-president López Mateo of Mexico is said to be one of the ten richest men in the world, but his wealth is not openly acknowledged, it was received under the presidential table), it is never financially creative.

Che Guevara, like Bolivar before him, dreamt of extending his political capital throughout Latin America. His ideas were central to the international political discourse of the sixties. No Latin American, on the other hand, has been able to manufacture and distribute a single line of products to compete in the world market. The Pacific Rim has produced more industrial and financial wizards in the last thirty years than Spain and Latin America in the last three hundred years. Koreans, overseas Chinese, say nothing of the Japanese (who asserted themselves in the world markets long after Spain had established a theological colonial empire that tentacled into Southeast Asia)—are all able to recognize the abstract power of money, the energy it can channel and invest throughout the world. Our appeal was in raw materials—from gold and silver to coffee and bananas—and it lasted as long as they were central to Western industrialization. In the eighties economic growth is in the transfer of technology and capital investment mainly to the Pacific Rim. Confucianist materialism is more productive than Loyola's army of faithful.

We have a dark, nocturnal sense of money; wealth is something you steal in the night, or something only worthy of display, like the hundreds of empty shoes owned by Imelda Marcos (the Philippines was the final frontier of Spanish ideology) or the jewelry displayed on so many Hispanics in the United States. You can always recognize a Spanish-speaking community by the proliferation of jewelry shops—as in Miami, Florida, or Union City, New Jersey.

A year ago *Forbes* magazine came out with a list of the richest men in Latin America. At the top of the list were Pablo Escobar Gaviria and Jorge Luis Ochoa Vázquez, both Colombians, both billionaires, both involved in the most powerful Spanish-speaking corporation in the world, with markets in both the United States and Europe, with investments in Hong Kong and Switzerland. They operate with faith in the subversive power of courage. Last November an American journalist, Tina Rosenberg, writing in the *Atlantic* on Medellín, Colombia *(Murder City)*, was surprised by the awe surrounding the drug barons: "Indeed, only listening to young Sandinistas in Nicaragua talk about Che Guevara have I heard anything comparable to the adoration that poor people in Medellín express for Don Pablo (Escobar Gaviria)." Both performed feats of courage, both have a place in the pantheon of Spanish heroes.

To-go-talking is as rewarding to a Spanish-speaking man or woman as to-go-shopping can be to their English-speaking counterparts. Language, conversation, is what we trade in the plaza. The plaza, the social space of Latin culture, constitutes itself wherever Spanish congregates. We exchange words to establish our position in the world and obtain recognition. To find an English equivalent one must go to the mall. Language in the mall is for pointing, requesting, showing needs, and satisfying desires. The mall is a bazaar and energy exchange center, crowded with products and images, a place to enjoy the warmth concentrated in bills and coins. The plaza is an empty space where things happen in thin air, where battles are lost or won, where authority and identity are achieved.

Whereas language is an instrument for those born in English, for those born in Spanish it's a supreme being—therefore relentlessly stubborn, obdurate. Spanish is locked into itself and into ourselves from the moment we appropriate the linguistic system during our first seven years on earth. The outlook of Spanish, nourished and grooved into our nervous system, our neurons by family and friends, can be studied following a periodicity similar to the epistemological stages established by Piaget. Instead of recognizing hidden objects or the changes of water levels in a bottle, the study would establish the hidden power of words and the changes in social approval between *cobarde* and *valiente*, or between *todo* and *nada*.

Since the pattern of meaning and behavior is built into the language, it produces and reproduces itself endlessly. That is why those born in Spanish are in agony. An agony that has not relented in modern times. Spanish has carried in its womb the values of feudalism into the postindustrial world. The three orders of feudal society, as Marc Bloch states, "those who prayed, those who fought and those who worked" are still interacting in our countries. Those who pray, apart from the *curas*, are the *políticos* and the *miembros del partido*. And we can easily recognize those who fight and those who work.

We have lost the battle of ideas; words cannot sustain values nor courage impose rigid *conceptualismo* in a world of relative freedoms and intensive production. Today alternatives are more decisive than the search for certainty; doubt is more productive than truth; individual freedom more comfortable than collective faith; courage is still able to stand up to superior number and weapons, as in Cuba and Nicaragua, but it cannot increase production nor propitiate scientific thinking and research. Fidel Castro moved the Cuban people with a promise of heaven on earth, but when it came to inanimate objects words left them cold. Manuel Sánchez Pérez, a former vice minister of *Comercio Exterior*, after a bleak economic report, was rebuked by Fidel Castro: "No se deje tupir por la realidad, joven" ("Young man, don't let reality deceive you"). Castro is still trapped in the power of words and the courage that established the roots of the present Cuban government. You cannot tease the economy into productivity, and civil society is inimical to absolutes.

Absolutes, unity, are essential to bring about social change, to face danger and survive catastrophe—not for everyday give and take. That is accomplished with diversity and space for experimentation. We have failed to understand the fulcrums of the world we must inhabit. More and more information to operate the planet is moving along the axis of Moscow, Bonn, London, New York, Los Angeles, and Tokyo, and less and less is exchanged with Latin America. Only by gutting Spanish will we be able to see around us, recognize the shape of things and the enormous amounts of energy stored in matter.

The unquestioned premises of language have created confusion and obstacles even in science. "Being guided by a fragmentary self-world view, man then acts in such a way as to try to break himself and the world up, so that all seems to correspond to his way of thinking." What physicist David Bohn sees as the distortion that language introduces into scientific thinking is eminently true of the way Spanish conditions us. "Man thus obtains an apparent proof of the correctness of his fragmentary self-world view though, of course, he overlooks the fact that it is he himself, acting according to his mode of thought, who has brought about fragmentation that now seems to have an autonomous existence, independent of his will and of his desire."

As the planet moves away from linguistic absolutes into visual thinking and insight and relies more on observation and corroboration, the value of language must decrease; we must move away from certainty, which is the main goal of thinking exclusively in language, and accept uncertainty as essential for survival. Spanish, the most self-centered Western language, should become aware of the golden cage in which singing changes nothing and divest itself of its baroque ballast. Only what is empty can be filled.

It would be naive to conclude in a note of hope, just because, as humans, we dislike bleak ends. Twenty years ago it seemed as if Latin America had a better chance than Spain to get out of the black hole of Spanish; now Spain seems more likely to accomplish this as the country integrates into the European community. That remains to be seen.

I have diagnosed the disease not only in others but in my own guts and mind. I see no end to the agony—unless we are all blown to pieces in a nuclear holocaust or exhaust the resources of the planet.

AA. Tell me a little about yourself, about the influences upon you.

GCS. Well, born in Calcutta in the middle of the war, 1942. Earliest memories are of the artificial famine created by the British military to feed the soldiers in the Pacific theater of the Second World War. It was obviously illegal to protest against this. As an extraordinary political move in response to this situation, was formed what became a major phenomenon, the Indian People's Theatre Association, IPTA. They took performance as the medium of protest. Obviously the British were not coming to check out street-level theatre: the actors were not professional actors. What they were performing was the famine and how to organize against it.

I was growing up as a middle-class child in the shadow of the famine. The extraordinary vitality of the Indian People's Theatre Association was in the air. A relationship between aesthetics and politics was being deployed by people who were taking advantage of the fact that aesthetics had been officially defined as autonomous by colonial ideology. They were, in other words, using the enemy's definition of aesthetics

Gayatri

Chakravorty

Spivak

Interviewed by
Alfred Arteaga

as having an autonomous sphere and sabotaging that in order to bring back the relationship between aesthetics and politics in a very direct way. The fine thing was that the plays were good; the songs were good. One still sings those songs, even on marches. That's something that colored my childhood more than I knew then.

One of the big memories is of negotiated political independence, very early on. My generation was on the cusp of decolonization. On our childhood and adolescent sensibilities was played out the meaning of a negotiated political independence. We were not adults; yet we were not born after independence. In a way, it's more interesting to have been in my generation than to have been a midnight's child, to have been born at independence, to be born free by chronological accident.

I come from the bottom layer of the upper middle class or the top layer of the lower middle class, depending on which side of the family you are choosing. I went to a missionary school, which is different from a convent. A convent is upper class and fashionable stuff. Mine was a cheap school, very good academic quality. By the time I was going, most of the teachers were tribal Christians, that is to say, Indian subalterns, lower than rural underclass by origin, neither Hindus nor Muslims, not even Hindu untouchables, but tribals—so called aboriginals—who had been converted by missionaries.

So that again, if the IPTA is one early experience, another early experience, which then I didn't know was going to influence me so strongly, was of learning—as a child from a good caste-Hindu family —from women who were absolutely underprivileged but who had dehegemonized Christianity in order to occupy a space where they could teach social superiors. The schooling was in Bengali, my mother tongue, until the last four years. Then, of course, it was hard to get us into English, since teachers and students were both Indian. But "English-medium" still has glamour for the Indian middle class, presumably because it is still a better weapon for upward class mobility.

And then B.A. from Presidency College. I think that the strongest influence on students of my class going to that kind of college was the intellectual left. It was, once again, a college known for academic excellence but not class-fixed, so that there was a sprinkling of students from working-class and rural, small bourgeois origins, as well as students from the upper middle, etc. It was a politically active institution. The atmosphere at the École normale on rue d'Ulm in Paris sometimes reminds me of my college. This was Calcutta, University of Calcutta. I left as a third-year graduate student to come to Cornell.

AA. How much English was there in your household?

GCS. Well no, there wasn't much English in the household. That's a characteristic. Even now for example, I will not write letters to my family in English. It's unthinkable, although they're all supereducated. It is sometimes assumed that, if one knows English well, then one would use English. That's not the case. One can know English as well as treasure one's own mother tongue. This is perhaps a Bengali phenomenon, rather than an Indian phenomenon, and there are historical reasons for this, or at least one can construct a historical narrative as a reason.

To an extent there was in conversation, in writing, in reading even, in the family situation, one could say, no English. But in school, of course, English was one of the languages; English was a language that we learned in class. And we knew very well that in order to get ahead in colonial, and immediately postcolonial, India, what you needed was English.

AA. I am interested in the ways diasporic intellectual workers describe themselves in light of their language use. For example, Jacques Derrida explained to me, in English, that he was raised in Algeria, a descendant of a Spanish Jewish family, but that he is not bilingual. Tzvetan Todorov, on the other hand, affirms the bilingualism and biculturalism of the Eastern European in the West. But it is an unequal bilingualism, weighted by time, distance, borders. How would you describe yourself?

GCS. From the point of view of language? I see myself as a bilingual person. As a bilingual person, I do translations from my native language. I think I would like a greater role in West Bengal as a public intellectual. Remaining in the United States was not at any point an examined choice, a real decision made. We won't go into the background now. I left India without any experience of what it was like to live and work in India. So I have kept my citizenship, and I'm inserting myself more and more into that. I have two faces. I am not an exile. I am not a migrant. I am a green-card-carrying critic of neocolonialism in the United States. It's a difficult position to negotiate, because I will not marginalize myself in the United States in order to get sympathy from people who are genuinely marginalized.

I want to have more of a role in the space where Bengali is a language for reading, writing. I write Bengali competently, with the same sort of problem making myself clear as I have in English. Mahasweta asks me to write more in Bengali. So reading, writing, public speaking, television: I want to get more involved. The cultural field in West Bengal is so rich that I'm a bit envious, you might say. It's working out slowly and I can now see myself, as a person with two fields of activity, always being a critical voice so that one doesn't get subsumed into the other.

AA. Do you think that had you remained in Calcutta, you would do as much work in English as you do now, working in the United States?

GCS. Probably so. I was an English honors student. English is my field. Remember, we are talking about a colonial country. I have colleagues there who have remained more wedded to "English," without the critical edge. There is sometimes a kind of resentment that I, living in the West, should be cutting the ground from under them, since for them, that's their specialty rather than a contested political field.

Recently I gave an interview for the BBC World Service regarding colonial discourse. The first question that the British questioner asked me was "Do you think your activities in this critical theory have anything to do with the fact that you were born in India?" And I told her, "Look, in fact, if you were born and brought up in India, you can have exactly the opposite view." So yes, I probably would have been more like a traditional, solid, British style (instead of maybe using the American style, who knows?) English scholar, probably a Yeats scholar.

AA. Is the choice of language, English or Bengali for example, particularly significant for the writer writing in India?

GCS. Quite significant because India is a multilingual country. I have talked a lot about the concept of enabling violation. The child of rape. Rape is something about which nothing good can be said. It's an act of violence. On the other hand, if there is a child, that child cannot be ostracized because it's the child of rape. To an extent, the postcolonial is that. We see there a certain kind of innate historical enablement which one mustn't celebrate but toward which one has a deconstructive position, as it were. In order for an all-India voice, we have had to dehegemonize English as one of the Indian languages. Yet it must be said that, as a literary medium, it is in the hands of people who are enough at home in standard English as to be able to use Indian English only as the medium of protest, as mockery, or as teratology; and sometimes as no more than local color, necessarily from above. So yes there is an importance of writing in English, high-quality writing.

AA. What are your thoughts on hybrid writing and speech, on a Bengalized English?

GCS. It's very interesting that you should ask me that, because that is the English that is an *Indian* language. It's not just *Bengalized*. You know there are over seventeen to nineteen languages, hundreds of dialects in India. The English I'm speaking of may be used, for example, on a bus by two people talking to each other, underclass people, who clearly share an Indian language, not English. They may at a certain point breaking into a kind of English sentence that you wouldn't understand. The situation changes as you climb up in class. And it is this imbrication of the dynamics of class mobility with proximity to standard English that would, as I have already indicated, make the project of hybrid writing in English somewhat artificial. And the writer who would be a serious user of hybrid English would probably write in the local language. That is the difference in India, that there are very well-developed literary traditions in some of the local languages. Many English words are, and continue to be, lexicalized in these languages in senses and connotations ex-centric to Standard English. You might say the choice to write pure or hybrid exists more realistically in those vernaculars. And the choice takes its place among other kinds of hybridizations: dialects, class-variations, underclass vernacular-mixings through internal migrant labor, multilingual irony. As in the case of South Africa, it would be difficult to find a clean analogy for resistant language-practice in the Indian case. Here as in many other instances of resistant cultural practice, I think the solidarity comes from exchange of information and bonding through acknowledgment of difference.

If we were a white country, might our hybrid English have been another English, as different from British as is American? What about the fact that we have flourishing, developing vernaculars. At any rate, the creative level of Indian English was always defined as a deviation. And the major vernacular literatures were somehow defined as *underdeveloped* because they had not followed the Hegel-Lukacsian line in form and content. This is by now so well-established, even internalized, that it seems hopeless to speculate about a counterfactual history. The idea of the European novel as the best form, and its harbingers and Cervantes and Defoe, is here to stay. To get back to Indian English, it is too late in the day to undertake the project of actually introducing it into public discourse. It already is there because, in fact, public Indian English is significantly different. It can seem comical to the users of "pure" Standard English—is there such a thing?—because it is unself-conscious. And our upper crust often joins in that laughter. The celebration of that intellectualized patois in international Indian literature, or subcontinental literature written in English, would be impractical for reasons that I have already given.

AA. Let me shift the focus from India to Ireland. Could you speak to the project of writing, as that of Joyce, Yeats, Beckett?

GCS. I hold on to the idea of dehegemonizing. I think I am more sympathetic with Joyce's stated deep irony. You remember Mother Grogan in *Ulysses?* Haines, the Englishman, who has learnt Irish, speaks to her in Irish, and she asks, "Is it German?" Yeats, in the event, transformed English. But in his stated politics, language politics, I find him less sympathetic than Joyce. It has to be self-conscious or nothing.

I will now draw an example not from India but from Bangladesh, because I've just had this discussion with a poet in Dhaka. When the British became territorial, rather than simply commercial, after the Battle of Plassey in 1757, they came in through Bengal. There was already an Islamic imperial presence in India located nearly a thousand miles away in Delhi, although the Nawab of Bengal was Muslim and there was a sizable, powerful Muslim minority, both urban and rural. In order to counteract Islamic domination, and I'm obviously simplifying, they played up the Hindu Sanskrit quality of Bengali. Bengali was the language they emphasized, because they had come through Bengal and established themselves in Bengal. There was therefore a colonial hype of Bengali as an Indic-Hindu language. In fact, of course Bengali had a strong Arabic-Pharsi element as well. Under the British, nearly all of it was erased, and subsequent Bengali nationalism also emphasized the Hindu element. (Curiously enough, the Hindu majority government of India has been playing the same game with Hindi, the national language, for some time.)

The liberation of Muslim-majority Bangladesh from Pakistan in 1971 was officially on linguistic-cultural rather than religious grounds. My friend the poet has this question: How do we restore the Islamic elements in Bengali without identifying with a program of religious fundamentalism? Bengali is my mother tongue too. So there we were: he born a Muslim; I born a Hindu; I Indian, he Bangladeshi; neither of us very religious, totally against fundamentalism, and neither of us at all interested in the crazy project of a separatist Bengal, a pipe dream that is occasionally brought out for sentimental or political rhetoric. I said to him that I thought that since language cannot be interfered with self-consciously, the only way to do it is absolutely self-consciously, that is to say, write manifestos, and so on. I have a great deal of sympathy with self-conscious tampering, because one knows that language works behind and beyond and beside self-consciousness.

AA. What about Beckett's writing in French?

GCS. I see it as a sort of self-distancing. When you began you were talking about identity. I have trouble with questions of identity or voice. I'm much more interested in questions of space, because identity and voice are such powerful concept metaphors that after a while you begin to believe that you are what you're fighting for. In the long run, especially if your fight is succeeding and there is a leading power-group, it can become oppressive, especially for women, whose identity is always up for grabs. Whereas, if you are clearing space, from where to create a perspective, it is a self-separating project, which has the same politics, is against territorial occupation, but need not bring in questions of identity, voice, what am I, all of which can become very individualistic also.[1] It seems to me that Beckett's project is that kind of self-separating project, that kind of clearing of a space. It is not possible to remain within the mire of a language. One must clear one's throat, if you're taking the voice metaphor, clear a space, step away, spit out the mother-tongue, write in French.

I don't have that relationship to English, no. No. First of all I shouldn't compare myself to Beckett. I am bilingual. Millions of Indians write in English. How many Irish write in French?

I think the South African writer J. M. Coetzee's relationship to English—"of no recognizable *ethnos* whose language of exchange is English"—is beautifully articulated with Beckett's distancing from *English*.[2] The Irish have a peculiar relationship with English too, after all.

AA. Would you speak about the *Satanic Verses?* What do you feel about the irony that while the *Satanic Verses* criticizes first world representation of the third, it, nevertheless, has become complicit in propagating such representational practices.

GCS. First off let me say that I have just published a piece on reading the *Satanic Verses* in *Third Text,* and I touch on exactly the kind of questions you are asking. The fact that it has become complicit is not Rushdie's fault. Rushdie was trying to create a postcolonial novel, from the points of view both of migration—being in Britain as black British—and of decolonization—being the citizen of the new nation, India, Islamic India.

Islamic India is strange too, because given what the minority does, its head ritually is turned toward Mecca outside the subcontinent. He's trying to deal with this. I've had a lot of conversations with people, Iranian friends, Palestinian friends, black British, British Muslim friends, etc., the Southhall Black sisters who are in Britain speaking up against the so-called fundamentalist reaction. If you read it from the point of view of "a secular Muslim," he is trying to establish a postcolonial readership—already in existence—who will in fact share a lot of the echoes that are in that book which you and I might miss. I, for